Twentieth-Century Science | **Physics**

Decade by Decade

Twentieth-Century Science | **Physics**

Decade by Decade

Alfred B. Bortz, Ph.D.

Set Editor: William J. Cannon

■ Facts On File
An imprint of Infobase Publishing

For Alex, 21st-century grandson

PHYSICS: Decade by Decade

Facts On File, Inc.
An imprint of Infobase Publishing
132 West 31st Street
New York NY 10001

ISBN-10: 0-8160-5532-7
ISBN-13: 978-0-8160-5532-6

Library of Congress Cataloging-in-Publication Data

Bortz, Alfred B.
Physics: decade by decade / Alfred B. Bortz
p. cm. — (Twentieth-century science)
Includes bibliographical references and index.
ISBN 0-8160-5532-7 (acid-free paper)
1. Physics—History—20th century. 2. Physics—Study and teaching. I. Title.
QC7.B58 2007
530.09′04—dc22   2006022921

Facts On File books are available at special discounts when purchased in bulk quantities for businesses, associations, institutions, or sales promotions. Please call our Special Sales Department in New York at (212) 967-8800 or (800) 322-8755.

You can find Facts On File on the World Wide Web at http://www.factsonfile.com

Text design by Dorothy M. Preston and Kerry Casey
Cover design by Dorothy M. Preston and Salvatore Luongo
Illustrations by Bobbi McCutcheon
Photo Research by Elizabeth H. Oakes

Printed in the United States of America

VB Hermitage 10 9 8 7 6 5 4 3 2 1

This book is printed on acid-free paper.

Contents

Preface

The 20th century has witnessed an explosive growth in science and technology—more scientists are alive today than have lived during the entire course of earlier human history. New inventions including spaceships, computer chips, lasers, and recombinant DNA have opened pathways to new fields such as space science, biotechnology; and nanotechnology. Modern seismographs and submarines have given earth and ocean scientists insights into the planet's deepest and darkest secrets. Decades of weather science, aided by satellite observations and computer modeling, now produce long-term, global forecasts with high probabilities (not certainties) of being correct. At the start of the century, science and technology had little impact on the daily lives of most people. This had changed radically by the year 2000.

The purpose of Twentieth-Century Science, a new seven-volume set, is to provide students, teachers, and the general public with an accessible and highly readable source for understanding how science developed, decade-by-decade, during the century and hints about where it will go during the early decades of the 21st century. Just as an educated and well-informed person should have exposure to great literature, art, music, and an appreciation for history, business, and economics, so, too, should that person appreciate how science works and how it has become so much a part of our daily lives.

Students are usually taught science from the perspective of what is currently known. In one sense, this is quite understandable—there is a great deal of information to master. However, very often, a student (or teacher) may ask questions such as "How did they know that?" or "Why didn't they know that?" This is where some historical perspective makes for fascinating reading. It gives a feeling for the dynamic aspect of science. Some of what students are taught today will change in 20 years. It also provides a sense of humility as one sees how brilliantly scientists coped earlier in the century with less funding, cruder tools, and less sophisticated theories.

Science is distinguished from other equally worthy and challenging human endeavors by its means of investigation—the Scientific Method—typically described as:

a) observations

b) hypothesis

c) experimentation with controls

d) results, and

e) conclusions concerning whether or not the results and data from the experiments invalidate or support the hypothesis.

In practice, the scientific process is not quite so "linear." Many related experiments may also be explored to test the hypothesis. Once a body of scientific evidence has been collected and checked, the scientist submits a paper, reporting the new work to a peer-reviewed journal. An impartial editor will send the work to at least two reviewers ("referees") who are experts in that particular field, and they recommend to the editor whether the paper should be accepted, modified, or rejected. Since expert reviewers are sometimes the author's competitors, high ethical standards and confidentiality must be the rule during the review process.

If a hypothesis cannot be tested and potentially disproved by experiment or mathematical equations, it is not scientific. While, in principle, one experiment can invalidate a hypothesis, no number of validating experiments can absolutely prove a hypothesis to be "The Truth." However, if repeated testing using varied and challenging experiments by diverse scientists continues to validate a hypothesis, it starts to assume the status of a widely accepted theory. The best friend a theory can have is an outstanding scientist who doubts it and subjects it to rigorous and honest testing. If it survives these challenges and makes a convert of the skeptical scientist, then the theory is strengthened significantly. Such testing also weeds out hypotheses and theories that are weak. Continued validation of an important theory may give it the stature of a law, even though it is still called a theory. Some theories when developed can revolutionize a field's entire framework—these are considered to be "paradigms" (pronounced "paradimes"). Atomic theory is a paradigm. Advanced about 200 years ago, it is fundamental to understanding the nature of matter. Other such paradigms include evolution, the big bang theory, and the modern theory of plate tectonics (which explains the origin of mountains, volcanoes and earthquakes) quantum theory, and relativity.

Science is a collective enterprise with the need for free exchange of information and cooperation. While it is true that scientists have strong competitive urges, the latter half of the 20th century has witnessed science becoming increasingly interdisciplinary. Ever more complex problems, with increasing uncertainty, are tackled and yet often elude precise solution.

During the 20th century, science found cures for tuberculosis, and polio and yet fears of the "dark side" of science (for example, atomic weapons) began to mount. Skepticism over the benefits of science and its applications started to emerge in the latter part of the 20th century even as its daily and positive impact upon our lives increased. Many scientists were sensitive to these issues as well. After atomic bombs devastated Hiroshima and Nagasaki, some distinguished physicists moved into the life sciences, and others started a magazine, now nearly 60 years old, *The Bulletin of the Atomic Scientists,* dedicated to eliminating the nuclear threat and promoting peace. In 1975, shortly after molecular biologists developed recombinant DNA, they held a conference at Asilomar, California, and imposed voluntary limits on certain experiments. They encouraged adoption of regulations in this revolutionary new field. We are in an era where there are repeated and forceful attempts to blur the boundaries between religious faith and science. One argument is that fairness demands equal time for all "theories" (scientific or not). In all times, but especially in these times, scientists must strive to communicate to the public what science is and how it works, what is good science, what is bad science, and what is not science. Only then can we educate future generations of informed citizens and inspire the scientists of the future.

The seven volumes of Twentieth-Century Science deal with the following core areas of science: biology, chemistry, Earth science, marine science, physics, space and astronomy, and weather and climate. Each volume contains a glossary. The chapters within each volume contain the following elements:

- background and perspective for the science it develops, decade-by-decade, as well insights about many of the major scientists contributing during each decade
- black-and-white line drawings and photographs
- a chronological time line of notable events during each decade
- brief biographical sketches of pioneering individuals, including discussion of their impacts on science and the society at large
- a list of accessible sources for Further Reading

While all of the scientists profiled are distinguished, we do *not* mean to imply that they are necessarily "the greatest scientists of the decade." They have been chosen to represent the science of the decade because of their outstanding accomplishments. Some of these scientists were born to wealthy and distinguished families, while others were born to middle- and working-class families or into poverty. In a century marked by two World Wars, the cold war, countless other wars large and small, and unimaginable genocide, many scientists were forced to flee their countries of birth. Fortunately, the century has also witnessed greater access to the scientific and engineering professions for women and people of color, and, with luck, all barriers will disappear during the 21st century.

The authors of this set hope that readers appreciate the development of the sciences during the last century and the advancements occurring rapidly now in the 21st century. The history teaches new explorers of the world the benefits of making careful observations, of pursuing paths and ideas that others have neglected or have not ventured to tread, and of always questioning the world around them. Curiosity is one of our most fundamental human instincts. Science, whether done as a career or as a hobby, is after all, an intensely human endeavor.

Acknowledgments

In writing this book, I had the assistance of many people who helped me find useful or necessary information. This included a number of still living scientists whose work was worthy of inclusion in a history of 20th-century physics but whose year of birth did not appear in any references available to me. Fortunately for them, I did not have to search for an obituary that would list their birth year. Rather I could find their e-mail addresses and ask them directly.

A few people and two organizations were particularly helpful, and I would like to acknowledge them here. To make sure I had assembled a good set of reference material, I exchanged e-mails and spent several hours in person with the staff of the library of the Center for the History of Physics at the American Institute of Physics. Director Spencer R. Weart and his staff were especially helpful in leading me to print and online resources about all areas of physics. Dr. Weart, in particular, directed me to resources dealing with the history of solid-state/condensed-matter physics, a critically important area that is often overlooked in popular histories of physics and physicists.

I am also grateful to the Fermilab Education Office, headed by Marge Bardeen, which includes the Lederman Science Education Center. Mrs. Bardeen always responded with the help I was looking for, and I enjoyed her friendly interactions. The education office provided me an efficient way to contacting Leon Lederman himself, and he directed me to the Academy of Achievement Web site, which turned out to be the perfect source of biographical information for developing the Lederman profile as scientist of the decade for the 1990s.

Marge Bardeen's husband, Bill, who also works at Fermilab, is the son of John Bardeen, scientist of the decade of the 1950s. Bill is an accomplished physicist in his own right. He graciously provided access to photographs in the Bardeen family archive, making it possible to portray the human side of John Bardeen, the only person to win two Nobel Prizes in the same field.

Likewise, Richard Muller of Lawrence Berkeley Laboratory directed me to his personal remembrance of his mentor, Luis Alvarez, part of which is quoted in the Alvarez profile as scientist of the decade of the 1980s.

Finally, I thank Facts On File, the publisher of this set of books on 20th-century science, for the opportunity to write this volume. I appreciate the guidance and input of Frank K. Darmstadt, executive editor, Amy L. Conver, copy editor, and the rest of the staff. I also appreciate the considerable illustrative talents of line artist Bobbi McCutcheon and photo research talents of Elizabeth Oakes. I enjoyed rediscovering the field in which I earned my doctorate in 1971. It was interesting to see as history ideas that were fresh discoveries when I was in college, and it was an adventure to explore and put into perspective the many new theories and changes in physics that have developed since then.

Introduction

The Nineteenth-Century Clockwork Universe

In the mid-1890s, physicists—scientists who study matter and energy—looked ahead to the 20th century with justifiable pride. The more they had studied the universe in the 19th century, the more orderly they had found it to be. Its behavior was thoroughly predictable through natural laws that they expressed in the precise language of mathematics. Though there were still a few important questions to be answered, most physicists were confident that the 20th century would be devoted to refining theories and making the critical measurements needed to complete the tapestry of their science.

They could not have been more wrong. Instead of tying up a few loose ends, physicists pulled on a few snags and watched the entire theoretical fabric of physics unravel. It would take most of the new century to reweave it. The process would redefine almost everything people thought they understood about matter and energy, space and time, and waves and particles. To understand those astonishing changes in physics during the 20th century, one must first examine the remarkable accomplishments of that science during the previous century, most notably in electromagnetism—including the electromagnetic nature of light—and the atomic theory of matter.

The Atomic Theory of Matter

In one sense, atomic theory was hardly new. The idea that matter is comprised of tiny, indivisible particles dated back more than 2,000 years to the ancient Greek philosophers Democritus and Leucippus, but it had been largely forgotten until meteorologist John Dalton (1766–1844) tried to make sense of what chemists had discovered about gases. In 1810, he published a landmark book called *A New System of Chemical Philosophy* in which he proposed a new theory of matter. Dalton proposed that matter consists of *elements* that combine in particular ratios to form *compounds*. The basis for the specific ratios, Dalton theorized, is that each element consists of tiny indivisible particles called *atoms*, and atoms combine to make *molecules*, the basic units of compounds.

Atomic theory quickly became the foundation of chemistry, and scientists regularly discovered new elements. They measured and cataloged each element's properties, such as freezing and boiling temperatures and density (mass or weight per cubic centimeter). They studied the elements' chemical behavior and deduced their atomic masses. As the number of known elements grew, scientists searched for a classification scheme—an arrangement of the elements so that those with similar chemical properties would group together.

In 1869, a Russian chemistry professor named Dmitry Mendeleyev (1834–1907) found that arrangement, a rows-and-columns grid that he called the *periodic table of the elements.* Beginning at the upper left with the lightest atom, hydrogen, he placed elements down the first column of his grid in the order of increasing atomic mass. Then he moved rightward from one column to the next, placing atoms with similar chemical properties next to one another in rows. (Today's periodic table, which appears in the Appendix, reverses the roles of rows and columns but otherwise follows Mendeleyev's approach.) Occasionally, to match chemical properties, he had to skip a space on the grid. He expected that those spaces would be filled later with undiscovered elements—and he was right. When those missing elements were found, their properties matched the predictions of the table.

The periodic table was a great achievement, but important questions remained. What distinguishes atoms of one element from those of another, and how do those differences result in the regularity of the periodic table? Answering those questions would have to wait until the 20th century.

Electromagnetism and Light

The 19th century also produced considerable knowledge of electricity, magnetism, and light. As that century began, physicists viewed electricity and magnetism as separate phenomena, and they were trying to choose between two competing 17th-century ideas about the nature of light. Was light a wave, as Dutch scientist Christiaan Huygens (1629–95) had argued, or was it a stream of particles, as the great English physicist Sir Isaac Newton (1643–1727) believed?

That question was settled quickly. In 1801, English scientist and researcher Thomas Young (1773–1829) performed an experiment that proved definitive. He split a beam of light in two and allowed both parts to illuminate a screen. Instead of seeing two bright regions as would have been expected from two streams of particles, he observed a phenomenon known as *interference*—a series of light and dark bands produced by overlapping waves.

Young's experiment immediately raised a new question. Light waves travel from stars through the vacuum of space, so what carries the wave? Some physicists proposed that all space was filled with a fluid called the *luminiferous ether.* The ether waved as light passed through it, yet offered no mechanical resistance to moving bodies, like planets. That explanation did not satisfy all scientists since it required the existence of something that filled the universe but had no detectable mechanical properties—not even mass—but it was a starting point.

In the 1820s and 1830s, a number of physicists, most notably the famed English researcher Michael Faraday (1791–1867), explored electricity, magnetism, and the relationships between them. They learned how to make an electromagnet and developed the first electric motors and generators. They also discovered that electricity was the force that bound atoms together in compounds. Physicists began to use the term *electromagnetism* and looked for ways to describe electromagnetic forces mathematically, just as Newton had done for *gravity* about 150 years earlier.

In 1859, a Scottish-born Cambridge University physics professor named James Clerk Maxwell (1831–79) developed a set of four mathematical equations based on the discoveries of Faraday and others. One was a formula for the forces that act on electric charges, another described the forces that act on magnetic poles, and two described the interrelationships between electricity and magnetism. Unexpectedly, *Maxwell's equations* also described waves of electromagnetic energy that could travel through empty space. The equations predicted the speed of those waves, which, remarkably, matched what other physicists had measured as the speed of light. The conclusion seemed inescapable: Light was an electromagnetic wave, and Maxwell's equations described the electrical and magnetic properties of the ether.

With Maxwell's equations and the periodic table, 19th-century physicists felt they were on the verge of a full understanding of nature. Every material object, no matter how large or small, is composed of indivisible atoms bound together by electric forces. On a larger scale, such as the solar system, gravitational attraction binds one body to another. In addition, the universe is awash in energy flowing as electromagnetic waves. Some great questions remained: Why do elements fit neatly into a periodic arrangement? What is the source of starlight? Are atoms and the ether real, and if so, how can they be detected? But overall, the universe seemed to be as predictable as clockwork and as orderly as a woven pattern, governed by precise mathematical laws of motion, gravitation, and electromagnetism.

Reweaving the Fabric of Physics

That precision and predictability turned out to be an illusion, and that is the major theme of the story of physics in the 20th century. A few seemingly loose ends turned out to be indicators of an unraveling fabric of ideas.

As the next chapter describes, the new century's first decade was marked by a series of remarkable discoveries. These included a reinterpretation of Newton's laws and Maxwell's equations in a way that eliminated the need for the ether. Mass and energy were shown to be different aspects

James Clerk Maxwell, who developed equations that described the relationships between electricity and magnetism and showed that light is an electromagnetic wave (AIP Emilio Segrè Visual Archives)

of the same physical phenomenon. Atoms were shown not only to exist, but also to be divisible. Remarkable experiments were about to reveal their internal structure. Likewise, the distinction between waves and particles was no longer clear. In the second and third decades of the century, quantum physics further blurred that distinction. More surprising, it replaced the clockwork universe with uncertainty.

It took the remainder of the century to weave a new pattern for the tapestry of physics. Today, in the early years of the 21st century, the pattern seems much clearer—except, again, for a few loose ends. As the closing chapters of this book discuss, some physicists are brashly declaring that they are in search of "the theory of everything," but the history of the century that just ended leaves them wary. They know there may be unseen universes hidden in the gaps of their knowledge.

Physics and Conservation Laws

How do physicists discover new perspectives? One of their most powerful guiding principles has been the realization that nature has certain conservation laws that state that certain quantities remain unchanged (conserved) in an interaction or process. As later chapters will show, conservation laws proved to be remarkably fertile for 20th-century physicists. In the 19th century, the following conservation laws proved useful:

- **Conservation of Momentum.** The oldest conservation law in physics results from two of Newton's three laws of motion. The third law, commonly known as the law of action and reaction, states that forces always occur in equal and opposite pairs. Whenever one body exerts a force on another, then the second body exerts exactly the same amount of force on the first, but in the opposite direction. For instance, while the Earth's gravitational attraction holds the Moon in its orbit, the

Moon's gravity pulls back on the Earth with equal intensity. Because the Earth is so much more massive than its satellite, the effect of the Moon's gravity on Earth is not to create an orbit but rather a wobble, which is most notable in the ocean tides.

Newton's second law states that when a force acts on a body, it produces a change in a quantity called momentum, which is commonly expressed mathematically as the product of mass and velocity. The longer the force acts on a body, the greater the change in the body's momentum. When two bodies exert equal and opposite forces on each other, they produce equal and opposite changes in momentum. Thus if no other forces are acting on them, the change in total momentum of the two bodies must be zero. Each body's individual momentum changes, but no matter how strong the force is between them or how long it acts, the total momentum remains the same at all times—or as physicists say, momentum is conserved.

- **Conservation of Mass.** Another of the great conservation laws deals with mass. Newton's first law of motion defines a quantity called inertia, or the tendency of a body to maintain its velocity unless a force acts on it. The measure of inertia is what physicists call mass, which is usually thought of as the amount of substance the body has. (In everyday language, people often speak of how much an object weighs, not how massive it is. But it is better to use the term *mass* for this reason: Weight is the force that Earth's gravity exerts on that object. On the Moon, it would weigh less, but its mass would be the same.)

One of the basic ideas behind the atomic theory of matter is that the total mass of the matter involved in a chemical reaction does not change. Atoms may rearrange, leading to different compounds, but the atoms themselves remain the same. As the 19th century was ending, physicists believed that the law of conservation of mass was fundamental.

- **Conservation of Energy.** Newton's laws of motion also lead to a quantity called energy, which can take two major forms called kinetic energy (energy of motion) and potential energy (energy of position). Both can result from a quantity called work, which is defined mathematically as the distance that a body moves multiplied by the force that acts in its direction of motion.

(continues)

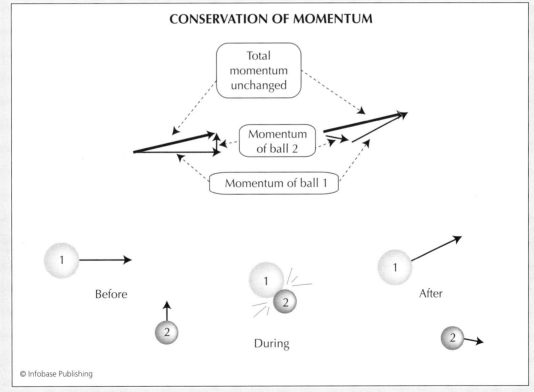

CONSERVATION OF MOMENTUM

Total momentum unchanged

Momentum of ball 2

Momentum of ball 1

1

Before

2

1
2

During

1

After

2

© Infobase Publishing

Newton's second and third laws of motion lead to the conclusion that when two bodies interact, the momentum of each individual body may change but their total momentum does not. In this glancing collision of two balls of different masses, each changes direction and speed, but their total momentum remains the same.

(continued)

Work can produce kinetic energy by making a body go faster, or it can produce potential energy in many ways, for example by stretching or compressing a spring or lifting a mass. The spring has the potential to make an object move when it returns to its normal length. The mass can fall back down, gaining kinetic energy along the way.

One of the great accomplishments of 19th-century physics was recognizing the relationship between energy and heat and developing a new conservation law. When two bodies interact, their total momentum is conserved, but their total kinetic and potential energy may change. For example, if two identical cars traveling at the same speed collide head-on, the resulting crumpled mass would immediately come to a dead stop. Before the collision, each car has the same amount of momentum, but in opposite directions. Thus their total momentum is zero both before and after they collide. As expected, momentum is conserved.

What about the energy? Unlike momentum, energy does not have a direction. The large amount of kinetic energy before the collision seems to be lost, and the crunched cars have no potential of springing apart on their own. But the collision generates a great deal of heat, which can be easily detected after the crash. By understanding heat as a measure of the total kinetic energy of the individual atoms in the car, it turns out that energy is conserved after all.

The branch of physics known as thermodynamics describes the way heat and energy are related to temperature. Physicists speak of three laws of thermodynamics, the first of which is a conservation law. It states that when heat is included, energy, like momentum, is conserved when bodies interact without any outside influence. Thermodynamics is closely related to a mathematical branch of physics that was developing in the late 19th century called *statistical mechanics*. Statistical mechanics enabled physicists to look at heat on the atomic level. It defined temperature as a measure of the average kinetic energy of the atoms or molecules in matter, whether they are moving freely and colliding as in a gas or liquid, or vibrating back and forth in a solid.

Statistical mechanics played an important role in the dramatic early discoveries of the first decade of the 20th century—including changes in physicists' understanding of the laws of conservation of mass and energy.

This book traces those remarkable developments of the 20th century decade by decade. Readers will see separate threads of physics developing and coming together in surprising ways. They will experience, as 20th-century physicists did, times of puzzlement, if not outright confusion. The feeling will probably be uncomfortable, but its solution lies in adopting a physicist's way of approaching the universe: thinking in terms of unification, such as the way Maxwell's equations combined electricity, magnetism, and light, or looking for conservation laws, as discussed in the sidebar on pages xx–xxii. Physicists always remain open to new perspectives. They do not deny unexpected observations, but rather consider new ways to interpret them. They do not allow arbitrary human conventions to stand in the way of discovery.

One such convention is the arbitrary division of history into centuries and decades. Because of that convention, this book and others in the

Twentieth-Century Science set have chapters that match the century's decades, starting with 1901–1910. But when important stories overlap those divisions, it is best to present some of the information in what might be considered the "wrong" chapter. That is certainly true in the first two chapters of this book. What is generally considered modern physics began in the second half of the 1890s, so chapter 1 opens then. Likewise, the early work leading to the discoveries of cosmic rays, the atomic nucleus, and the phenomenon of *superconductivity* all began before 1911. But discussion of that research is postponed until chapter 2, when it reached fruition.

1901–1910:
The Dawn of Modern Physics

1

As noted at the end of the Introduction, discoveries in the first decade of the 20th century shook the foundations of physics. The great transformations in that science resulted from the work of many innovative thinkers, but none had ideas that were more influential than those of a German-born Swiss patent clerk by the name of Albert Einstein (1879–1955). In 1905, he published three articles that changed the way physicists viewed space and time, matter and energy, and particles and waves. He reinterpreted both Newton's laws and Maxwell's equations in a way that eliminated the need for the ether. He showed that mass and energy are different aspects of the same physical phenomenon. He interpreted well-known experiments to demonstrate that atoms were real, not merely a useful concept for understanding chemistry.

Great ideas do not spring from nothingness. The stage for the discoveries of the early 20th century was set in the mid-to-late 1890s, when physicists were investigating the relationship between electricity and matter. They knew that electricity existed as positive and negative charges and that it was like atoms—tiny, indivisible bits of charge of a certain size—not like a fluid that could be parceled out in any amount. Atoms could be electrically neutral, or they could exist as electrically charged ions.

But what was electricity, and how was it related to matter? Research into *cathode rays* seemed most likely to produce insight into this question. Cathode rays were curious beams that occurred in sealed glass tubes from which most of the air had been removed. Inside the tubes were two electrodes—a negative cathode and a positive anode—with a large voltage (electrical pressure) between them. When the cathode was heated, it emitted a beam that caused the remaining air around it to glow. If that beam struck the tube, the glass would also glow.

Curious Findings

On November 8, 1895, German physicist Wilhelm Röntgen (1845–1923) was studying cathode rays when he discovered an odd phenomenon. He knew that cathode rays could cause a fluorescent glow, and so he had a fluorescent screen in his laboratory to study them. But this day, he was not using that screen. He had placed it far from the cathode-ray tube and covered it with black cardboard, but in the darkened laboratory, Röntgen noticed that it was glowing. What could be causing that?

After a number of experiments, Röntgen discovered that cathode rays were causing an unknown form of radiation, which he called X-rays, to be emitted from the anode. X-rays could pass through certain types of matter—such as the glass of the cathode-ray tubes—but not others, and they would darken a photographic plate. (X-rays are now known to be a high-energy form of electromagnetic waves.)

Early the next March, French physicist Henri Becquerel (1852–1908) discovered that a compound of uranium also produced radiation that darkened a photographic plate. At first, he thought that he had found another source of X-rays, but he soon discovered that "uranium rays" were a different phenomenon altogether. Becquerel's discovery was soon called *radioactivity*, and other physicists and chemists quickly got into the act, including Polish-born chemist Marie Curie (1867–1934) in France and Gerhardt Schmidt in Germany. Working separately in 1898, each of them discovered radioactivity in thorium. Later that year, Marie Curie and her husband, Pierre Curie (1859–1906), discovered two previously unknown radioactive elements, radium and polonium, in uranium ore.

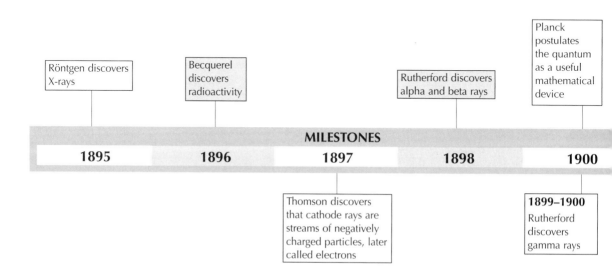

| Röntgen discovers X-rays | Becquerel discovers radioactivity | | Rutherford discovers alpha and beta rays | Planck postulates the quantum as a useful mathematical device |

MILESTONES

| 1895 | 1896 | 1897 | 1898 | 1900 |

Thomson discovers that cathode rays are streams of negatively charged particles, later called electrons

1899–1900
Rutherford discovers gamma rays

Radioactivity also caught the attention of Joseph John ("J. J.") Thomson (1856–1940), the director of the world-famous Cavendish Laboratory at Cambridge University in England. As soon as he heard about Becquerel's discovery, he decided to investigate those mysterious rays. He assigned the task to Ernest Rutherford (1871–1937), a dynamic young graduate student who had arrived from New Zealand the previous autumn. By 1898, Rutherford had discovered two distinct forms of radioactivity and named them after the first two letters of the Greek alphabet. *Alpha rays* could be stopped by just a few sheets of aluminum foil, but *beta rays* were much more penetrating. Both were charged particles—alphas carrying a positive charge and betas carrying a negative charge.

Meanwhile Thomson was in the midst of his own carefully crafted experiments to determine whether cathode rays are a wave or particle phenomenon. In 1897, he announced his findings: Cathode rays are a stream of tiny particles that carry negative electric charge. He called the particles corpuscles, and he assumed that each corpuscle carried nature's basic unit of electric charge. His measurements and that assumption led him to this astonishing conclusion about the particles' size: A corpuscle's mass was less than a thousandth of that of the hydrogen atom, the smallest atom on the periodic table. (Present-day measurements put that value at less than 1/1,800.) As scientists learned more about the behavior of these corpuscles in atoms, they became known as *electrons*.

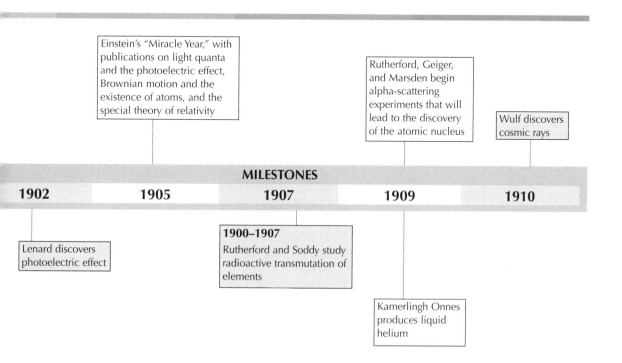

Einstein's "Miracle Year," with publications on light quanta and the photoelectric effect, Brownian motion and the existence of atoms, and the special theory of relativity

Rutherford, Geiger, and Marsden begin alpha-scattering experiments that will lead to the discovery of the atomic nucleus

Wulf discovers cosmic rays

MILESTONES

1902   1905   1907   1909   1910

Lenard discovers photoelectric effect

1900–1907 Rutherford and Soddy study radioactive transmutation of elements

Kamerlingh Onnes produces liquid helium

Marie Curie, shown here with her husband, Pierre Curie, with whom she shared the 1903 Nobel Prize in physics (AIP Emilio Segrè Visual Archives)

There were two possible explanations. Either his assumption about the corpuscle's single unit of charge was wrong and it actually had more than 1,000 units of negative electricity, or its mass was indeed very tiny. A charge of more than a 1,000 units did not make sense, so Thomson and other physicists concluded that corpuscles were particles much smaller than atoms.

Mysterious rays and subatomic particles were not the only surprises in physics as the 19th century drew to a close. In 1900, the familiar glow of heated objects led German physicist Max Planck (1858–1947) in an unexpected direction that led to a Nobel Prize in physics in 1918. Using statistical mechanics to describe the different vibration rates of atoms of a heated object, Planck calculated the *spectrum* of the light it would emit—that is, how the intensity of the glow would vary for different colors—and compared his calculations to measured spectra of its so-called *blackbody radiation* at different temperatures.

The measurements were familiar: The object emitted no visible light when it was cool but became dull red when heated to a few hundred degrees. At higher and higher temperatures, it glowed bright red, then orange. If it could have been heated to the temperature of the Sun, it would have glowed yellow. Those colors were not pure, but rather mixtures of light at different wavelengths, like those Sir Isaac Newton discovered in sunlight in his famous experiments 200 years earlier.

Planck presented the spectra as graphs. From left to right along the horizontal axis, colors went from infrared to red, across the visible spectrum to violet, and beyond to ultraviolet. The vertical direction represented intensity. The numerical value along the horizontal axis was the light's frequency or the rate at which wave crests would pass by a given point. Frequency increases from infrared to ultraviolet, passing through the visible red-to-violet colors in between. Each spectrum reached a peak at a particular frequency that corresponded roughly to the color people would see. Then the intensity dropped off sharply at higher frequencies.

*Ernest Rutherford and J. J.
Thomson many years after their
pioneering work on cathode
rays and radioactivity* (AIP
Emilio Segrè Visual Archives,
Bainbridge Collection)

Planck's calculations produced good news and bad news. The good news was that the calculated spectra matched the measured spectra especially well in the infrared area; the bad news was that it failed to predict the peak. In fact, his computations predicted an ever-growing intensity for higher frequencies. So Planck looked for an idea of how to change his statistical mechanical model to correct the high-frequency problem (which scientists in later years called the "ultraviolet catastrophe").

His approach went against Maxwell's equations in a minor way. Those equations allow electromagnetic waves to have any intensity from very dim to very bright and everywhere in between. That means light energy is like a fluid that can be measured out in any amount. Planck decided to treat light energy like atoms or grains of sand instead. If the grains are small, the energy can be measured out almost like a fluid, as if controlled by a dimmer switch. But large grains produce noticeable gaps between different levels of brightness, like a three-way bulb.

Max Planck, whose study of the light emitted by hot bodies led to the idea of the quantum (AIP Emilio Segrè Visual Archives)

Planck called an energy grain a *quantum* (plural: *quanta*). To preserve the good match between his prediction and measurements in the infrared, he knew he needed small quanta at low frequencies. But to eliminate the problem in the ultraviolet, he needed large quanta at high frequencies. He started with the simplest possible way to do that. He wrote a formula that expressed the energy of a quantum as a multiplier times its frequency.

Remarkably, when Planck chose the right multiplier, the shape of his calculated spectrum matched the measured spectrum at all frequencies from infrared through ultraviolet. Planck originally thought that he might need a different multiplier for each temperature, but he discovered the same multiplier worked at all temperatures.

Today that multiplier is known as *Planck's constant*. Planck realized that number said something important about the nature of light, but he did not know what. He had invented the quantum as nothing more than a clever computational trick, but he had stumbled onto something that seemed to be real. The 19th century had opened with Young's experiment that established light as a wave phenomenon. Now, in that century's last year, Planck's theory was hinting that light might be a stream of particles after all. The two results contradicted each other, but physicists could not deny either of them. Resolving the contradiction would take physics down unanticipated paths in the 20th century.

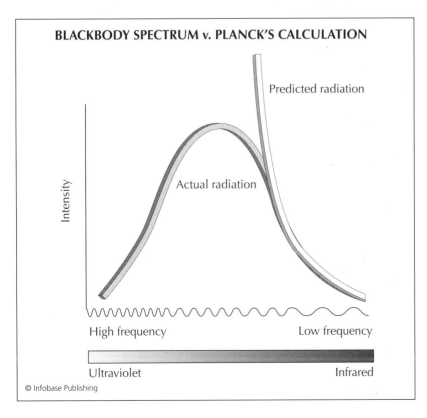

BLACKBODY SPECTRUM v. PLANCK'S CALCULATION

Predicted radiation

Actual radiation

Intensity

High frequency

Low frequency

Ultraviolet

Infrared

© Infobase Publishing

Planck's calculation of the spectra of light emitted by a heated body agreed with measured spectra in the longer infrared region but was spectacularly wrong in the ultraviolet. He introduced the quantum to eliminate the discrepancy, even though it did not fit the wave theory of light.

New Century, New Perspectives

At first, the discovery of a subatomic particle and the reemergence of the wave-or-particle question about the nature of light did not seem to threaten early 20th-century physicists' comfortable picture of their science. It still rested on the solid foundation of Newton's laws of motion and gravitation and Maxwell's equations of electromagnetism. Conservation of mass and energy were still two of its bedrock principles.

But the foundations and bedrock were about to be shaken. Physics was about to be transformed, and the person who would be most responsible was a virtual unknown in 1901, Albert Einstein. Having completed his college degree from the Zurich Polytechnic Institute the previous year at the age of 21, Einstein began the new century looking for a job, and he was not having much luck. Some of his professors realized that he was very smart, but he was also so unconventional that they were reluctant to hire him as an assistant or to recommend him for good jobs. Einstein took two temporary teaching jobs before finding permanent work as a technical expert, third-class, in the Swiss Patent Office in 1902.

That job turned out to be ideal. It was not very demanding, and it allowed him plenty of time to think about the great questions of physics while working for a doctoral degree from the University of Zurich. In 1905, he not only completed his doctoral dissertation, but he also wrote three papers (articles) that were published in the scientific journal *Annalen der Physik* (*Annals of Physics*). Each of the papers was on a different subject, and each was a masterpiece.

Quanta and the Photoelectric Effect

Einstein's first paper, "On a Heuristic Point of View Concerning the Production and Transformation of Light," dealt with Planck's quanta and a puzzling experimental discovery known as the *photoelectric effect*. In 1902, Philipp Lenard (1862–1947) found that light shining on a metal electrode could, under some circumstances, cause electrons to be emitted. Every metal behaved differently, but all had one puzzling feature—a threshold frequency for the light, below which the effect disappeared.

The photoelectric threshold for each metal was different, ranging from blue for some metals to ultraviolet for others. Below the threshold, no electrons were emitted, no matter how bright the light. Above the threshold, even the dimmest light could free electrons from the surface.

Einstein recognized the photoelectric threshold as evidence that Planck's quanta were more than mathematical inventions. They were actual particles—bundles of light energy—which later became known as *photons*. He explained it as follows: To free an electron from a metal requires a certain amount of energy called the work function. Planck's

Albert Einstein was a 26-year-old patent clerk in Bern, Switzerland, in 1905, when he published three articles that transformed physics. (Hebrew University of Jerusalem Albert Einstein Archives, courtesy AIP Emilio Segrè Visual Archives)

constant relates the energy of a quantum of light to its frequency. For a quantum to boost an electron out of a metal, its energy exceeds the work function, which means its frequency must be high enough. Above the frequency threshold, no matter how dim the light, each quantum has enough energy to free an electron. Below the threshold, no matter how many quanta there are, none has enough energy to knock an electron loose.

It was not difficult to test Einstein's conjecture. The farther above the frequency threshold the photons were, the more energy they would be able to give to the emitted electrons. When physicists did experiments to determine the dependence of that excess energy on frequency, they found the results matched Einstein's prediction. Thus the photoelectric effect was undeniable evidence that light is a stream of particles—Planck's quanta. Yet other phenomena, like Young's demonstration of interference,

PHOTOELECTRIC EFFECT

Light source

Prism

Monochromatic light

Collector

Metal sheet

Electrons

Phototube
(evacuated)

+   −

Voltage

Ammeter

Photons below threshold frequency

Photons above threshold frequency

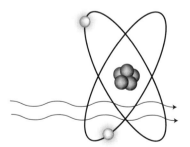

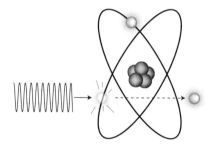

Pass through with no effect no
matter how bright the light

Knocks electron from its orbit no
matter how dim the light

(Opposite page) Einstein explained a puzzling phenomenon called the photoelectric effect by recognizing that light was made of actual packets of energy. That is, the quantum Planck had proposed was more than a mere mathematical convenience. Physicists now call the light quantum a photon.

demonstrated light's wave nature with equal certainty. As bothersome as that seemed, Einstein took the only attitude that a physicist can: Nature is what it is, and it is up science to find ways to describe it. Sometimes scientists need to find new tools or vocabulary. Sometimes they need to ask different questions. In this case, asking an either-or question about the nature of light was the wrong approach, because experiments were showing it to be both. Now the question was how that could be so.

Brownian Motion and the Reality of Atoms

Einstein's second 1905 paper, "On the Movement of Small Particles Suspended in Stationary Liquids Required by the Molecular-Kinetic Theory of Heat," used statistical mechanics to analyze other scientists' observations of a phenomenon known as *Brownian motion*. About 80 years earlier, Scottish botanist Robert Brown, after whom the effect is named, observed pollen grains suspended in a fluid through a microscope. Brown noticed that the grains moved jerkily along irregular paths. In the years after that, other scientists made precise measurements of Brownian motion and reported their results.

Einstein realized that those irregular jogs were the result of collisions with the molecules of the fluid. He calculated how far and how fast the particles would be expected to move between collisions, and how the details of the zigs and zags would be affected by changes in temperature. His compared his calculations to experimental measurements and found that they matched. Though single atoms and molecules had still not been observed, Einstein's calculations provided direct evidence that they existed.

The Special Theory of Relativity

Einstein's third 1905 paper is the best known to nonscientists. Called "On the Electrodynamics of Moving Bodies," it laid out his theory of relativity and changed the way physicists viewed space and time.

The theory developed from Einstein's perspective on the luminiferous ether. He realized that the ether, if it exists, is more than a medium in which electromagnetic waves flow. It also provides a fixed background—a *frame of reference*—against which all motion in the universe can be measured. A particular point in the universe could be designated the origin, where three perpendicular axes (plural of axis) meet. Those axes could be designated x, y, and z (or east-west, north-south, and up-down). Any

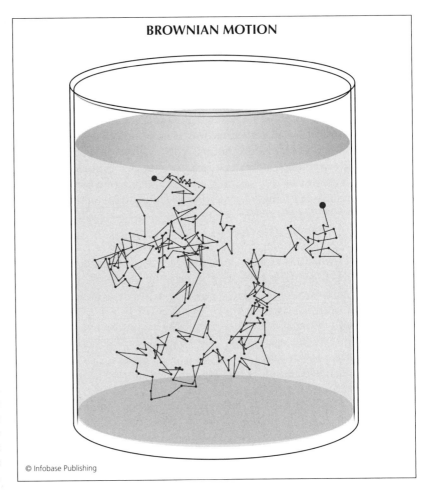

BROWNIAN MOTION

© Infobase Publishing

Einstein explained the random paths followed by tiny particles suspended in fluids, known as Brownian motion, as the result of collisions with the atoms or molecules of the fluid, providing the first direct observational evidence of atoms and molecules.

point in the universe would be defined by three numbers, specifying its distance from the origin along the three axes.

To describe the path of a moving object, a person would only need the values of those three numbers at different times. Any wave or object could move with respect to that frame of reference, but the ether itself would remain stationary. That makes the ether an *absolute* frame of reference. Earthbound scientists can only measure the *relative* motion of an object with respect to their instruments. To determine the absolute motion of that object, they would need to measure the absolute motion of those instruments with respect to the ether. For years, scientists had been trying to do that, but they were always unsuccessful.

For example, they tried to detect slight differences among the speeds of light beams that travel along the direction of Earth's motion, opposite to that direction, and perpendicular to that direction. Very sensitive measurements failed to find any differences. Some people interpreted the failure to detect such differences as evidence that the ether does not exist. Einstein went a step further. He said that the nonexistence of the ether means that the universe has no absolute frame of reference. The motion of one object or wave can only be measured relative to another, but not with respect to the universe itself.

Einstein's view of relativity was a natural extension of earlier scientific thought. At first, people viewed the Earth as the unmoving center of everything. Then they realized that Earth was one planet moving in a larger solar system. The natural human reaction was then to place the Sun at the center of the universe. But by Einstein's time, astronomers could tell that the stars were moving with respect to one another. They no longer had reason to think that the Sun—or any other star—occupied a special place in the universe. From that perspective, it was easier to give up the idea of an absolute frame of reference.

That led Einstein to state this basic principle of physics: If two observers are moving at constant velocity with respect to one another, neither observer's frame of reference is preferable to the other's. It is impossible to make any observation that determines that one is moving while the other is absolutely at rest in the universe.

That simple principle produces some surprising consequences. As noted in the Introduction, Maxwell's equations predict the existence of electromagnetic waves that travel at a definite speed. That means that two observers, regardless of their relative motion, must measure the same speed for a beam of electromagnetic radiation.

But that statement does not match everyday experience. Suppose a major league baseball pitcher is standing on the roof of the engine of a train traveling at 50 mph (80 kph), and suppose he throws a 100 mph (161 kph) fastball in the direction of the train's travel. A person on the ground would measure its speed to be 100 + 50 = 150 mph (241 kph). If he threw it backward, the person on the ground would measure its speed to be 100 - 50 = 50 mph in the opposite direction.

But things are different when the baseball is replaced by a flashlight. The relativity principle predicts the same speed of light—the speed specified by Maxwell's equations—for both the observer on the ground and the pitcher on the train, no matter how fast the train is going or in which direction the pitcher points the flashlight. That is exactly the effect scientists were seeing when they tried and failed to measure differences in the speed of light as the Earth moves at more than 66,000 mph (106,000 kph) around the Sun in its orbit.

Einstein's theory of relativity leads to a number of phenomena that occur at high relative speeds but seem odd when judged by everyday human experience. It forces physicists to change the way they view space and time, and that affects the mathematical interpretation of Newton's laws of motion and Maxwell's equations.

For example, measuring an object's length requires a determination of where its endpoints are *at the same time*. That means the measurement of length requires the observer to have synchronized clocks in different places. Clocks can be synchronized by transmitting an electromagnetic "the time is now" message outward from a central transmitter. When that message, traveling at the speed of light, reaches a clock, the clock automatically sets itself according to its distance from the transmitter.

But there is a complication: Observers moving in frames of reference with respect to each other do not agree on synchronization. Consider the flashlight on the train as an example. Suppose that the observer on the ground and the pitcher have extremely accurate, identical meter sticks and clocks. Before the experiment begins, the observer and the pitcher synchronize their clocks by setting off a flash at the middle of the train. Because of the train's motion, the observer notices that the flash reaches the clock at the back of the train before it reaches the clock at the front. It has to, because in the observer's frame of reference, light travels less than half a train length before the back of the train meets the flash and more than half a train length before the flash reaches the front.

To the pitcher, the light travels exactly the same distance to the ends of the train and therefore reaches them at the same time. In his frame of reference, the two clocks are properly synchronized, but in the observer's, the one at the back is set too late, and the one in the front is set too early. Looking at the same situation from the frame of reference of the pitcher, he sees the observer moving in the opposite direction, and the observer's clocks are out synchronization for him in the same way his are out of synchronization for the observer.

Since the principle of relativity states that neither frame of reference is better than the other, both are correct in their observations. In other words, the pitcher's and the observer's conclusions about synchronization differ, depending on their relative motion. From the simple assumption that no frame of reference is absolute comes the unexpected result that synchronization is relative!

Similar analysis leads to startling conclusions about length of meter sticks and the rate a clock ticks. Objects moving in a frame of reference are shortened along the direction of motion compared to the same objects at rest. Clocks moving in a frame of reference run more slowly than the same clocks at rest. The observer and the pitcher look at each other, and each notes that the other has shortened meter sticks and clocks that run more slowly than if they were at rest. Yet when both observe the same experiment with those different-length meter sticks and those differently synchronized clocks running at differing rates, they agree on the laws of nature. Otherwise, one reference frame would be preferred above the other.

A "thought experiment," one of Einstein's favorite techniques, may clarify this. Suppose the pitcher stands at the back of the caboose and shines the light forward toward a detector at the front of the train, which he has measured to be one light-microsecond (lms), or 1,000 light-nanoseconds (lns) long. (A light-microsecond is the distance light travels in a microsecond, about 984 feet, or 300 meters, in everyday units. A light-nanosecond is 1/1,000 of that distance.) The train travels at half the speed of light with respect to the ground. The pitcher and the observer both record the time and place the light turns on (event A) and the time and place when the light reaches the detector (event B). Then they compare notes.

The pitcher says the light took one microsecond to reach the front of the train. As the diagram on page 16 shows, the observer sees things very differently. The observer measures the moving train to be shorter, approximately 86.6 percent as long as it is to the pitcher, or 866 lns. The pitcher, of course, notices nothing unusual about his surroundings. According to the observer, that is because the pitcher's meter sticks have been shortened too.

The light beam travels at the speed of light, but in the observer's frame of reference, the front of the train is moving ahead at half that speed. The light from event A catches up with the front of the train (event B) after 1,732 nanoseconds, during which the beam has traveled two train lengths, or 1,732 lns. Because of the difference in clock rates, the observer judges that the pitcher's clocks ticked off 1.5 microseconds during that time, but the pitcher measured only one microsecond because the two clocks were incorrectly synchronized by 0.5 microsecond (the pitcher's microseconds, not the observer's).

None of the observer's disagreements with the pitcher violate the laws of nature. They only clash with human concepts of space and time that developed from experiences at relative speeds much less than the speed of light. If the observer and the pitcher lived in a world where relative speeds were often a significant fraction of the speed of light, then their everyday experience would include meter sticks whose length depends on the way they are moving, clocks that run at different rates when moving at different speeds, and no absolute synchronization.

The observer and the pitcher agree that event A occurs when and where the flashlight is turned on at the back of the train—though their two sets of instruments give different measured values for the place and time. Likewise, they agree that event B occurs when and where the light reaches the detector at the front of the train, though again with different numbers that specify position and time. Despite the differences between the measured numbers, they agree on this: The light beam travels at the speed predicted by Maxwell's equations. That is a law of nature, and it must be the same in both frames of reference.

Relativity also produces a surprise when the observer and the pitcher interpret a simple electrical experiment. Suppose each is conducting the same experiment on identical laboratory setups, measuring the electrical forces between two charged balls. Because a moving electric charge is an electric current, and because an electric current produces a magnetic

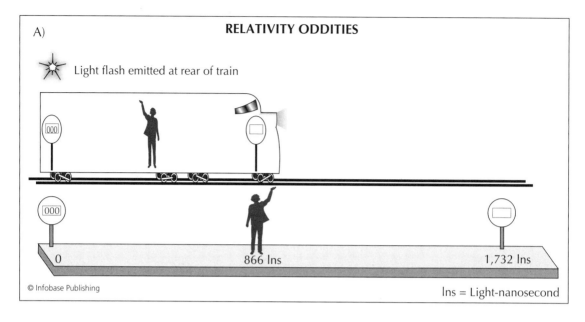

RELATIVITY ODDITIES

Light flash emitted at rear of train

000

000

0   866 lns   1,732 lns

© Infobase Publishing

lns = Light-nanosecond

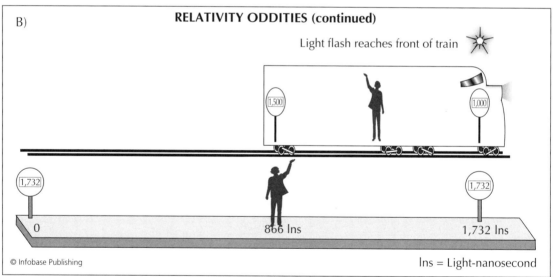

RELATIVITY ODDITIES (continued)

Light flash reaches front of train

1,500   1,000

1,732   1,732

0   866 lns   1,732 lns

© Infobase Publishing

lns = Light-nanosecond

field, each looks at the other's experiment and observes not only an electric force but also a magnetic one. When the relativity principle is applied to Maxwell's equations, the electric and magnetic fields are no longer separate entities but rather a single electromagnetic field that may appear to be more electrical or more magnetic, depending on the

(Opposite page) *Einstein's two simple assumptions for the special theory of relativity (the speed of light is the same for all observers and no frame of reference is preferable to another when they move at a constant relative velocity) lead to a number of high-speed phenomena that seem odd when judged by everyday human experience. Here, as seen by an observer in a railroad station at rest with respect to this book, a train passes left-to-right through the station at half the speed of light. It carries a statue of Albert Einstein that was made in an identical fashion to one in the station. Part A shows that a light flashes as the back of the train passes the left edge of the platform, triggering clocks on the platform and train at that point to start at zero. Part B shows that the light reaches the right end of the platform at the same time as the front of the train reaches that point. That event triggers another pair of clocks to turn on with different time settings. Because observers on the train and the platform must measure the same speed of light despite their relative motion, they are unable to agree about the synchronization of their clocks, the rates those clocks tick, or the length of the objects measured along the direction of relative motion. Each observer notes that the other's clocks run slowly and that lengths are compressed (which is why the statue on the train is thinner). Because neither frame of reference is preferred, both are correct in that observation! This is explained in detail in the main text of this chapter.*

relative motion between the observer apparatus and the person making the measurement.

The theory of relativity's most dramatic surprise of all came, not in Einstein's first paper on the subject, but in a postscript to it entitled "Does the Inertia of a Body Depend on Its Energy Content?" which was published later in 1905. The postscript extended the first paper's analysis of the meaning of mass, which is the measure of a body's inertia. Electromagnetic energy must travel at the speed of light, but anything with mass can never achieve that speed, no matter how strong the force acting on it and no matter how long that force acts. The higher an object's speed in an observer's frame of reference, the more force must be applied to increase that speed by a given amount. The work done on it causes its inertia—or mass—to increase.

When Einstein looked at his new version of the laws of motion and compared them to Newton's, he found that conservation of momentum still holds when the increasing mass is taken into account. But conservation of mass needs to be modified, as does conservation of energy. The main point of the postscript is expressed by the famous equation $E=mc^2$, which states that mass and energy are two aspects of the same phenomenon. Mass and energy can be transformed into each other, and thus are not necessarily conserved separately. However, they are still conserved when considered together. Thus relativity combines those two conservation laws into one.

At this point, readers may wonder about the word *special* in the heading of this section. The theory of relativity discussed here is for the special case of two frames of reference moving at a constant relative velocity. A general theory of relativity would have to take into account acceleration or changing relative velocities. That proved to be quite difficult, but Einstein eventually succeeded in doing so, as will be discussed in chapter 2.

The Divisible Atom

Einstein was not the only physicist making remarkable discoveries in the first decade of the 20th century. Building on the 1897 discovery of the electron, J. J. Thomson and others were busy exploring the subatomic world. Thomson continued to use the term *corpuscle* to describe the electron for many years. But no matter what he called it, he knew that its discovery had opened many new avenues of research in physics for the new century. Some researchers investigated the electron itself, while others concerned themselves with the role of the electron in matter. For instance, if electrons, which are negatively charged, are part of electrically neutral atoms, then atoms must also contain positive charges. Since electrons are so light, the remaining positively charged matter must contain most of the atom's mass.

It soon became apparent that an element's *atomic number*, which specifies its position in the periodic table, corresponds to the number of electrons in its atoms—or equivalently, the electric charge on the positive part of the atom (though they did not yet know what that positively charged part was like). The *atomic masses* of the different elements are also related to the atomic number, but not in a simple proportion. Hydrogen is the lightest atom and has atomic number one, but a helium atom, with atomic number two, has four times the mass of hydrogen. Heavy atoms, such as lead with atomic number 82 and an atomic mass about 207 times that of hydrogen, are even further out of proportion. No one knew why that should be so.

Scientists also realized that electrons were responsible for an atom's chemical behavior. An atom's *valence* is a property that describes the way it reacts with other atoms. Valence is related to the number of electrons it contributes to chemical reactions and dictates the particular combinations of atoms that form molecules. Elements in the same column of the periodic table have the same valence. Though they did not yet understand why, physicists and chemists recognized that most elements have not only valence electrons but also other electrons that do not participate in chemical reactions. It was also becoming clear that electric currents in metal wires are a flow of electrons. Why some substances, such as metals, conduct electricity while others do not was not yet understood, but it was obvious that some electrons are not as tightly bound to their atoms or molecules as others.

Among physicists at the turn of the 20th century, Ernest Rutherford quickly emerged as a leading figure in understanding both radioactivity and the internal structure of atoms. In 1898, he became a professor at McGill University in Montreal, Canada, where he continued the research he had begun with Thomson in England. He soon found a third form of radioactivity, even more penetrating than beta rays, which he naturally called *gamma radiation*, with properties that resembled those of X-rays.

In late 1900, he joined forces with McGill chemist Frederick Soddy (1877–1956), and they began the new century trying to understand some of the very strange chemistry that went along with radioactivity. For example, Rutherford and Soddy chemically separated radioactive atoms of a different element from a sample that was mainly thorium. The remaining material was much less radioactive at first, but then the same kind of radioactive atoms that they had removed reappeared, as if from nowhere. Other experiments with different radioactive materials yielded similarly puzzling results.

As they analyzed their radioactive samples, they often found the same chemical elements in different materials, but with different atomic masses. It took a few years of careful work to understand what was happening. Radioactivity was giving scientists hints about the internal structure of atoms. Rutherford and Soddy realized that radioactivity takes place when that positively charged portion of the atom—whatever it is—emits something. Their results indicated that when a "parent" atom emits an alpha particle, its atomic number decreases by two; that is, it changes, or transmutes, into a "daughter" element two atomic numbers below it on the periodic table. Furthermore, its atomic mass decreases by four, which led them to suspect that an alpha particle is a helium atom without its electrons.

Rutherford's earlier research had shown that beta rays are electrons. When the positive part of a radioactive atom emits a beta particle, the resulting daughter has one more unit of positive charge than the parent. So *transmutation* by beta emission results in an element that is one atomic number higher on the periodic table. The mass of the electron is so tiny that the daughter and the parent have the same atomic mass even though they are chemically distinct. For both alpha and beta radiation, the daughter atom is often more radioactive than the parent. That explains the increase in radioactivity that Rutherford and Soddy observed in their work with thorium and other radioactive elements.

Rutherford and Soddy's results also explained the different masses that had been noticed for chemically identical elements. Two atoms had the same chemical behavior, and were thus the same element, if they had the same electrical charge. But they could still have different masses. (Soddy later called these *isotopes*. By 1913, he realized that different isotopes also exist for nonradioactive atoms, which explained fractions in some measured atomic masses such as chlorine's 35.5. We now know that naturally occurring chlorine, atomic number 17, has two isotopes: a more common one with 35 mass units and a less common one with 37 mass units.)

In 1908, Rutherford was awarded the Nobel Prize in chemistry for his work on transmutation. (Soddy won it later, in 1921, for his explanation of isotopes.) Meanwhile, physicists were having lively discussions about

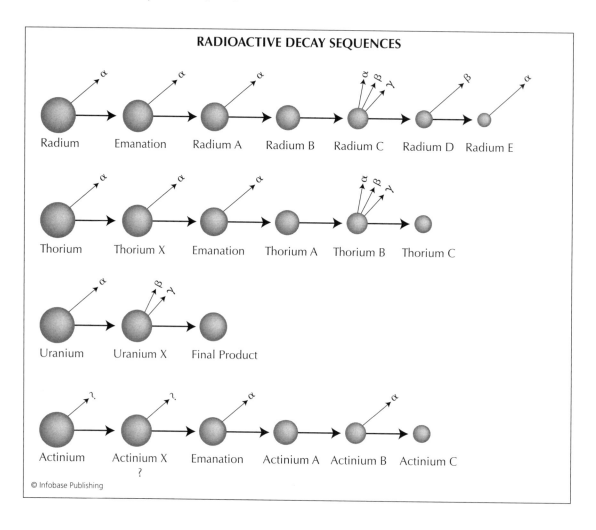

RADIOACTIVE DECAY SEQUENCES

Radium — Emanation — Radium A — Radium B — Radium C — Radium D — Radium E

Thorium — Thorium X — Emanation — Thorium A — Thorium B — Thorium C

Uranium — Uranium X — Final Product

Actinium — Actinium X ? — Emanation — Actinium A — Actinium B — Actinium C

© Infobase Publishing

Ernest Rutherford and Frederick Soddy produced this diagram of different radioactive decay sequences. Today the "daughter" atoms are known to be different elements in the periodic table. For example, the radioactive "emanation" is radon gas.

the internal structure of atoms. What was the positively charged matter like, and how were electrons mixed with it to make atoms?

One popular idea was J. J. Thomson's "plum pudding" model, which pictured atoms like a favorite British dessert. (If Thomson were American, he might have called it the raisin bread model instead.) It envisioned an atom as a serving of pudding with its positive charge spread evenly throughout its bulk, while tiny, negatively charged electrons were sprinkled within it like plums or raisins.

Other physicists had different ideas, picturing atoms as hard, little balls that somehow contain lightweight negatively charged electrons and an equal number of heavier, positively charged subatomic particles. No matter what model they thought was better, none of the physicists felt certain of their preference. Thus they were eager for someone to find a way to look inside the atom. Rutherford, who in 1907 had returned to

England as professor at the University of Manchester, had an idea of how to do that.

His plan was to use alpha particles as bullets, which he would shoot at thin metal foils. By measuring how their paths change as they pass through, he could deduce what kinds of structures they had encountered. Soft plum pudding would have little effect on the bullets, and their direction would barely change. But if the alphas struck hard, little balls, he would expect the alphas to be diverted—or scattered—from their original direction.

The first order of business in Manchester was to confirm his suspicions about the nature of alpha radiation. His assistant Hans Geiger (1882–1945) developed an instrument to detect the passage of high-energy charged particles and to count them. That device, the forerunner of the modern Geiger counter used to measure the intensity of radioactivity, proved to be the key to showing that alpha particles were indeed helium atoms without electrons.

Then, in 1909, Rutherford and Geiger began their *scattering* experiments. They quickly found that almost all of the alpha particles passed through metal foils with little or no change in direction. That pattern fit with Thomson's plum pudding model, but they were careful not to jump to that conclusion. Geiger's detectors were very precise, so they were able to compare the total number of alpha particles that struck their target on one side to the number that they detected on the other side. A very small fraction of the alphas escaped detection after hitting the foil, and they needed to understand what happened to them.

Rutherford considered several possibilities. Perhaps an occasional alpha particle was striking a detector and not registering. That seemed plausible, but the detectors had been perfectly reliable in other tests. Another possibility was that a few alpha particles were scattering more than Rutherford and Geiger had anticipated. Those particles may have gone far off to the side where there were no detectors. Since such large-angle scattering seemed very unlikely, Rutherford had Geiger concentrate his efforts on the detection techniques.

Meanwhile, he decided that looking for large-angle scattering, even if unsuccessful, would be good practice for Ernest Marsden (1889–1970), a young student just learning the laboratory's research techniques. Much to everyone's surprise, Marsden not only detected alpha particles scattered far off to the side, but he even detected some scattered back toward the source. Rutherford later described that result as "almost as incredible as if you had fired a 15-inch shell at a piece of tissue paper and it came back and hit you."

Following up on Marsden's discovery took more than another year, which meant that the first decade of the new century ended with Rutherford and his team in hot pursuit of a mystery. There was something unexpected inside those tiny particles called atoms, but they had not quite figured out what their results were telling them.

Scientist of the Decade: Albert Einstein (1879–1955)

"That person is an Einstein!" That expression, used to describe a creative genius, is a testament to the lasting influence of Albert Einstein the physicist, who transformed his science through his ability to find a new perspective from which to view old observations. But throughout the 20th century and even today, popular images have also portrayed Einstein as eccentric. He is the vest-wearing, bicycle-riding professor with a German accent, preoccupied by equations and unaware of the chalk on his clothing, his wild gray hair blowing in the wind.

But the life story of Einstein is more complex because he not only lived through tumultuous changes in world culture and politics, he also had a lasting influence on them. Born in Ulm, Germany, on March 14, 1879, Einstein's unusual way of looking at the world had always caused him problems in school. Because his thoughts were often elsewhere, some teachers thought he was slow. In his teens, he attended a *Gymnasium* (gim-NAH-zium, the German word for high school) in Munich, but he rebelled against its authoritarian approach. His disrespectful attitude led teachers there to say he would never amount to anything.

When a business failure drove his father to move the family to Milan, Italy, young Albert at first remained behind to complete his courses at the *Gymnasium*, but soon he left to rejoin his family. He could have graduated by continuing to study in Italy, but in 1896, exasperated with German culture, he signed a document giving up his German citizenship and with it any right to earn a diploma.

Albert Einstein's distinctive appearance and expressive face made him a photographer's favorite throughout his life. (AIP Emilio Segrè Visual Archives)

Even so, he took the college entrance examinations for the Zurich Polytechnic Institute in Switzerland, but he failed. He enrolled in a Swiss high school in Aarau and flourished in its more relaxed environment. With better preparation, he retook the exams and got into Zurich Poly on the second try. He found the course material at the institute interesting, but not the lectures. So he skipped most of his classes and read important books on his own. He passed the necessary examinations to earn a degree in the fall of 1900.

After graduating, he expected to be hired as an assistant to one of his physics professors, but the

New Techniques, Technologies, and Observations

The new perspectives of the first decade of the 20th century came about largely because physicists are inclined to extend the limits of their observations. That is also true of people who apply scientific discoveries in technology. The remarkable science noted in this chapter occurred

job never came. It should not have been surprising. A physics professor had once told him, "You are a smart boy, Einstein, a very smart boy. But you have one great fault: you do not let yourself be told anything."

Einstein took two temporary teaching jobs before finding permanent work as a technical expert, third-class, in the Swiss Patent Office in 1902. The job allowed him plenty of time to think about the great questions of physics and to study for his doctorate at the University of Zurich. In 1905, he completed his doctoral thesis and published three remarkable papers (articles) in the scientific journal *Annalen der Physik* (*Annals of Physics*) that transformed physics, as this chapter describes.

Those papers, plus his doctoral thesis that was published in 1906, brought Einstein fame in the world of physics. He took a series of professorships that began at the University of Zurich in 1909, then at Karl-Ferdinand University in the Czech capital of Prague, and then back to Zurich Poly. In 1913, Max Planck and Walter Nernst (1864–1941), another leading German physicist, offered Einstein the chance to establish and lead a physics institute in Berlin. He was reluctant to go back to Germany, but the position was too important to turn down. In Berlin, he was soon doing work that would bring him world fame. He extended his theory of relativity to include gravity, and it led to the conclusion that light rays bend in a gravitational field.

According to that theory, a beam of starlight passing close to the Sun would not go straight but would be deflected toward the Sun by an amount large enough to be measured here on Earth. It was an astonishing prediction but difficult to test because the faint starlight would be invisible in the Sun's glare—except on the rare occasion of a total solar eclipse. In 1919, two teams of physicists on opposite sides of the South Atlantic Ocean (off West Africa and in Brazil) observed some stars during an eclipse and measured exactly the bending that Einstein had predicted. Major newspapers splashed the discovery and Einstein's name around the world.

Einstein won the Nobel Prize in physics in 1921, not for the theory of relativity that brought him world recognition, but for his explanation of the photoelectric effect. His fame became very important later in his life. He was a Jew by birth, though he preferred to call himself a "deeply religious nonbeliever" and spoke not of a personal God but of "unbounded admiration for the structure of the world so far as science can believe it." In the 1930s, people with Jewish ancestry faced persecution under Adolf Hitler's Nazi government in Germany, so Einstein knew it was time to leave his native country again. His well-known name opened doors to brief stays in Belgium, England, and California before he settled at the Institute for Advanced Study at Princeton University in New Jersey.

During World War II, Einstein was a leader among scientists who persuaded United States president Franklin D. Roosevelt to develop the atomic bomb before the Nazis could. But his political inclinations were always those of a pacifist. After the war, he used his personal acclaim to become a powerful voice against further research into nuclear weapons and in favor of world peace. He remained in Princeton until his death on April 17, 1955.

in parallel with equally dramatic technological achievements. The first transatlantic radio communication occurred in 1901, and in 1903, on the outer banks of North Carolina, two bicycle-building brothers by the name of Wright demonstrated powered human flight.

Planck was not the only scientist studying spectra in the new century. When the light of glowing gases was spread out into spectra, each substance produced its own distinctive set of bright lines at particular wavelengths (a *line spectrum* as opposed to a *continuous spectrum* such as blackbody radiation). Some scientists were discovering patterns among those wavelengths, but they had no theories about why those patterns existed. They expected those theories to come from better understanding of the subatomic world and had good reason to expect such understanding to come in the next decade.

In the Netherlands, the laboratory of Heike Kamerlingh Onnes (1853–1926) was leading the world in the study of very low temperature phenomena. Researchers there had liquefied all of the gases in air. Helium had the lowest boiling temperature of all, approximately - 452°F (-269°C) or a mere 7.7°F (4.3°C) above absolute zero, a limiting temperature that thermodynamics said could be approached but never achieved. In the next decade, this technological and scientific achievement would lead to an astonishing discovery: the phenomenon of superconductivity.

Meanwhile in 1910, a Jesuit priest by the name of Theodor Wulf (1868–1946) studied radiation in the air from the top of the Eiffel Tower and found more than expected. He suspected the excess was coming not from the Earth but rather from elsewhere in the universe. He proposed to study these *cosmic rays* by launching balloons to heights greater than ever achieved but left the work to others in the decade to come.

The first decade of the new century had come to an end with unexpected new perspectives. It had begun with the expectation of tying up loose ends. But now physicists knew that they would have to unravel some old ideas in order to being weaving a new tapestry of understanding of the universe.

Further Reading

Books

Bodanis, David. *E=mc²: The Biography of the World's Most Famous Equation.* New York: Walker, 2001, and reissued 2005, with a new foreword by Simon Singh. A term-by-term discussion of the elements of Einstein's best-known formula.

Bortz, Fred. *The Electron.* New York: Rosen Publishing, 2004. An easy-to-read history of the electron and its applications.

———. *The Photon.* New York: Rosen Publishing, 2004. An easy-to-read history of the photon and its applications.

Calaprice, Alice. *The Einstein Almanac.* Baltimore, Md.: Johns Hopkins University Press, 2005. An overview of Einstein's life and work in concise snippets.

———, ed., with a foreword by Freeman Dyson. *The New Quotable Einstein.* Princeton, N.J.: Princeton University Press, 2005. Einstein's human side as shown in his often witty and warm letters to colleagues, friends, family, and lovers.

Calder, Nigel. *Einstein's Universe: The Layperson's Guide.* New York:
    Penguin, 2005. A reissue of a 1979 guide to relativity, with a new
    author's note and afterword.

Close, Frank, Michael Marten, and Christine Sutton. *The Particle Odyssey:
    A Journey to the Heart of Matter.* New York: Oxford University Press,
    2002. A detailed and colorfully illustrated overview of the discovery of
    subatomic particles.

Cropper, William H. *Great Physicists: The Life and Times of Leading Physicists
    from Galileo to Hawking.* New York: Oxford University Press, 2001. The
    life and times of many great physicists, including Maxwell, Einstein,
    Planck, Marie Curie, and Rutherford.

Einstein, Albert, with a new introduction by Brian Green. *The Meaning of
    Relativity.* 5th ed. 1954. Reprint, Princeton, N.J.: Princeton University
    Press, 2005. A readable presentation of Einstein's most famous theory in
    his own words.

Kragh, Helge. *Quantum Generations: A History of Physics in the Twentieth
    Century.* Princeton, N.J.: Princeton University Press, 1999. An in-depth
    history of 20th-century physics and physicists.

Lightman, Alan. *The Discoveries: Great Breakthroughs in 20th Century Science,
    Including the Original Papers.* New York: Pantheon, 2005. Includes
    Planck's paper on the quantum, Einstein's papers on the photoelectric
    effect and relativity, and commentary on their significance.

Rigden, John S. *Einstein 1905: The Standard of Greatness.* Cambridge, Mass.:
    Harvard University Press, 2005. Accessible discussion of Einstein's three
    1905 masterworks.

Suplee, Curt. *Physics in the 20th Century.* New York: Harry N. Abrams,
    1999. A pictorial history of 20th-century physics.

Web Sites

American Institute of Physics, Center for History of Physics. Available
    online. URL: http://www.aip.org/history. Accessed March 27, 2006.
    Follow pull-down menu for special online exhibits on Albert Einstein,
    Marie Curie, the electron, and radioactivity, among other topics, or
    browse for a variety of written resources and images.

Nobelprize.org. Available online. URL: http://nobelprize.org. Accessed
    March 27, 2006. The official Web site of the Nobel Foundation contains
    brief biographies of Nobel Prize winners, summaries of their prize-win-
    ning work, and their acceptance speeches.

The Science Museum. Available online. URL: http://www.sciencemu-
    seum.org.uk. Accessed March 27, 2006. A British online science
    education resource that includes useful exhibits on Atomic Firsts;
    Life, the Universe, and the Electron; Marie Curie and the History of
    Radioactivity; and many other topics discussed in this book.

The Science Shelf, Books for the World Year of Physics 2005. Available
    online. URL: http://www.scienceshelf.com/WorldYearofPhysics.htm.
    Accessed April 26, 2006. This page on the book review site of Fred

Bortz has brief comments about a number of books published in recognition of the World Year of Physics, plus links to reviews of a number of other physics books for nonspecialist readers.

World Year of Physics 2005. Available online. URL: http://www.physics2005.org. Accessed March 27, 2006. An online resource developed in honor of the centennial of Albert Einstein's "Miracle Year."

2

1911–1920:
New Views of Matter

The year 1910 marked the centennial of the publication of John Dalton's *A New System of Chemical Philosophy*, which described the atomic nature of matter. A hundred years of advances in chemistry had demonstrated the power of the simple idea that all matter was made of atoms.

Still no one had figured out what made atoms of one element different from those of another. The different chemical properties seemed to be related to the number of electrons in the atoms of the different elements, but electrons were too much light to explain the large differences in atomic masses. Most of an atom's mass was made of something else that was still not understood. Since atoms are electrically neutral, that unknown matter had to carry a positive electric charge equal to the negative charge of all that atom's electrons. But what was that positively charged matter, and how did nature build atoms from it and electrons?

The second decade of 20th-century physics would be dominated by that question, and many of the most important and surprising discoveries would come from the University of Manchester laboratories of Ernest Rutherford.

The Discovery of the Nucleus

Ernest Rutherford never won a Nobel Prize in physics, perhaps because his greatest accomplishment came only three years after he had won the 1908 Nobel Prize in chemistry. In 1911, after puzzling over the surprising results of Geiger's and Marsden's alpha-scattering experiments, he announced his interpretation of their measurements to the world.

Rutherford concluded that atoms should be described neither by Thomson's plum pudding model nor by the hard-ball model favored by other physicists, but by a model that resembled a planetary system held together by electricity rather than gravity. The results of Geiger's and Marsden's alpha-scattering experiments—that their alpha particles scattered only slightly with the striking exception of a small fraction that went far off to the side or even backward—told him that atoms are mostly empty space with most of their mass concentrated in a tiny central core called the *nucleus* (plural: *nuclei*). According to Rutherford's new picture of the atom, its electrons orbit the nucleus like Earth, and its sister planets go around the Sun. Remarkably, Rutherford's atoms were even emptier than the solar system. To compare: The Sun contains about 99.8 percent of the mass of the solar system, and its diameter is about 1/700 as large as the orbit of Neptune (the most distant planet). The nucleus has more than 99.9 percent of the atom's mass, but its size is truly minuscule. Even the largest nuclei have less than 1/10,000 the diameter of their atoms.

That structure explains why most positively charged alpha particles pass through atoms without being scattered much. Most of them pass too far from the nucleus to feel much of its influence. However, by chance, about one alpha particle in 8,000 comes near enough to the nucleus to feel an electrical force so powerful that the alpha scatters to the side—or even backward in the case of a very rare direct hit.

As is usual in science, a breakthrough like Rutherford's nuclear model of the atom opens up many new questions. The most serious difficulties were these: (1) an orbiting electron is accelerated, which means it should be radiating electromagnetic waves, and (2) the masses of different atomic nuclei are not proportional to the positive charge they carry.

To clarify the first point, when physicists speak of a body's velocity, they are referring to both its speed and direction. When they speak of its acceleration, they are referring to the rate that its velocity changes, taking both speed and direction into account. An orbiting planet is accelerated toward the Sun by the force of gravity, and, by the same analysis, an

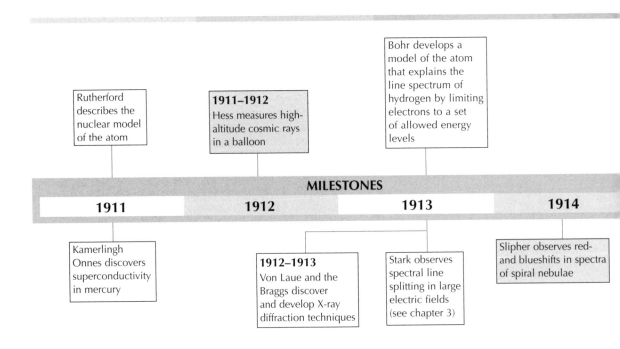

Bohr develops a model of the atom that explains the line spectrum of hydrogen by limiting electrons to a set of allowed energy levels

Rutherford describes the nuclear model of the atom

1911–1912
Hess measures high-altitude cosmic rays in a balloon

MILESTONES

| 1911 | 1912 | 1913 | 1914 |

Kamerlingh Onnes discovers superconductivity in mercury

1912–1913
Von Laue and the Braggs discover and develop X-ray diffraction techniques

Stark observes spectral line splitting in large electric fields (see chapter 3)

Slipher observes red- and blueshifts in spectra of spiral nebulae

orbiting negatively charged electron is accelerated toward the positively charged nucleus by electrical attraction. In both cases, the orbiting body constantly falls *toward* the central body but never falls *into* the central body because its motion is in another direction.

In the case of the planets, that is a stable situation. However, for an accelerated electron, Maxwell's equations, even as modified by Einstein, predict that it will radiate electromagnetic waves. The energy of those waves will come from its kinetic energy (energy of motion), which means it should steadily slow down and spiral into the nucleus within a tiny fraction of a second. Since most atoms are stable, something had to be wrong with either the laws of electromagnetism or Rutherford's model.

The new model changed but did not answer an old question about atoms. Scientists used to puzzle over the difference between atomic number and atomic mass in the periodic table. Now that they knew an atom's mass was mainly in its nucleus, they asked the same questions about nuclei. Why do helium nuclei have a mass of four times that of hydrogen nuclei when they only have twice the charge, and why do lead nuclei have a charge of 82 units and a mass of 207?

Rutherford's nuclear model offered no immediate insights on those questions, but it still offered significant advantages in understanding other phenomena such as radioactivity. Rutherford now could identify alpha particles as helium nuclei and beta particles as electrons. He could describe radioactivity as a process of nuclear disintegration or decay, in which a parent nucleus emits either a helium nucleus or an electron and

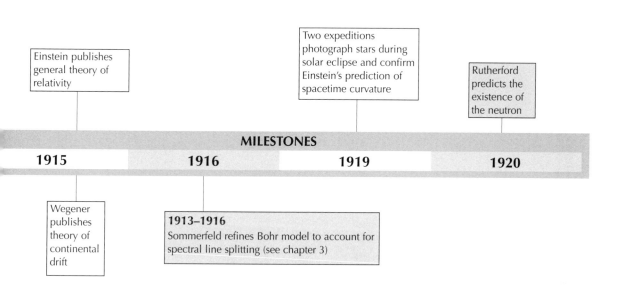

Einstein publishes general theory of relativity

Two expeditions photograph stars during solar eclipse and confirm Einstein's prediction of spacetime curvature

Rutherford predicts the existence of the neutron

MILESTONES

1915   **1916**   **1919**   **1920**

Wegener publishes theory of continental drift

1913–1916
Sommerfeld refines Bohr model to account for spectral line splitting (see chapter 3)

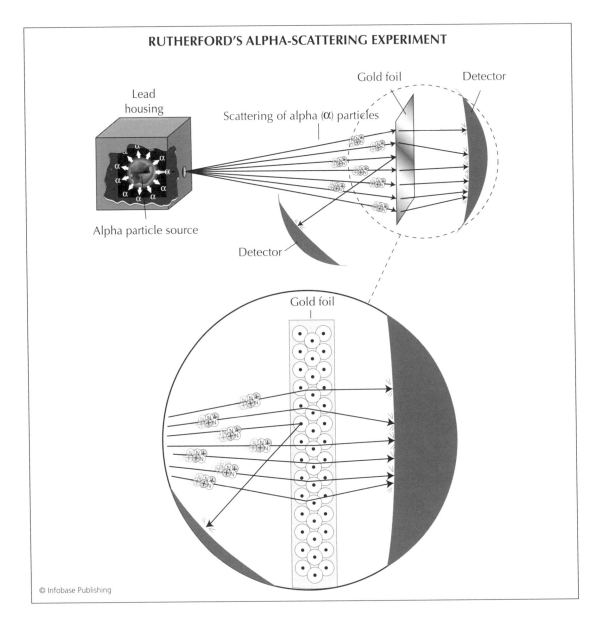

RUTHERFORD'S ALPHA-SCATTERING EXPERIMENT

Gold foil

Detector

Lead housing

Scattering of alpha (α) particles

Alpha particle source

Detector

Gold foil

leaves behind a daughter nucleus of a different element. (Gamma rays are never emitted alone but always as successors to *alpha* or *beta decays*.)

The Bohr Model of the Atom

The first significant refinement of Rutherford's nuclear model came in 1913, when a 28-year-old, Copenhagen-born physicist named Niels Bohr

(1885–1962) published a series of papers that quickly drew considerable attention. The main purpose of these articles was to propose a theoretical way out of the problem of electromagnetic radiation from orbiting electrons, but their impact turned out to be much wider than that. They moved Planck's quantum from the limited realm of light's interaction with matter to the broad arena of atomic structure.

Planck discovered the quantum while analyzing the continuous spectra in the glow of hot bodies like the filaments of incandescent lightbulbs. Bohr took note of the line spectra produced when electricity passes through low-pressure gas in a tube, producing a glow, such as the distinctive red of neon lights. Why do electrically excited gases emit quanta of only certain frequencies? What underlies the mathematical patterns in those frequencies, such as a series of spectral lines from

(Opposite page) The alpha-scattering experiment of Rutherford, Hans Geiger, and Ernest Marsden produced an astonishing discovery: A thin metal foil causes a small fraction of the high-energy alpha particles to scatter far off to the side or even backward. From that result, Rutherford concluded that most of an atom's mass is contained in a tiny, positively charged nucleus with negatively charged electrons orbiting it.

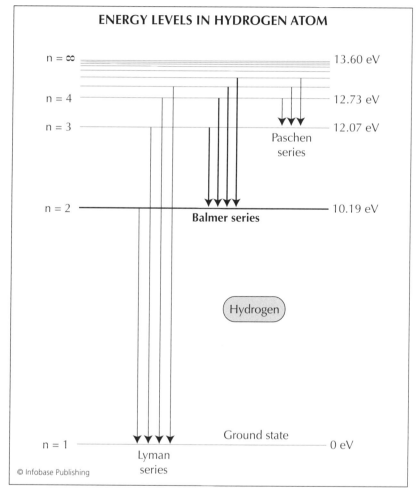

Niels Bohr developed a theory that explained the line spectrum of hydrogen as the result of electrons making transitions between allowed energy levels and emitting quanta of light with energy equal to the difference between the levels.

hydrogen identified 30 years earlier by a Swiss schoolteacher, Johann Balmer (1825–98)?

Bohr began his analysis by assuming that line spectra were the result of emissions from individual atoms. Could the pattern of frequencies in those emissions shed light on why electron orbits are stable in apparent violation of the laws of electromagnetism? What if the laws of physics dictated that only certain orbits were stable? With a single electron, hydrogen was a particularly easy atom to analyze. The formulas for gravitational and electrical attraction have the same mathematical form with charge replacing mass and an electrical constant replacing a gravitational one. Both state that the force decreases as the separation increases in an inverse square relationship. If the separation doubles, the force decreases to one-fourth (one part in two times two) of its previous value; if the separation triples, the force decreases by a factor of nine (three times three); and so forth.

The calculations were essentially the same as for the orbit of a planet (the electron) around the Sun (the hydrogen nucleus) without the complicating influences of other bodies. The laws of motion and electromagnetism predict a simple mathematical relationship between the size of an electron's orbit and the time it takes to make a round trip. That relationship is akin to the second of 17th-century astronomer's Johannes Kepler's (1571–1630) three laws of planetary motion. That law is an equation relating a planet's distance from the Sun to the length of its year.

Bohr's model of the atom also had equivalents of Kepler's first and third laws, but Bohr added one more that Kepler did not need: a restriction on what orbital periods were permitted. Bohr stated that electronic orbits are stable only if their energy is equal to an integer times the product of Planck's constant and the orbital frequency. It was as if the solar system restricted planetary orbits so that no body in orbit around the Sun could have a period of 365 or 366 days, but only the exact length of Earth's year (365.24 days).

In the Bohr model, electrons made transitions between allowed energy levels by emitting or absorbing a quantum of light having energy equal to the difference between the levels. The Bohr model could therefore compute a set of allowed frequencies of emitted light. Remarkably, they matched the hydrogen spectrum precisely. The Bohr theory was also successful, but less so, in predicting the line spectra of more complex atoms, just as Kepler's laws are not precisely valid when the influence of other planets needs to be considered. The theory's successes, however, suggested that the laws of electromagnetism did not apply to electrons in atoms, as long as their orbits met special conditions. Physicists were not entirely comfortable with that, but clearly, Bohr's analysis, like Planck's before it, was telling them something fundamental about the atomic world.

Inside the Nucleus

Rutherford and his team continued their alpha-scattering research until 1913, using different sources of alpha particles and foils of different metals to refine their conclusions. By then, the nuclear model of the atom was well established. But what made nuclei of one substance different from another? Two numbers were clearly important, electric charge and mass. The nucleus's positive electric charge corresponds to the identity of the nucleus as a particular chemical element, or where it fits in the periodic table. When surrounded by a number of electrons equal to that charge, it is a neutral atom, and the electrons are responsible for that atom's chemical behavior.

The nuclear mass, as Soddy pointed out, might differ between two isotopes of the same element. But mass, like charge, seemed to come in basic units. The simplest nucleus was hydrogen, with one unit of charge and one unit of mass.

When World War I broke out in 1914, fundamental physics research was one of the casualties as students were called to military service or other wartime duties. Rutherford himself became involved with submarine detection, but he also had time to continue work in the laboratory. He decided to follow up on an intriguing finding by Marsden, who had bombarded hydrogen gas with alpha particles.

When an alpha particle collides with a heavier, fixed nucleus of a metal atom, it changes direction but loses little of its energy. However, when the target is hydrogen gas, the collision resembles a billiard shot with an extra heavy cue ball. Both the alpha particle and the hydrogen nucleus rebound from the collision. If it is a near-direct hit, the hydrogen nucleus may go off at an even higher speed than the incoming alpha particle had.

By that time, Rutherford had begun calling hydrogen nuclei *protons* to signify that they are fundamental subatomic particles like electrons. Furthermore, those experiments had taught him how to distinguish protons from alpha particles when they struck his detecting screen. The ability to recognize protons soon proved to be very useful. When Rutherford began bombarding nitrogen gas with alpha particles, he detected protons even though he had started out with no hydrogen. His conclusion was that the collision caused the nitrogen nucleus to break apart and release a proton. That conclusion was generally correct, although scientists were not able to describe the exact nuclear transformation until the 1920s, namely this: an alpha particle (charge 2, mass 4) combined with a nitrogen nucleus (charge 7, mass 14) to produce a proton (charge 1, mass 1) and an uncommon but stable isotope of oxygen (charge 8, mass 17). Rutherford detected the proton but not the oxygen nucleus.

From what Rutherford observed, it made sense to think that all nuclei might be built up from protons. That would account for the charges of nuclei but not their larger masses. It also raised questions about what held a nucleus together. Two or more protons in such a confined space as the nucleus would repel one another with an enormously large force. Some physicists suggested that the nucleus might contain a certain number of additional protons and that same number of electrons, but Rutherford disagreed. He argued that a negatively charged electron and a positively charged proton within a nucleus would be so strongly attracted to each other that they would be inseparable, essentially forming a single neutral particle.

In 1920, he theorized that such "neutral doublets" were the third type of fundamental atomic building blocks after electrons and protons. He called this proposed particle a *neutron*. He noted that its mass would be very close to that of a proton. Thus an isotope's atomic number, which determined its place in the periodic table, was its number of protons, while its atomic mass was its total number of protons and neutrons.

It would be 1932 before neutrons were detected and even later before the force that binds the nucleus together was understood, but by the end of the second decade of the 20th century, Rutherford had provided the correct description of the makeup of atoms: electrons surrounding a massive but minuscule nucleus of protons and neutrons.

He probably would have phrased that differently, because physicists at that time spoke of electrons orbiting—not merely surrounding their nuclei. Developments in quantum theory in the 1920s, however, would lead physicists to a new view of electron orbits and of electrons themselves.

Atoms in Solids

While Rutherford's work dealt with individual atoms, matter is made up of many atoms interacting with one another. The properties of compounds can be very different from those of the atoms that join to form the molecules, and the properties of the same substance in liquid or solid form is very different in its gaseous state. Today physicists speak of *condensed matter* to distinguish the solid and liquid states, in which each atom or molecule is constantly influenced by its neighbors, from gases, in which atoms or molecules move almost independently from one another except when they collide; but for most of the 20th century, they focused attention separately on solids and liquids. As later chapters will make clear, research in what was then called *solid-state physics* produced a number of significant technological advances.

In broad terms, the distinction between a solid and a liquid is the arrangement of its atoms or molecules. Long before the 1910s, it was clear to scientists that most solids formed *crystals*. Gemstones and minerals were the most striking examples, but even common salt and sand had obvious sharp edges and could be cut (cleaved) more easily along certain directions than others. A number of different crystal types were recognized and described according to the pattern of the cleavage planes. A few substances, such as glass, did not have preferred directions. These were called *amorphous*, meaning "without form."

It was reasonable and natural to assume that a solid's crystalline behavior reflected a regular pattern in the way its atoms or molecules joined together and that liquids and amorphous solids did not have such regularity. So physicists began looking for tools that would enable them to discover the arrangements within crystals. They needed something that would be sensitive to something as small as the spacing between atoms in solids.

That something turned out to be X-rays. In 1912, German physicist Max von Laue (1879–1960) demonstrated that crystals would diffract, or spread out, a beam of X-rays. His discovery was similar to Thomas Young's 1801 discovery of interference in light. X-rays were coming to be understood as electromagnetic waves with wavelengths as small as the size of an atom. Building on this discovery, British physics professor William H. Bragg (1862–1942) and his son William L. (Lawrence) Bragg (1890–1971) developed techniques to deduce the internal arrangements of atoms or molecules in crystalline solids from the *X-ray diffraction* patterns that resulted when a beam of X-rays passed through them.

Physicists quickly recognized the importance of these discoveries. Laue was awarded the Nobel Prize in physics in 1914, followed by the Braggs a year later.

Astronomy and Cosmology

While many physicists were concerning themselves with phenomena at the smallest scale—the subatomic realm—others were looking at the largest objects in the universe, even the universe itself. The 1910s saw the first glimmerings of a subfield of physics that would become increasingly important throughout the 20th century. *Cosmology*, the study of the universe itself, relies on astronomical observations, but it is as distinct from astronomy as atomic physics is from chemistry. By the end of the century, cosmologists would find their questions leading them as often to the sub-subatomic as to the astronomical.

The first significant cosmological questions emerged from Albert Einstein's continuing work on relativity. His 1905 work in the field dealt with a special circumstance—namely, frames of reference whose relative motion is constant. As noted in the preceding chapter, that is why the work became known as the special theory of relativity. But what about the more general case, when the relative motion of two bodies or frames of reference is changing?

GENERAL RELATIVITY THOUGHT EXPERIMENT

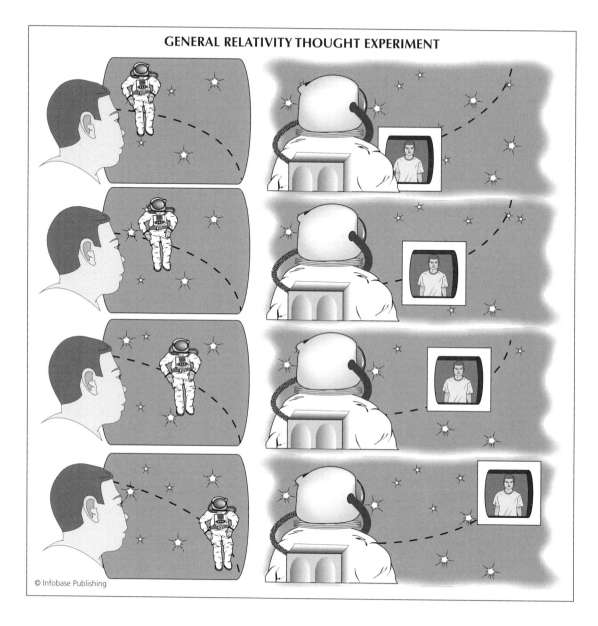

The General Theory of Relativity

Developing what has become known as general relativity took Einstein into unusual mathematical territory. Again, a thought experiment provides a useful window into the analysis. Suppose an observer in a laboratory is making measurements of the motion of falling bodies. The bodies are in a vacuum chamber, so there is no air resistance. They are also electrically neutral and nonmagnetic. The only force acting on them is gravity, and the observer's goal is to measure the effect of gravity.

The observer notes that their velocity changes in a particular way, which is the same for all such bodies regardless of differences in their mass. Their speed and direction parallel to the ground are unchanged, but their vertical motion is increasingly in the downward direction, changing at a rate of 32 feet per second (9.8 m/s) every second. The conclusion is clear. The observer and the laboratory are in a gravitational field with acceleration 32 feet per second per second, or one "g."

But an observer on the falling body would see it differently. To that observer, the lab observer and the laboratory are accelerating upward at one g. In fact, without looking outside the laboratory, neither observer would be unable to perform any experiment that distinguishes whether the laboratory is in a gravitational field or is an accelerated frame of reference.

Pursuing this line of thought led Einstein to unify space and time into a four-dimensional *spacetime*. People are used to envisioning position as defined by a three-dimensional space as a grid of imaginary meter sticks stretching to infinity in three directions, which can be specified at a given point on Earth as east-west, north-south, and up-down. Mathematicians like to call those directions the x, y, and z axes.

But there is a fourth dimension, time or the t axis, through which everything and everyone moves at the rate of one second per second. All observers measure the motion of a light beam through space at one light-second per second no matter whether the observers are accelerated or not, or equivalently, no matter what gravitational fields the observers are in.

To envision spacetime as Einstein described it, imagine a four-dimensional grid with markings along the x, y, z, and t axes. In human experience, people use different units of measurement for space (x, y, z) and time (t), but space and time can be combined into a single four-dimensional set of axes with the same units by multiplying time or dividing distance by the speed of light.

Einstein asked himself about the effect of mass in spacetime. He found an effect that could be envisioned as similar to what happens when a ball is placed on a taut rubber sheet. The ball stretches the sheet in its immediate surroundings. When two balls are on the sheet close together, the depressions they create merge, and they roll toward each other. Suddenly, gravitational attraction becomes the result of the distortions mass causes in the fabric of spacetime.

What does this mean for light? In mathematical terms, a light beam follows a channel in a spacetime distorted by gravity. Photons have no mass, otherwise they would have to travel slower than the speed of light according to the special theory of relativity, but Einstein's general theory of relativity leads to this conclusion: Massless entities are still affected by gravity.

That astonishing result says that a flashlight beam on Earth curves ever so slightly toward the ground, but the curvature is far too small

(Opposite page) *Einstein generalized the theory of relativity to include relative accelerations with thought experiments like this one. An observer in the lab sees an astronaut following a parabolic path downward like a falling ball on Earth, while the astronaut sees the observer to be following a parabolic path upward. They can make no measurements to distinguish whether the astronaut is falling under the influence of gravity or the laboratory is accelerating upward at that rate. Thus a gravitational field is equivalent to an accelerated frame of reference. Pursuing this idea led Einstein to combine space and time into a four-dimensional spacetime that distorts in the presence of mass. He concluded that gravity is the result of that distortion and thus affects light as well as matter.*

to be measured by our most sensitive scientific instruments. Still, when Einstein published his general theory of relativity in 1915, physicists were determined to test the prediction. Fortunately, the solar system provided a way to do that on rare occasions: during total solar eclipses.

If starlight on its way to Earth passes close to the Sun, solar gravity is large enough to divert the light's path by a measurable amount. During total solar eclipses, astronomers can see and measure the pattern of stars that would normally be invisible against a bright sky. Though such eclipses happen once or twice a year, they occur along narrow paths as the Moon's shadow sweeps across the Earth's surface. Totality lasts only a few minutes in any one place, so observing a total solar eclipse also requires a bit of good luck. Passing clouds can spoil an opportunity to see and photograph an event that people might travel halfway around the world to experience.

In the mid-1910s, wartime conditions also made it difficult to get equipment to the right places at the right times. It was not until 1919

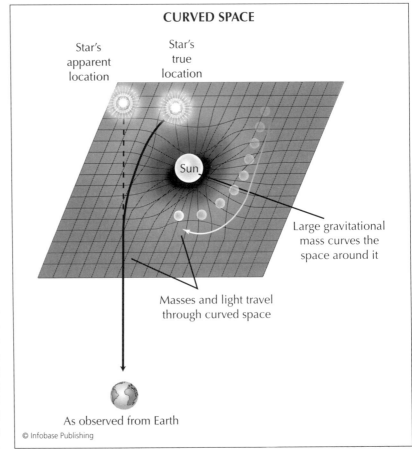

CURVED SPACE

Star's apparent location

Star's true location

Sun

Large gravitational mass curves the space around it

Masses and light travel through curved space

As observed from Earth

© Infobase Publishing

Einstein became world famous when one of the remarkable predictions of his general theory of relativity was shown to be correct during a total eclipse of the Sun in 1919. Stars in nearly the same direction as the Sun, normally hidden in the Sun's glare, became visible from Earth. Light from a star that passed close to the solar disk bent toward the Sun. Thus the star appeared to be shifted outward from its expected position. Astronomers measured the shifts during that eclipse and found they matched Einstein's predictions.

that two expeditions on opposite sides of the Atlantic Ocean—one on the Island of Principe off West Africa led by British astrophysicist Arthur Eddington (1882–1944) and the other in Sobral in northern Brazil led by British astronomer Andrew Crommelin (1865–1939)—were successful in photographing the stars near the solar disk. By comparing their observations to others at the time of year when those same stars are visible at night, they detected exactly the shift predicted by general relativity. Newspaper headlines around the world announced the confirmation that gravity affected the path of light. Einstein, as the scientist who made that improbable prediction on the basis of experiments he did in his head, became world-famous.

Of course, the bending of starlight was just one consequence of the even more sweeping idea that mass causes a curvature in the fabric of spacetime. In 1917, as he was exploring the implications of his new mathematical description, Einstein discovered that his theory predicted a universe that was steadily expanding or contracting. That troubled him. Geologists and biologists had been trying to determine the age of the Earth. Though there was still considerable disagreement as to the exact age of the planet, all agreed that it was many millions and possibly billions of years old. If the universe had been expanding for that long, most other stars would be too far from Earth to be seen. If it had been contracting, it would have long ago collapsed on itself. Yet the universe seemed to be quite stable.

Einstein also noticed that the mathematical solution to his equations included an apparently arbitrary value called the *cosmological constant*. Different values of that constant would lead to different rates of cosmic expansion or contraction. One particular value would lead to stability, and that was the one that nature had apparently settled on.

Discoveries in the 1920s would lead Einstein to view the cosmological constant as unnecessary, and he went to his grave believing it to be his "greatest mistake." But at the end of the 20th century, the cosmological constant made a comeback, and physicists began the 21st century hoping for another Einstein to come along to make sense of it all.

The Discovery of Galaxies

When Einstein spoke of the cosmos or the universe in 1917, his view of it was very different from the modern one. Besides stars and planets, telescopes revealed that the universe included some fuzzy objects known as spiral nebulae. Today we know that they are galaxies containing many millions or billions of stars, but then they were oddities awaiting explanation.

In 1914, American astronomer Vesto Slipher (1875–1969) was observing spiral nebulae at the Lowell Observatory in Flagstaff, Arizona. His telescope was equipped with a *spectroscope*, which enabled him to analyze starlight to identify the elements in the stars. Being a very hot body, the star emits a continuous spectrum like the one that led Max Planck to discover the quantum. However, the outer layers of stars contain gases that are cooler than the regions emitting most of the light. These cooler gases absorb those wavelengths of light that they themselves would emit as line spectra. That produces an absorption spectrum, dark lines on a bright background, like a photographic negative of the gases' emission spectra. From that absorption spectrum, Slipher would be able to determine the chemical elements present in those outermost stellar layers.

When he compared the line spectra of the spiral nebulae to known elements, he found an unexpected difference. The spacing of the lines matched the spectra of the expected elements, but the lines were shifted to slightly different wavelengths. The spectrum of the great nebula in Andromeda, which we now know is the nearest major galaxy to our own Milky Way, was shifted slightly toward the blue. Most of the others were redshifted.

Slipher realized that the shift was due to the Doppler effect, which is familiar to most people when it occurs in sound. When an emergency vehicle approaches and zips past a person with siren screaming, the siren's pitch drops. The pitch corresponds to the wavelength or frequency of sound waves passing the person's ears. Wave crests are compressed together when the vehicle is approaching, resulting in a higher pitch. As the vehicle moves away, the crests are spread out, and the pitch is lower.

Slipher realized that the blueshift in the spectrum of the Andromeda nebula meant that it is moving rapidly in our direction, while the redshifts signified that the other nebulae were moving away, also at very high speed. When Arthur Eddington heard about Slipher's results, he realized that the objects were probably also at vast distances from Earth and suggested that they were galaxies, vast systems of stars. That implied that the cosmos was far larger than anyone had previously considered. Almost all the lights in our night sky were stars in our own galaxy, which was only one of many in a vast universe.

Cosmic Rays

Austrian Victor Hess (1883–1964) was discovering the cosmos in a different way in the 1910s. He acted on Theodore Wulf's suggestion to do high-altitude measurements of the particles that seemed to be streaming through Earth's atmosphere from above. Ten times in 1911 and 1912, he loaded himself and radiation detectors into balloons that carried him to altitudes greater than 16,400 feet (5,000 m) above sea level.

This was quite a risky venture, but the instruments required a human operator, so he went. Above 3,300 feet (1,000 m), he discovered a significant increase in radiation compared to that at the surface. The higher he went, the more radiation he found. At 16,400 feet (5,000 m), he detected three to five times as much radiation as at sea level.

Victor Hess after his 1912 balloon flight, during which he discovered cosmic rays from space (National Geographic, courtesy Pierre Auger Observatory)

Hess concluded that powerful radiation, cosmic rays, streams down to Earth from outer space. Identifying this radiation would take many years, but it would eventually lead to profound new ideas about the subatomic world. As a result, Hess was awarded the Nobel Prize in physics in 1936.

New Theories, Techniques, and Technologies

While Einstein was exploring the frontiers of spacetime, Rutherford was probing the internals of atoms, Hess was capturing cosmic rays, and

Scientist of the Decade: Ernest Rutherford (1871–1937)

By most criteria, Ernest Rutherford could not have been more different from Albert Einstein. Einstein was the eldest of two children of an urban, European intellectual family. Rutherford was the fourth of 12 children growing up in rural New Zealand. Einstein explored new theories at a desk in a small office. Rutherford explored new phenomena in some of the world's best-equipped laboratories. Einstein's intellect was unappreciated before he burst to prominence. Rutherford seemed destined for success from the beginning of his schooling. Einstein did not win the Nobel Prize in physics until 16 years after his most significant work. Rutherford won the Nobel Prize in chemistry before he made what is arguably his greatest contribution to physical science.

The two physicists were also vastly different in appearance and manner. Einstein was unremarkable in stature, quiet, and modest. Rutherford was physically imposing, exceptionally ambitious, and had a booming voice. Yet they shared a goal to explore the essentials of physics without preconceived ideas. That open-mindedness enabled both men to recognize the unexpected. It led Einstein to reinterpret the laws of motion; the meaning of space and time; the nature of matter, energy, waves, and particles. It guided Rutherford's probe of the most basic components and structures of matter.

Rutherford was born in 1871 near the town of Nelson on New Zealand's South Island. He was an excellent student who, with financial sacrifices from his parents and scholarship aid, was able to afford a good local secondary school (Nelson College) and then to study at Canterbury College in Christchurch. There he showed not only an exceptional talent for experimental science but also an interest in working on the latest discoveries.

German physicist Heinrich Hertz (1857–1894) had recently learned to produce the electromagnetic waves that we now call radio, and Rutherford decided to measure their effect on magnetized steel needles. That work led him to invent a sensitive detector of the so-called Hertzian waves that had traveled over a long distance. This radio receiver soon became an important component in the communications revolution known as wireless

Ernest Rutherford, whose work led to an understanding of the internal structure of atoms (Smith Collection, Rare Book & Manuscript Library, University of Pennsylvania)

telegraphy that was sweeping the world and made Rutherford a prominent candidate in the 1895 competition for a major research scholarship to study in England. Unfortunately, the scholarship committee ranked him second to a chemist. But a stroke of good fortune soon followed. The chemist decided to marry and stay in New Zealand. Rutherford was offered the award and decided to work at Cambridge University's renowned Cavendish Laboratory led by J. J. Thomson.

Rutherford immediately set to work on more wireless experiments and continued to produce important results. But as his work became more significant technologically, it became less interesting as science. So he and Thomson began looking for a new field in which he might contribute. When word came of Röntgen's discovery of X-rays, they had their answer.

As part of his study of cathode rays that would soon lead to the discovery of the electron, Thomson had been investigating the phenomenon of *ionization*—the creation of electrically charged atoms—in gases. He could create uncontrollable high-voltage sparks or glows, but he was not able to create a steady ionic current that he could control and measure.

Röntgen had reported that when X-rays passed through gases, the application of an electric field to those gases would cause small electric currents to flow. Thomson suspected those currents were a stream of *ions*—exactly what he was looking to study. He assigned Rutherford the task of finding out if he was right. Rutherford confirmed Thomson's conjecture and immediately knew what to do next. He would see if the newfound phenomenon of radioactivity would also produce ions in gases. It did, so he set out to learn what radioactivity was and how it interacted with matter.

He began by putting aluminum foil between a piece of uranium and an ionization detector, adding one layer at a time. Each of the first few layers measurably reduced the ionization, but eventually, he reached a point where adding a single layer made little difference, even though a significant amount of the original radiation was still passing through. Rutherford concluded that radioactivity must have at least two components, one much more penetrating than the other. He named the two components alpha and beta rays after the first two letters of the Greek alphabet, with alpha rays being the component that was more easily blocked.

By 1898, Rutherford's name was becoming known throughout the world of physics, and he was offered a professorship and his own research laboratory at McGill University in Montreal. He soon began working with a young electrical engineer, R. B. Owens, who was studying radioactivity from thorium as Rutherford had done with uranium. Owens observed a peculiar effect: thorium radiation was sensitive to air currents in the lab.

Rutherford suspected that thorium was producing a radioactive gas. He designed experiments to test that hypothesis and found that he was correct. He also discovered two new mysteries. First, as that gas, which we now know was radon,

emitted alpha radiation, solid radioactive material began to accumulate on the walls of its container. Second, as he studied the radioactivity from the solid deposits, he found not only alpha and beta radiation but also a third, even more penetrating form of radioactivity, which he called gamma radiation.

These remarkable discoveries all took place within two years of Rutherford's arrival at McGill. By the summer of 1900, he was ready for a vacation. He traveled back to New Zealand to see his family and to marry his understandably impatient fiancée, who had endured numerous delays of her wedding date while her husband-to-be was in the midst of a brewing revolution in physics.

In September, Rutherford returned to Montreal with his bride. As he settled into a new home life, he knew he needed an additional person in his laboratory. He sought a skilled chemist to help him sort out the changes in chemical makeup that accompanied radioactive emissions. As noted in chapter 1, he teamed with Frederick Soddy, who demonstrated that they were observing chemical transformations unlike any ever seen. It was not the rearrangement of atoms to form new chemical compounds but rather radioactive transmutation of one element into another.

During the same years in which Einstein was challenging fundamental assumptions about space, time, matter, and energy, Rutherford was challenging the fundamental assumption of chemistry that one atom could not be changed into another. His description of transmutation earned him the Nobel Prize in chemistry in 1908, but his greatest accomplishments—the discovery of the atomic nucleus and the proton and the prediction of the neutron—lay ahead. (See chapters 1–4 for details.)

In addition to Rutherford's remarkable scientific achievements, he was also noted for his leadership that enhanced the quality of research wherever he worked. As noted in chapter 1, he was lured back to England from McGill in 1907 to lead a research program at the University of Manchester. He left Manchester in 1919 to succeed J. J. Thomson as Cavendish professor at Cambridge University, the most prestigious physics professorship in Britain. He remained at Cambridge until his death in 1937.

The laboratory for low temperature research of Heike Kamerlingh Onnes (front row, center) in Leiden, the Netherlands. In this laboratory, helium was liquefied (1908) and superconductivity was discovered (1911). (Kamerlingh Onnes Laboratorium, Leiden, courtesy AIP Emilio Segrè Visual Archives)

astronomers like Slipher and Eddington were redefining the limits of the cosmos, other physicists were probing different frontiers.

Superconductivity

For example, Heike Kamerlingh Onnes was investigating what happens to matter at the lowest temperatures ever achieved on Earth. Liquefying helium had been an outstanding accomplishment—it would earn him the Nobel Prize in physics for 1913—but that was merely the first step in his research. By 1911, it was time to immerse materials in liquid helium and measure properties such as electrical conductivity. Electric currents in metals were recognized to be flowing electrons, and physicists were striving to understand the internal structures of solids that affected the flow. They suspected that the thermal vibrations of atoms were a major impediment to current, and thus they expected that *electrical resistance* would steadily decrease as they cooled metals toward absolute zero.

As Kamerlingh Onnes cooled a thin wire of mercury, its electrical resistance decreased steadily in agreement with the theory until suddenly, at just below the temperature where helium became liquid, the mercury seemed to lose all of its resistance at once. He found he could start current flowing in a loop of mercury, cool it to below what is now called the critical temperature, remove the source of voltage, and the current would continue to flow.

As long as he kept the wire cool enough, the electrons kept flowing, even for hours, without a battery. But as soon as he allowed the temperature to rise above the critical temperature, the current would stop. Kamerlingh Onnes had discovered superconductivity. He investigated many different metals and found that superconductivity was a common phenomenon. The critical temperature varied from one metal to another, but it was always extremely low.

As remarkable as the discovery of superconductivity was, no one could develop a theory to explain the phenomenon until a 1957 discovery that led to a Nobel Prize. Thirty years after that, superconductivity surprised physicists again. This time, researchers observed the phenomenon at unexpectedly high (but still frigid) temperatures in a class of ceramics. That experimental result led to another Nobel Prize—and physicists still have not come up with a fully satisfactory theory for what causes it in those materials.

Continental Drift

In a decade full of discoveries in physics that changed the world, one proposed new theory about a changing world was widely criticized— even ridiculed. In 1915, German climatologist and geophysicist Alfred Wegener (1880–1930) published the first edition of *The Origin of the Continents and Oceans*, which laid out the theory of continental drift. Wegener relied on evidence from maps, geology, and paleontology. But because he was unable to propose a mechanism for the drifting of Earth's continents, proponents of existing theories prevailed in academic arguments.

Decades later, after Wegener's death, discoveries about Earth's interior validated his ideas, which turned out to be as revolutionary in his area of physics as Einstein's, Rutherford's, Bohr's, and Kamerlingh Onnes's were in theirs.

Further Reading

Books

Bodanis, David. *E=mc²: The Biography of the World's Most Famous Equation.* New York: Walker, 2001, and reissued 2005, with a new foreword by Simon Singh. A term-by-term discussion of the elements of Einstein's best-known formula.

Bortz, Fred. *The Neutron.* New York: Rosen Publishing, 2004. An easy-to-read history of the neutron and its applications.

———. *The Proton.* New York: Rosen Publishing, 2004. An easy-to-read history of the proton and its applications.

Calder, Nigel. *Einstein's Universe: The Layperson's Guide.* New York: Penguin, 2005. A reissue of a 1979 guide to relativity, with a new author's note and afterword.

Close, Frank, Michael Marten, and Christine Sutton. *The Particle Odyssey: A Journey to the Heart of Matter.* New York: Oxford University Press, 2002. A detailed and colorfully illustrated overview of the discovery of subatomic particles.

Cropper, William H. *Great Physicists: The Life and Times of Leading Physicists from Galileo to Hawking.* New York: Oxford University Press, 2001. The life and times of many great physicists, including Nernst, Einstein, Bohr, and Rutherford.

Einstein, Albert, with a new introduction by Brian Green. *The Meaning of Relativity.* 5th ed. 1954. Reprint, Princeton, N.J.: Princeton University Press, 2005. A readable presentation of Einstein's most famous theory in his own words.

Kragh, Helge. *Quantum Generations: A History of Physics in the Twentieth Century.* Princeton, N.J.: Princeton University Press, 1999. An in-depth history of 20th-century physics and physicists.

Lightman, Alan. *The Discoveries: Great Breakthroughs in 20th Century Science, Including the Original Papers.* New York: Pantheon, 2005. Includes Rutherford's paper on the atomic nucleus, von Laue's paper on X-ray diffraction and crystal structures, Bohr's paper on electron energy levels, and commentary on their significance.

Suplee, Curt. *Physics in the 20th Century.* New York: Harry N. Abrams, 1999. A pictorial history of 20th-century physics.

Web Sites

American Institute of Physics Center for History of Physics. Available online. URL: http://www.aip.org/history. Accessed March 27, 2006. Follow pull-down menu for special online exhibits on Albert Einstein, Marie Curie, the electron, and radioactivity, among other topics, or browse for a variety of written resources and images.

Nobelprize.org. Available online. URL: http://nobelprize.org. Accessed March 27, 2006. The official Web site of the Nobel Foundation contains brief biographies of Nobel Prize winners, summaries of their prize-winning work, and their acceptance speeches.

The Science Museum. Available online. URL: http://www.sciencemuseum.org.uk. Accessed March 27, 2006. A British online science education resource that includes useful exhibits on Atomic Firsts; Life, the Universe, and the Electron; Marie Curie and the History of Radioactivity; and many other topics discussed in this book.

The Science Shelf, Books for the World Year of Physics 2005. Available online. URL: http://www.scienceshelf.com/WorldYearofPhysics.htm. Accessed April 26, 2006. This page on the book review site of Fred Bortz has brief comments about a number of books published in recognition of the World Year of Physics, plus links to reviews of a number of other physics books for nonspecialist readers.

World Year of Physics 2005. Available online. URL: http://www.physics2005.org. Accessed March 27, 2006. An online resource developed in honor of the centennial of Albert Einstein's "Miracle Year."

3

1921–1930:
The Quantum Revolution

Few decades are as tumultuous as the 1920s turned out to be, both in physics and the world at large. The decade began in the aftermath of World War I, then called the Great War, and ended with a worldwide economic collapse that is still known as the Great Depression.

Although the war ended in 1918, its consequences had dramatic effects in international relations for many years. Though some people spoke

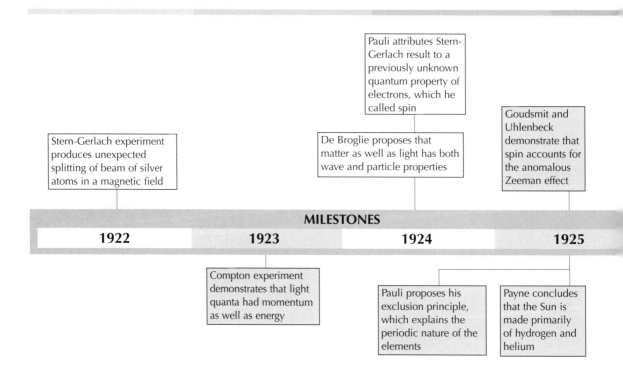

Pauli attributes Stern-Gerlach result to a previously unknown quantum property of electrons, which he called spin

Goudsmit and Uhlenbeck demonstrate that spin accounts for the anomalous Zeeman effect

Stern-Gerlach experiment produces unexpected splitting of beam of silver atoms in a magnetic field

De Broglie proposes that matter as well as light has both wave and particle properties

MILESTONES

| 1922 | 1923 | 1924 | 1925 |

Compton experiment demonstrates that light quanta had momentum as well as energy

Pauli proposes his exclusion principle, which explains the periodic nature of the elements

Payne concludes that the Sun is made primarily of hydrogen and helium

of it as "the war to end all wars," the 1919 Treaty of Versailles failed to achieve that objective. In redrawing the map of Europe, it created deep international resentments that continued to seethe. Rabid nationalism colored the relationships among citizens of different countries. It even divided physicists who, before the war, had eagerly cooperated in the pursuit of knowledge.

Despite such political obstacles, and despite the remarkable changes that had already transformed physics during the first two decades of the century, new ideas about the nature of matter and energy came faster than ever in the 1920s. Fueling that acceleration was the realization that the quantum was at the core of understanding the physical universe.

Astonishingly, the greatest developments in quantum physics emerged from Germany, a badly defeated, political outcast nation whose economy was in shambles. The sciences of physics and chemistry flourished there in the 1920s as they had before the war—despite the barring of German scientists from major international conferences for several years after hostilities ended. With a sense of national pride, Einstein was touted as a German genius when he won the 1921 Nobel Prize in physics (for his explanation of the photoelectric effect as a quantum phenomenon), even

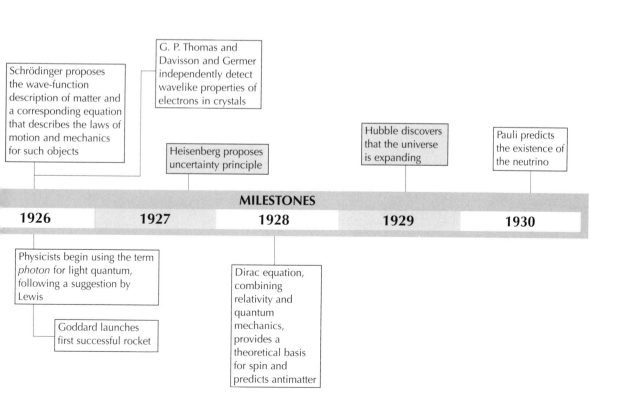

Schrödinger proposes the wave-function description of matter and a corresponding equation that describes the laws of motion and mechanics for such objects

G. P. Thomas and Davisson and Germer independently detect wavelike properties of electrons in crystals

Heisenberg proposes uncertainty principle

Hubble discovers that the universe is expanding

Pauli predicts the existence of the neutrino

MILESTONES

| 1926 | 1927 | 1928 | 1929 | 1930 |

Physicists begin using the term *photon* for light quantum, following a suggestion by Lewis

Goddard launches first successful rocket

Dirac equation, combining relativity and quantum mechanics, provides a theoretical basis for spin and predicts antimatter

though he had once given up German citizenship. Ironically, he would renounce it again in the 1930s as a Jew fleeing Nazi persecution.

From the Bohr Atom to Quantum Mechanics

Much of the development of quantum physics was driven by efforts to understand the line spectra of various elements. Bohr's atomic theory was remarkably successful at predicting the hydrogen spectrum under normal circumstances, but it needed to be modified to explain the phenomenon of *spectral line splitting*. Applying electric and magnetic fields causes some lines in the hydrogen spectrum to split into clusters of lines, each with a frequency slightly different from the original. As the strength of the applied field increases, the shift in frequency becomes larger.

The electron orbits of Bohr's basic theory were described by a single quantum number, n, and the frequency of a given line in the spectrum could be calculated from the n-values of the orbits before and after the electron's transition. To explain line splitting, Arnold Sommerfeld (1868–1951), a physics professor at the University of Munich in Germany, extended the Bohr model of electrons in atoms in a particularly important way. Chronologically, Sommerfeld's extension belongs in chapter 2, since he did much of this work between 1913 and 1916, but it is included here for a unified presentation of the flowering of quantum physics. Sommerfeld's innovation was to add the equivalent of Kepler's first planetary law to Bohr's theory; namely, that their orbits are ellipses. Circular orbits, which Bohr was using in his calculations, are special cases when the two axes of the ellipse are equal.

Sommerfeld's calculations considered Bohr's n to be the "principal" *quantum number* but added a second "azimuthal" quantum number, k, which corresponds to the elongation of the ellipse. For circular orbits, k is zero, but Sommerfeld's theory also allowed for larger values of k and thus more elongated orbits. His mathematics permitted elliptical orbits described by k-values that are whole numbers less than n. For instance, instead of having a single circular orbit for $n=3$, Sommerfeld's mathematics permitted a circle for $k=0$ and two ellipses with elongations corresponding to $k=1$ and $k=2$. He soon added a third "magnetic" quantum number, m. Envisioning the nucleus as a sphere with a north-south axis, the theory permits m to take on whole-number values from zero through k. The m-values correspond to different inclinations of the electron's orbit between polar and equatorial. The value of m is either positive or negative, depending on whether the orbit is clockwise or counterclockwise when viewed from above the north pole.

In the absence of an applied electric or magnetic field, all electron orbits in a hydrogen atom with the same principal quantum number have the same energy no matter what their k- and m-values. Thus, for example, all electrons that drop from orbits with $n=3$ to orbits with $n=2$ produce light quanta of the same frequency. But in the presence of an electric field, the orbital energies, and thus the frequency of resulting the light quanta, depend on the elongation of the elliptical orbits (as specified by their k-values) before and after the orbital transition. That results in spectral line splitting in high electric fields, a phenomenon first observed by German physicist Johannes Stark (1874–1957) in 1913 and not explained successfully until Sommerfeld's computations.

The magnetic quantum number accounts for spectral line splitting in magnetic fields, first noted by Dutch physicist Pieter Zeeman (1865–1943) in sodium light in 1896. The Bohr-Sommerfeld theory explains the Zeeman effect in hydrogen this way: An orbiting electron can be considered a tiny loop of electric current and therefore acts as an electromagnet. The direction of the orbit, clockwise or counterclockwise (corresponding to positive or negative values of m), determines the direction in which that tiny electromagnet's north and south poles point. In the presence of an applied magnetic field, a clockwise orbit has a different energy from an otherwise identical counterclockwise one, because it takes work to align the electromagnet's poles against the field direction. The greater the field, the more pronounced the difference. The Zeeman effect is also greatest when the inclination of the electron's orbital plane (corresponding to the values of m) is closest to equatorial and least when it is closest to polar.

Three quantum numbers were sufficient to explain most line spectra, but some puzzles remained. One of these was the so-called anomalous

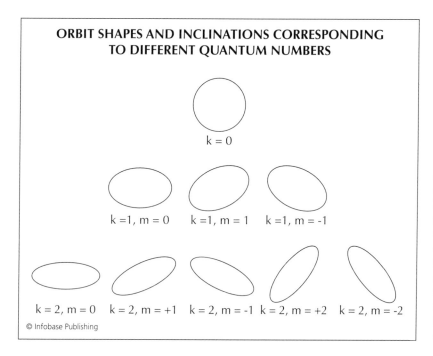

ORBIT SHAPES AND INCLINATIONS CORRESPONDING TO DIFFERENT QUANTUM NUMBERS

$k = 0$

$k = 1, m = 0$ $k = 1, m = 1$ $k = 1, m = -1$

$k = 2, m = 0$ $k = 2, m = +1$ $k = 2, m = -1$ $k = 2, m = +2$ $k = 2, m = -2$

© Infobase Publishing

To explain spectral line splitting, Arthur Sommerfeld refined Bohr's atomic theory by including two new quantum numbers beyond the principal quantum number n: the azimuthal quantum number, k, corresponding to the elongation of the ellipse; and the magnetic quantum number, m, corresponding to the angle the long axis of the ellipse makes with an external magnetic field.

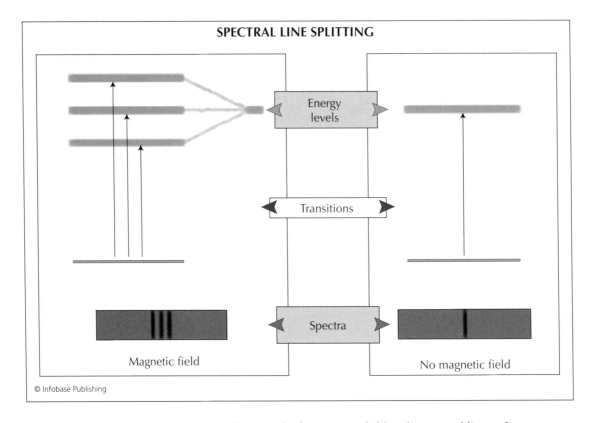

In the presence of an electric or magnetic field, electron energy levels for each value of the principal quantum number, n, split into sets of energy levels, which results in corresponding sets of lines in the atomic spectrum. One type of splitting became known as the anomalous Zeeman effect because it could not be explained by the azimuthal and magnetic quantum numbers, k and m, alone. It led Wolfgang Pauli to propose the property of spin, its corresponding quantum number s, and the exclusion principle that explained the periodic table of the elements.

Zeeman effect, in which magnetic fields split spectral lines of some atoms into more branches than could be explained by n, k, and m alone. An even more striking result arose from an experiment by German physicists Otto Stern (1888–1969) and Walther Gerlach (1889–1979) in 1922. They passed a beam of silver atoms through a magnetic field that got stronger from bottom to top along the vertical direction. If the total magnetization of each atom was the sum of the m-values of all 47 of its electrons, they expected that the magnetic field would spread the narrow beam into a wide band. Instead, it split into two bunches, each as narrow as the original beam. The magnetization of each silver atom apparently was the same. If it was aligned with the magnetic field, the atoms deflected in one direction; if it was opposite to the field, they deflected in the opposite direction.

A number of theoretical physicists, most notably Austrian-born Wolfgang Pauli (1900–58) at the University of Hamburg, Germany, struggled to explain that result. In 1924, Pauli proposed that the magnetism of an electron results not only from its orbital motion like a planet around the Sun but also from its "spin" or the rotation around its own axis. The Stern-Gerlach experiment suggested that an electron has a *spin* quantum number, s, that can take on only the values $+\frac{1}{2}$ and

-½, commonly envisioned as spin up and spin down. In a silver atom, 46 of the 47 electrons in the silver atom seemed to group themselves into 23 up-down pairs whose opposite magnetizations added up to zero. The one left over would give the atom a net spin of ½, which could be either up or down.

The next year, Samuel Goudsmit (1902–78) and George Uhlenbeck (1900–88) of the University of Leyden in the Netherlands demonstrated mathematically that electron spin could account for the anomalous Zeeman effect. With evidence accumulating that spin was a real physical property of electrons, Pauli made this daring assumption about the apparent pairing of spin-up and spin-down electrons in an atom: No two electrons in an atom can have the same quantum state, that is, the same set of four quantum numbers (n, k, m, s). He called this the exclusion principle, and it led to his winning the 1945 Nobel Prize in physics. According to Pauli's theory, the electrons in an atom fill energy levels as spin-up/spin-down pairs from the lowest energy upward, starting with $n=1$, $k=0$, $m=0$; then $n=2$, $k=0$, $m=0$; then $n=2$, $k=1$, $m=0$; then $n=2$, $k=1$, $m=+/-1$; and so forth. The $n=1$ level would thus hold one pair of electrons. The next level, with principal quantum number $n=2$, fills up with eight electrons. The $n=3$ level holds 18 electrons, eight having $k=0$ or 1, and 10 having $k=2$.

Pauli began to see a pattern that reminded him of the periodic table of the elements. The noble gases helium, neon, argon, krypton, xenon, and radon have 2, 10, 18, 36, 54, and 86 electrons, which correspond to filled energy levels up to certain n/k values. Helium, for example, had two $n=1/k=0$ electrons, one with spin up and the other with spin down. Neon is helium plus all possible $n=2$ electrons. Argon is neon plus the $n=3$ electrons with $k=0$ or 1, and so forth. These noble gases can be thought of as closed *shells* of paired electrons. Other elements have electrons outside of those closed shells, which determine their chemical valence and influence the way they form compounds and crystals. For example, the alkali metals (sodium, potassium, rubidium, cesium, francium) all have one electron more than a closed shell and behave very similarly in chemical interactions. Likewise, the halide nonmetals (fluorine, chlorine, bromine, iodine, and astatine) are one electron short of being closed shells.

Thus Pauli's innovations of the spin quantum number, s, and the exclusion principle did much more than explain magnetic effects such as the anomalous Zeeman effect and the Stern-Gerlach experiment. They also shed light on a half-century old puzzle; they were the natural laws underlying the periodic behavior of the elements. With Sommerfeld's and Pauli's refinements, the Bohr model of the atom had come a long way. Still, many physicists were troubled by a major unsolved problem in atomic theory, one that had plagued them ever since Rutherford first proposed the planetary model. According to Maxwell's equations, orbiting electrons should radiate electromagnetic waves. Why should that requirement be suspended for certain orbits? Likewise, the exclusion principle itself seemed arbitrary. Spectral evidence made it clear that no two electrons could occupy the same quantum state, but nothing in the theory suggested why that should be so.

To answer the radiation question, they turned to a revolutionary idea proposed in 1924 by a young Frenchman named Louis de Broglie (1892–1987). De Broglie began by noting that physics had recently undergone a radical reinterpretation of the nature of electromagnetic energy (such as light). For centuries, they had been asking an either-or question: Is light a wave or a stream of particles? Young's famous 1801 experiment had convinced them that light was a wave phenomenon, and Maxwell's equations showed that light waves were electromagnetic. That view held firmly until the very last year of the 19th century, when Planck's mathematical invention—the quantum—suggested that light had a particle nature. Soon afterward, the discovery of the photoelectric effect led Einstein to declare that the answer to the either-or question about light was "both."

If electromagnetic waves such as light could behave like streams of particles, did those particles carry momentum as well as energy? Einstein's theory of relativity said they did, but it was not until 1923 that the momentum of light quanta was observed in an experiment. American physicist Arthur Holly Compton (1892–1962; Nobel Prize in physics, 1927) was studying a narrow beam of X-rays passing through blocks of graphite. All the incoming X-rays had the same frequency, but the outgoing X-rays did not. The graphite spread out the beam, and the outgoing X-rays had lower frequencies than the incoming one. The farther the X-ray beam scattered away from its original direction, the greater was the reduction in its frequency. It was as if he had shined pure violet light through a piece of glass and produced a spread-out spectrum with violet in the center and bands of color spreading outward starting with blue, progressing through green, yellow, orange, and finally reaching red on the outside.

X-rays were clearly scattering from something and giving up increasing amounts of energy as the scattering angle got larger. What were they interacting with in the graphite, and how were they interacting? Compton decided that the interaction could be considered a collision between two particles, an X-ray quantum moving at the speed of light and an electron moving so much slower that he could consider it to be at rest. For the quantum, he used the energy given by Planck's law and the momentum predicted by relativity theory. He then applied the principles of conservation of momentum and energy to compute the relationship between energy of the outgoing quantum and its direction. His result matched what he saw in his experiment. Thus Compton's experiment had demonstrated that light quanta had momentum as well as energy like any other kind of particle. (By 1926, scientists were calling the light quantum a photon, following usage suggested by American chemist Gilbert Lewis [1875–1946].)

With the light quantum's dual wave-particle nature firmly established, de Broglie proposed that the same wave-particle duality is true of electrons or anything else physicists normally characterize as particles. He then developed a theory that used electron waves to eliminate the problem of non-radiating orbits. He rewrote Planck's formula for light quanta in a different form. His formula related the wavelength to a quantum's momentum rather than its energy. Next he applied that

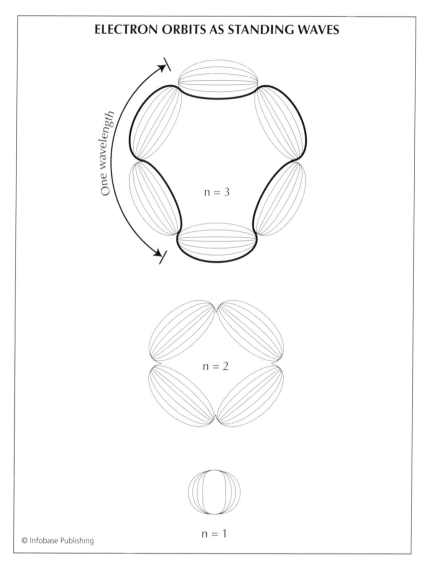

ELECTRON ORBITS AS STANDING WAVES

One wavelength

n = 3

n = 2

n = 1

© Infobase Publishing

Louis de Broglie set physicists on a new path when he extended the dual wave-particle nature of light to matter as well. He proposed that an electron had a wavelength that depended on its momentum, and the allowed orbits of electrons in atoms corresponded to standing waves like the tones produced by a musical instrument.

formula to electrons, and the result was striking. For a hydrogen atom, the circumference of Bohr's lowest-energy electron orbit was exactly equal to that electron's wavelength. For the second-lowest orbit, the circumference was two wavelengths, and so forth. The circumference of Bohr's nth orbit was exactly n wavelengths of an electron in that orbit.

If electrons have wave properties, it makes sense for electrons to settle into orbits that contain whole numbers of wavelengths. Similar *standing wave* or *resonance* phenomena are common in the physical world. For instance, an organ pipe produces a fundamental tone that corresponds to a wavelength equal to the distance between its two openings. It also produces overtones that give it its distinctive timbre, a mixture of notes with shorter wavelengths that fit exactly two, three, four, or a larger whole number of times into that distance.

If the electron is a standing wave rather than an orbiting body, it does not need to move to maintain its place in the atom, and thus it is not accelerated. Without acceleration, there is no radiation. De Broglie's idea had eliminated a serious objection to the planetary model of the atom, but at the cost of replacing electron particles with electron waves. Most physicists struggled with that idea because it went against their intuition about the particle makeup of matter. Still, they had already accepted the dual nature of light because their experiments told them it was so. Before discounting de Broglie's theory, they knew it was time to see where it might lead.

They followed it in two directions: a mathematical path and an experimental one. In 1926, German physicist Erwin Schrödinger (1887–1961) found a way to express the equations of motion, or mechanics, in a form that accommodated waves. Instead of describing the position of a particle as a point in space, he described it as a *wave function*. The wave function is a mathematical expression that when graphed is a set of wiggles that are concentrated around a particular point in space. That point would be the position of the object if it were a particle. But the wiggles spread out from that point, indicating that the object has a broader, wavelike presence. Just as Newton's and Einstein's laws of motion predict the exact path of a particle, Schrödinger's equation allows physicists to describe the corresponding wave function and how it changes over time.

The equation proved to be very successful, and many physicists adopted the wave-function interpretation that removed the distinction between particles and waves. In the new way of viewing things, particles and waves are the same, though people perceive them differently. Objects that people call particles have tightly confined wave functions. If the wave functions are spread out, then people observe them as waves instead. But, by the late 1920s, no matter how people perceived them, the behavior of wave functions was known to obey the laws of a new branch of physics known as *quantum mechanics*.

Erwin Schrödinger built on de Broglie's wave-particle duality to formulate an equation that is central to quantum mechanics. (AIP Meggers Gallery of Nobel Laureates)

Understanding the Quantum Universe

Even though quantum mechanics provided a theoretical foundation, many physicists could not accept the dual nature of electrons without experimental confirmation. That did not take long to emerge. The first signs came in 1926, when American physicists Clinton Davisson (1881–1958) and Lester Germer (1896–1971) found some puzzling results in an experiment to study the crystal structure of nickel. They were bouncing electrons from the surface of a piece of the metal and found unexplained variations in their results. At a scientific conference, Davisson described his experiments to other physicists, and some suggested that he might be seeing wavelike behavior. He went back to his laboratory and refined the experiment. The next year, Davisson and Germer had the answer. The nickel atoms formed layers in the crystal, and they were clearly observing interference patterns produced by reflections of electron waves from different layers.

At the same time, British physicist George P. Thomson (1892–1975), son of the famous J. J. Thomson, was doing experiments with electron beams passing through very thin crystals. He, too, observed interference. In an oddity of history, Thomson, whose father had won the 1906 Nobel Prize in physics for demonstrating that cathode rays were not waves but a stream of particles, shared the same prize in 1937 with Davisson for discovering that those same particles had wave properties after all.

As is often the case in theoretical physics, there was more than one mathematical way to describe quantum phenomena. While Schrödinger was developing his wave mechanics, another German physicist named Werner Heisenberg (1901–76) had already begun using a different technique based on matrices (singular: matrix) and vectors. A matrix is a rows-and-columns arrangement of numbers or mathematical expressions, and a vector is a set of numbers or expressions arranged in a row or column. The most familiar kind of vector describes the distance and direction from one point in space to another by three numbers corresponding to the difference along the east-west, north-south, and up-down axes.

Whatever was calculated by Schrödinger's equation could also be calculated by the Heisenberg formulation, but the different mathematical methods produced different physical insights. The Heisenberg method does not require particles to have wavelike natures, but it leads to similar conclusions. In 1927, Heisenberg produced one of the most profound conclusions about the quantum universe and gave new significance to Planck's constant. It is known as the *uncertainty principle*, and it continues to guide physicists into new territory even today.

Briefly, Heisenberg noted that the quantum nature of the universe imposes limits on how precisely the position and momentum (or velocity) of an object can be measured. Any measurement of an object's position or velocity is uncertain because no instrument is perfect, but that's not what the uncertainty principle is about. The uncertainty principle means that there is a natural limit to how precisely those quantities can be measured at the same time, no matter how well-made the instruments.

One way to look at the uncertainty principle is this: The act of measurement affects the quantity being measured. To measure the position or momentum of a body, an instrument must interact with the body—which

Werner Heisenberg's matrix approach to quantum mechanics complemented Schrödinger's equation and led to the famous uncertainty principle that often carries his name. (AIP Emilio Segrè Visual Archives, Segrè Collection)

means exerting at least a very small force on it. That interaction changes both the position and momentum of the body, introducing an uncertainty in both. The problem cannot be solved by making the interaction weaker. While that would reduce the amount of uncertainty caused by the interaction, it would also produce a weaker signal, which would increase the uncertainty of the instrument itself. Another way to think of it is to consider what it means to measure both position and momentum of an object at the same time. To measure momentum means measuring the rate its position is changing. To increase the precision of an instrument that determines the object's position, the instrument must detect the particle over a very short time interval. A short interaction requires more intensity, which causes a greater uncertainty in the object's measured momentum. Likewise, an instrument that measures the momentum more precisely needs to interact with the object over an interval of time, thus leading to a greater uncertainty in its position.

Heisenberg expressed the uncertainty principle in mathematical terms, but it can be stated as follows: The uncertainty in position times the uncertainty in momentum is never less than Planck's constant. For an electron in an atom, the uncertainty of its position corresponds to its orbit size or its wavelength, so for all practical purposes, it can be considered a wave. Trying to treat that electron as a particle by measuring its position more precisely would have a strange result. The uncertainty principle would force such a large uncertainty in the electron's momentum that its orbit would be impossible to determine. Heisenberg's approach does not force a wave-particle duality, but it has the same result.

Heisenberg also found a similar relationship between the uncertainty in an object's energy and the time interval needed to measure that energy. Later in the century, physicists would use that principle as they developed cosmological theories to describe the origin of the universe from apparent nothingness. It would also guide them in their understanding of the nature of the fundamental forces binding atoms and nuclei together. For this work, Heisenberg was awarded the Nobel Prize in physics in 1932.

The mathematics of Heisenberg and Schrödinger also led to an explanation of the exclusion principle. When physicists used the equations to determine wave functions of systems of spin-½ particles like the electrons in an atom, the only possible solutions had no more than one electron in each quantum state. The exclusion principle followed directly from the addition of spin to the set of quantum numbers needed to describe an electron's state in an atom.

Besides their work on quantum theory in the 1920s, Heisenberg and Pauli were also making major contributions to understanding the magnetic properties of matter. Heisenberg's work was especially important for understanding the phenomenon of *ferromagnetism*, or the ability of materials such as iron to develop permanent magnetism. Pauli worked on paramagnetism, which is a common property of many materials when placed in a magnetic field. They become magnetized in proportion to the strength of the applied field, but the magnetism disappears as soon as the field does.

Both of those forms of magnetism result from the electron's spin. The applied field creates a force that tends to align the spins, which leads to paramagnetic behavior. But in certain crystal alignments, Heisenberg noted, the electrons' magnetic poles would align with each other, producing regions where the magnetism persists even after the field that created the alignment was removed. That phenomenon is the source of ferromagnetism.

Relativity, Spin, Beta Decay, and Predicted Particles

When Schrödinger developed his wave equation, he began with the same mathematical relationship between energy and momentum that came from Newton's laws of motion. As successful as the theory seemed to be, physicists realized that it still needed to be modified for the same reason that Einstein had to restate Newton's laws in his theory of relativity. Furthermore, Schrödinger's equation, when applied to electrons, addressed their orbital motion, corresponding to quantum numbers n, k, and m, but it said nothing at all about spin.

Theoretical physicists wondered if those two deficiencies might be related, and in 1928, British physicist Paul A. M. Dirac (1902–84) came up with a relativistic wave equation that showed they were. Even though Dirac had not included spin in his calculations, his equation, when applied to an electron in a magnetic field, predicted that spin would exist—a very satisfying result. But that was not its only prediction. Every wave function that satisfied Dirac's formulation was four-dimensional instead of three-dimensional, combining space and time into spacetime the way general relativity did. Furthermore, each wave-function solution was paired with another that also satisfied the Dirac equation. The second solution represented a particle that was identical to the first in every way but carried an opposite charge. Today we call such particles *antimatter.*

Dirac, like most physicists, reacted to this odd prediction by calling it a mathematical fluke that had nothing to do with the real universe. He was wrong! His comment turned out to be eerily similar to Max Planck's reaction to his mathematical invention of the light quantum in 1900. Five years after Planck's mathematical invention of the quantum, Einstein realized that quanta of light were real and had already been detected in the photoelectric effect. Similarly, as the next chapter notes, the first particle of antimatter, a positively charged antielectron (or positron), was discovered in 1932, four years after Dirac developed his equation. The next year, he and Schrödinger shared the Nobel Prize in physics.

Before the third decade of the century ended, Pauli would also predict an undiscovered subatomic particle. In his case, it did not result from a mathematical oddity but rather from his quirky imagination. That occurs often in physics, where quirkiness and originality frequently go hand in hand, especially when experimental results cry out for a new way of viewing the physical world. In this case, the experiments were studies of the energy beta particles emitted from radioactive materials. When a particular radioactive substance emits alpha particles, they all carry the same energy. The same is true of gamma rays. But beta decay is different: The emitted particles have a range of energies from near zero to a maximum value.

Because the law of conservation of energy was so well established, physicists realized that the energy of the emitted radiation must correspond to a change in the mass of the radioactive nucleus. The nucleus transforms itself during the emission, starting as one isotope with a particular mass and ending up as a different isotope with a smaller mass, and the loss of mass shows up as the energy of the emitted radiation.

So why is the energy of all the emitted beta particles not the same? Pauli came up with what he called "a desperate remedy" in a letter he wrote to the attendees of a 1930 conference in Tübingen, Germany. He wrote the letter because he was unable to attend the meeting, but he wanted to discuss his idea. His premise was that in beta decay, the nucleus splits into three parts, not two, but the third piece had not yet been detected. The undetected particle would have to be electrically neutral and have very little mass. Furthermore, because quantum mechanics had led physicists to new conservation laws, including conservation of spin, the unknown particle would have to carry spin ½. Finally, it would have to pass through matter easily with interactions so rare that they had yet to be seen. In his letter, Pauli admitted, "At the moment, I don't trust myself enough to publish anything about this idea," but he thought the people at the conference might come up with a way of detecting these tiny, electrically neutral particles that he called "neutrons." (The much more massive neutron that Rutherford had predicted had not yet been detected, so the name was still unclaimed by any known subatomic particle.) It was a provocative suggestion that would bear fruit in the next decade—but by then the particle would have a different name, the *neutrino*.

Subatomic Physics

Though the flowering of quantum mechanics dominated physics in the 1920s, important work was also going on in other areas. Cambridge University's Cavendish Laboratory, under the direction of Rutherford, continued its leadership in the study of subatomic phenomena. In particular, Cavendish scientists improved the equipment and techniques to observe the paths of radioactive emissions and other subatomic particles. The lab had been a leader in those techniques since at least 1911, when Charles T. R. Wilson (1869–1959) developed the first *cloud chamber*. He based it on a discovery he made on a meteorological project in the late 1890s. He wanted to understand the way water droplets form in the atmosphere, so he built a chamber filled with very humid air, then caused it to cool rapidly by expanding it. He noticed that the droplets formed most readily around ions. Since radioactive emissions ionize the air they pass through, the cloud chamber revealed their paths.

The cloud chamber became an important tool in the 1920s as Cavendish scientists developed improved ways of controlling and automating its operation, and Wilson's invention was recognized with the Nobel Prize in physics in 1927. While some physicists continued to use it to study radioactivity and collisions between nuclei and alpha particles or protons, others were discovering different applications. In particular, in 1930 at Caltech (the California Institute of Technology), Professor Robert Millikan (1868–1953; winner of the 1923 Nobel Prize in physics for a 1909 experiment that measured the electric charge carried by electrons) assigned a research student named Carl Anderson (1905–91) the task of developing a cloud chamber to study cosmic rays. The results, to be described in the next chapter, were remarkable.

Stars, Galaxies, and Rockets

Two discoveries in astronomy during the 1920s turned out to be particularly important for the direction of physics later in the century. American astronomer Edwin Hubble's (1889–1953) systematic survey of the sky led him to powerful conclusions. In 1927, after seeing distant galaxies in every direction, he realized that the Sun must also be part of a galaxy, and all the stars of the night sky are also part of that galaxy seen from the Earth's vantage point. The Milky Way, which stretches across Earth's night sky and gives the galaxy its name, is a band of distant stars at the galactic edge. As Hubble measured the spectra of other galaxies, he discovered that, with the notable exception of nearby galaxies such as the Andromeda nebula and the Magellanic clouds, the light of all the others was redshifted. The size of a galaxy's redshift tells astronomers how fast it and the Milky Way are moving apart. Hubble discovered that more distant galaxies had greater redshifts than closer ones and thus were receding faster. Furthermore, the speed of recession was proportional to the distance: Comparing the redshift of two galaxies, one twice as far away from the Milky Way as the other, the more distant one was receding twice as fast; those three times as distant receded at three times the speed.

In 1929, Hubble concluded that the proportionality between redshift and distance was evidence that the universe was expanding. Perhaps Einstein's cosmological constant was not necessary after all. At that point in the century, it was still too soon to state that conclusion firmly. However, it was clear that Hubble's discovery had opened up a whole new field of inquiry, now known as cosmology, or the study of the universe itself.

Meanwhile, at Harvard University, Cecelia Payne (1900–79; later Payne-Gaposchkin) was working on her Ph.D. under the supervision of noted astronomer Henry Norris Russell (1877–1957). Her analysis of the solar

Understanding Wave Functions

Erwin Schrödinger's famous wave equation is based on a particular way of describing the motion of a body in a force field, such as a planet moving in the gravitational field of the Sun or an electron moving in the electric field of a nucleus. In both cases, the force field can be thought of as a conical well with curved sides of a particular shape called a hyperbola. The body can be viewed as a ball rolling without friction along the inside walls of that well. Without friction, the body's total mechanical energy (potential plus kinetic) is conserved.

Solving the equations of motions mathematically, physicists find certain allowed paths that the body may follow, depending on its total mechanical energy. A mass of any size from a tiny grain to a giant planet, moving under the influence of the Sun's gravity but without enough energy to escape the solar system, will follow an elliptical path. Mathematically, the mass is represented as a particle with a definite position and momentum at a definite time. The resulting solutions to the equations are ellipses of all sizes and elongations. Thinking in terms of a ball rolling along the inside of a well with curved walls, it can have a circular orbit if it stays at a particular level. Or it can move inward and outward on an elliptical path, slowing down as it climbs the walls until it reaches its maximum distance, then speeding up as in moves inward. Eventually, it reaches a minimum distance where its speed is fast enough for it to climb outward again. More energetic particles move in larger ellipses, but all shapes and elongations of the ellipses, with all energies up to escape energy, are possible. (If the energy is greater than the escape energy, it follows a hyperbolic path that goes outward indefinitely.)

However, in the quantum realm, physicists were finding that electrons could not be considered particles. They could get away with describing bodies orbiting the Sun as having a definite position and momentum because the quantum wavelength, according to de Broglie's formula, was unimaginably smaller than the body itself. (The larger the momentum, the smaller the wavelength; so planets have much smaller wavelengths than subatomic particles.) But electron wavelengths are comparable to the size of their orbits, which means their wave nature dominates within the atom. By representing the electrons as fuzzy wave functions instead of sharp particles, Schrödinger's equation provided physicists with a way to determine the allowed orbits. They

spectrum led her to the conclusion that the Sun was made primarily of hydrogen and helium. That conclusion conflicted with earlier research by Russell and other notable scientists, who had determined that the Sun consisted primarily of iron. So in 1925, when the time came for her to present her thesis (a book-length discussion of her research project) for approval by a committee of professors, she faced an unfriendly audience. They could not dispute that her conclusion was in agreement with her data, but they forced her to add a statement to the thesis that some other phenomenon was probably responsible. If she had defied them and insisted that the Sun was not mostly iron, she would not have been awarded the degree.

That story sheds as much light on the secondary status of female scientists at that time as it does on the physics of stars. Had Cecelia Payne been male, it is unlikely that she would have been asked to back

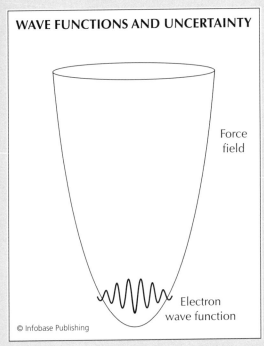

WAVE FUNCTIONS AND UNCERTAINTY

Force field

Electron wave function

© Infobase Publishing

Schrödinger's equation describes particles by their wave functions, which means they cannot be precisely located in space nor can their momentum be precisely determined. Heisenberg's matrix analysis produces the same conclusion in the form of the uncertainty principle.

found that only certain orbits and energy levels were possible. Corresponding to each orbit was a wave function that described the electron not as a particle having a definite momentum at a definite position but rather a wavelike entity with a certain probability of being measured in a given region. Likewise, the electron's wave function yielded a certain probability of its momentum being within a certain range.

In an atom, the possible wave functions were standing waves, like the tones of an organ pipe or a violin string. The wavelike electron is likely to be found anywhere in its orbital region. In intermediate circumstances, such as in the case shown here, the electron still has wavelike properties, but the peak in the wave function makes it possible to treat it more like a particle. Chances are much greater that the electron will be detected near the peak of its wave function, but it is still possible to find it near one of the wave function's tails. The importance of this will become apparent in chapters 5, 6, and 9.

away from her conclusions. The treatment of her thesis is a black mark on Russell's otherwise distinguished career. But to his credit, he later acknowledged his error and set about to repair the damage. As soon as he saw other research that bolstered Payne's original conclusions, he became a powerful advocate of her work, which ultimately led to a deep understanding of the life cycle of stars and the origins of the elements.

The 1920s will also be remembered for the birth of rocketry. Scientists in many countries were actively trying to develop chemical rockets, but Robert Goddard (1882–1945) of the United States is credited with the first successful launch in 1926. Rocketry would have profound implications later in the century, both in military applications and civilian space exploration.

Scientist of the Decade: Wolfgang Pauli (1900–1958)

Choosing a featured scientist from among all the notable physicists whose work contributed to quantum theory is not an easy task, especially since many of them continued to contribute to physics in later years. However, historical records and correspondence of that period leave little doubt that most physicists considered Wolfgang Ernst Pauli to be in a class by himself.

Pauli was born in Vienna, Austria, on April 25, 1900, the son of Wolfgang Joseph Pauli, a professor of physical chemistry at the University of Vienna, and Bertha Schütz Pauli, a newspaper correspondent from a prominent Vienna musical family. Wolfgang Joseph, whose name was originally Pascheles, had grown up in a respected Jewish family from Prague. Religion was not important in his life, and he knew he would have an easier time in his academic career if neither his name nor his religious practice was Jewish. So he changed his name to Pauli and converted to Roman Catholicism when he became a professor in Vienna.

Young Wolfgang was a brilliant student and often found his classes at the Döblinger Gymnasium less than challenging. When they became particularly dull, he would read Einstein's recently published papers on general relativity. He published his first paper in a physics journal on that subject at the age of 18, two months after

Wolfgang Pauli, discoverer of electron spin and the exclusion principle. His brilliance earned him a distinguished professorship while still in his twenties. (AIP Emilio Segrè Visual Archives, Goudsmit Collection)

graduation. That fall, he began studying quantum mechanics with Arnold Sommerfeld at the University of Munich, who assigned the gifted student the task of writing an encyclopedia article

Further Reading

Books

Bortz, Fred. *The Neutrino.* New York: Rosen Publishing, 2004. An easy-to-read history of the neutrino and its significance.

Cassidy, David. *Uncertainty: The Life and Science of Werner Heisenberg.* New York: W. H. Freeman, 1991. An interesting personal history of Heisenberg's life and science, with the theme of uncertainty in both.

Chown, Marcus. *The Magic Furnace: The Search for the Origin of Atoms.* New York: Oxford University Press, 2001. A readable history of the quest to

on relativity. He worked on the article while doing his doctoral research, completing his thesis in 1921 and the 237-page encyclopedia entry two months later. Sommerfeld called it "simply masterful," an opinion that Einstein shared.

Later that year, Pauli joined the research group of noted professor Max Born at the University of Göttingen, also in Germany, where Born judged him "undoubtedly a genius of the highest order." A year later, Pauli moved to Neils Bohr's Institute in Copenhagen, Denmark. Both Bohr and Pauli loved a good argument about physics. They agreed that a critical conversation was the best way to refine an idea, and Pauli was quickly gaining a reputation as a critic who spoke his mind quite directly. Even after Pauli moved to Hamburg and then, at age 28, to a distinguished professorship at the Swiss Technical University (ETH) in Zurich, he and Bohr conducted a remarkable correspondence, in which they continued to rely on each other for criticism.

Pauli was not one to watch his sharp tongue when discussing work he viewed as substandard, and some of his comments are legendary. After reading a paper that he judged of little value and poorly written, he commented, "It is not even wrong." And he once told another colleague, "I do not mind if you think slowly, but I do object when you publish more quickly than you think."

Still, he was unfailingly honest in his opinions and often could see more deeply into a theory than the physicist who devised it. When it came to new ideas in quantum mechanics, no one considered the work complete without Pauli's approval. Even when he was not present, they would ask each other, "What would Pauli think?"

Pauli's most significant contribution to physics was the exclusion principle, which still carries his name, but there was a running joke among physicists about "the Pauli effect." If he showed up in a laboratory, equipment would fail inexplicably. Coincidences like that seemed to follow him, including at a memorable conference when other physicists had rigged a chandelier to come crashing down when he entered the room. The rigging got stuck, and the joke was on the ones who planned to play it.

After joining the ETH, with the exception of five years at the Institute for Advanced Study at Princeton University during World War II, Pauli continued to live and work in Zurich until his death on December 15, 1958. Soon after that, physicists invented one last Pauli story. They described Pauli's first meeting with God, in which he asked for an explanation for the value of a particular physical constant. God went to the blackboard and started writing. Pauli studied the equations and soon began to shake his head.

understand the composition of the universe, including a discussion of the work of Cecelia Payne-Gaposchkin.

Close, Frank, Michael Marten, and Christine Sutton. *The Particle Odyssey: A Journey to the Heart of Matter.* New York: Oxford University Press, 2002. A detailed and colorfully illustrated overview of the discovery of subatomic particles.

Cropper, William H. *Great Physicists: The Life and Times of Leading Physicists from Galileo to Hawking.* New York: Oxford University Press, 2001. The life and times of many great physicists, including Bohr, Rutherford, Pauli, Heisenberg, Schrödinger, de Broglie, Dirac, and Hubble.

Gribbin, John, with Mary Gribbin. *Stardust: Supernovae and Life; The Cosmic Connection*. New Haven, Conn.: Yale University Press, 2001. Covers similar material as Marcus Chown's *The Magic Furnace* (above), with a greater emphasis on science and a lesser emphasis on history.

Kragh, Helge. *Quantum Generations: A History of Physics in the Twentieth Century*. Princeton, N.J.: Princeton University Press, 1999. An in-depth history of 20th-century physics and physicists.

Lightman, Alan. *The Discoveries: Great Breakthroughs in 20th Century Science, Including the Original Papers*. New York: Pantheon, 2005. Includes Heisenberg's paper on the uncertainty principle and Hubble's paper on the expansion of the universe, plus commentary on their significance.

Moore, Walter. *Schrödinger: Life and Thought*. Cambridge: Cambridge University Press, 1989. A biography that captures the human and scientific complexities of the man who captured the wave-particle duality of matter and energy in a famous equation.

Suplee, Curt. *Physics in the 20th Century*. New York: Harry N. Abrams, 1999. A pictorial history of 20th-century physics.

Web Sites

American Institute of Physics, Center for History of Physics. Available online. URL: http://www.aip.org/history. Accessed March 27, 2006. Follow pull-down menu for special online exhibits or browse for a variety of written resources and images.

Nobelprize.org. Available online. URL: http://nobelprize.org. Accessed March 27, 2006. The official Web site of the Nobel Foundation contains brief biographies of Nobel Prize winners, summaries of their prize-winning work, and their acceptance speeches.

The Science Museum. Available online. URL: http://www.sciencemuseum.org.uk. Accessed March 27, 2006. A British online science education resource that includes useful exhibits on many topics discussed in this book.

The Science Shelf, Books for the World Year of Physics 2005. Available online. URL: http://www.scienceshelf.com/WorldYearofPhysics.htm. Accessed April 26, 2006. This page on the book review site of Fred Bortz has brief comments about a number of books published in recognition of the World Year of Physics, plus links to reviews of a number of other physics books for nonspecialist readers.

World Year of Physics 2005. Available online. URL: http://www.physics2005.org. Accessed March 27, 2006. An online resource developed in honor of the centennial of Albert Einstein's "Miracle Year."

4

1931–1940:
Particles and Politics

As the 1920s ended and the 1930s began, the physics spotlight shifted from the theorists, who had developed quantum mechanics, to the experimentalists and observational scientists who were discovering the subatomic world. Meanwhile, the political skies were darkening in Europe as Adolf Hitler (1889–1945) and the National Socialist (Nazi) Party took power first in Germany and then in Austria. The party's philosophy of racial purity was well known, but most intellectuals doubted Hitler could turn hatred of so-called inferior people and races into national policy.

They were tragically wrong. The economic woes of the Great Depression and the humiliation of Germany's defeat in the Great War left many ordinary Germans looking for a scapegoat. An undercurrent of anti-Semitism—prejudice against Jews—had long simmered in Europe, so it was easy for Hitler to point the finger of blame at them. Anti-Semitic sentiments soon became law. Jews were barred from certain professions and stripped of many of their rights as citizens. In the face of Nazi intimidation and power, even those who held no ill will against Jews remained silent. By 1938, Nazi mobs were destroying Jewish homes and businesses, and the government was seizing Jewish property. In 1939, Hitler's army began invading neighboring countries, and the world was once again at war.

As had been the case 20 years earlier, the open culture of physics research was in conflict with nationalism. Many of the leading physicists in the German-speaking regions of Europe were Jewish (like Einstein) or had Jewish ancestry (like Pauli). As Hitler's power grew during the 1930s, many of them fled to England, Scandinavia, or the United States. Those physicists who remained in Germany, including Heisenberg, had to accommodate their work to the goals of the Third Reich, as the German government came to be known. New technologies based on applications of physics took on profound importance for both sides as the world moved toward war. Perhaps the most significant discovery was nuclear fission, observed in a German laboratory and explained by a recently exiled member of the team, a Jewish-born woman physicist by the name of Lise Meitner (1878–1968).

Inside the Nucleus

Wolfgang Pauli's famous letter to the 1930 Tübingen conference (see chapter 3) was addressed directly to Lise Meitner and Hans Geiger and indirectly to the other "Radioactive Ladies and Gentlemen" in attendance. And although the attendees included the world's greatest experts in experiments dealing with beta decay, not one of them was able to devise an apparatus to detect the elusive particles that he called neutrons.

Still, if those undetected particles did not exist, physicists faced an even more desperate alternative: abandoning the law of conservation of energy at the subatomic level. Pauli's proposal may have seemed outrageous, but it was the best they had. So while experimentalists pondered how they might catch those tiny sprites of matter, theorists worked on refining their theories of beta decay in nuclei.

As is often the case in science, the first hints of the solution came from work that seemed to be unrelated. For more than a decade, Ernest Rutherford had used the term *neutron* differently. His neutrons were not the tiny particles that Pauli had proposed but rather neutral particles comparable in mass to protons. In his theory, neutrons and protons accounted for the mass of a nucleus. Most physicists rejected that idea, believing that nuclei were composed of protons and electrons. The pres-

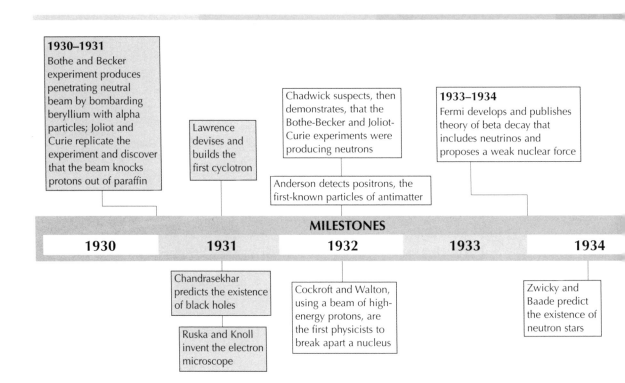

1930–1931
Bothe and Becker experiment produces penetrating neutral beam by bombarding beryllium with alpha particles; Joliot and Curie replicate the experiment and discover that the beam knocks protons out of paraffin

Lawrence devises and builds the first cyclotron

Chadwick suspects, then demonstrates, that the Bothe-Becker and Joliot-Curie experiments were producing neutrons

1933–1934
Fermi develops and publishes theory of beta decay that includes neutrinos and proposes a weak nuclear force

Anderson detects positrons, the first-known particles of antimatter

MILESTONES

1930	1931	1932	1933	1934

Chandrasekhar predicts the existence of black holes

Ruska and Knoll invent the electron microscope

Cockroft and Walton, using a beam of high-energy protons, are the first physicists to break apart a nucleus

Zwicky and Baade predict the existence of neutron stars

ence of electrons within the nucleus accounted for the phenomenon of beta decay, they said. Rutherford disagreed. He was still convinced that confining a proton and an electron within a minuscule nucleus would result in such an enormous electrical attraction that they would unite as a single neutral particle.

A 1930 experiment by German physicist Walther Bothe (1891–1957) and his student Herbert Becker provided the first hint that Rutherford might be right, although they did not recognize it at the time. They bombarded the light metal beryllium with a beam of alpha particles and detected a highly penetrating neutral beam coming out. They presumed that beam to be gamma rays. The French husband-and-wife team of Irène Curie (1897–1956; daughter of Pierre and Marie Curie) and Frédéric Joliot (1900–58) followed up the Bothe-Becker experiment. They, too, assumed the outgoing beam was gamma rays but were surprised to discover that it was able to knock protons out of paraffin, a compound rich in hydrogen. They published their results in January 1932, and Rutherford's colleague James Chadwick (1891–1974) at the Cavendish Laboratory immediately suspected that the beam was made of neutrons. To test this idea, he allowed the neutral emission to collide with hydrogen, helium, and nitrogen gases. By measuring the recoil of the molecules of those gases, he was able to determine the momentum

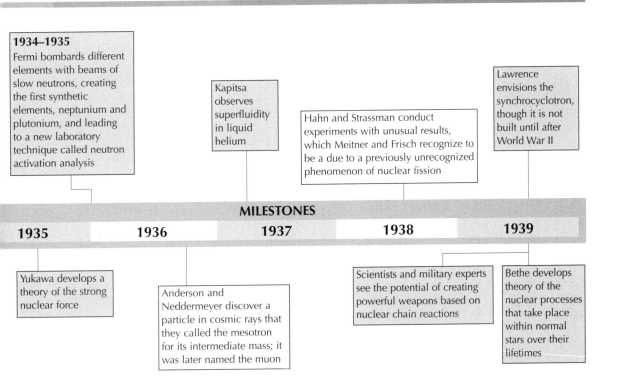

1934–1935
Fermi bombards different elements with beams of slow neutrons, creating the first synthetic elements, neptunium and plutonium, and leading to a new laboratory technique called neutron activation analysis

Kapitsa observes superfluidity in liquid helium

Hahn and Strassman conduct experiments with unusual results, which Meitner and Frisch recognize to be a due to a previously unrecognized phenomenon of nuclear fission

Lawrence envisions the synchrocyclotron, though it is not built until after World War II

MILESTONES

1935   1936   1937   1938   1939

Yukawa develops a theory of the strong nuclear force

Anderson and Neddermeyer discover a particle in cosmic rays that they called the mesotron for its intermediate mass; it was later named the muon

Scientists and military experts see the potential of creating powerful weapons based on nuclear chain reactions

Bethe develops theory of the nuclear processes that take place within normal stars over their lifetimes

and energy transferred by the beam. The result was clear: The beam was composed not of gamma-ray photons but of electrically neutral particles with a mass comparable to that of a proton. For discovering the neutron, Chadwick won the Nobel Prize in physics in 1935, the same year the Joliot-Curies shared it for chemistry.

The basic makeup of atoms was known at last. At the heart of an atom was a nucleus composed of protons and neutrons that determined its atomic number and atomic mass. Surrounding that nucleus were electrons that determined its chemical behavior. However, major questions about nuclei still remained unanswered. What held them together; what caused some of them to emit alpha, beta, and gamma radiation; and where did the electrons of beta radiation come from?

Before physicists understood the makeup of the nucleus, gravity and electromagnetism were sufficient to explain all known interactions between physical bodies. But a few simple calculations told them that the gravitational attraction among the protons and neutrons of a nucleus would be vastly overwhelmed by the much greater electrical repulsion between protons. There had to be a previously unrecognized nuclear binding force.

That force might explain alpha decay: Sets of two protons and two neutrons might bind together with particular intensity and then break away as a unit from the parent nucleus. But it said nothing about beta decay. Italian physicist Enrico Fermi (1901–54), working at the University of Rome, was the first to come up with a theory about beta decay. It included Pauli's "neutron," which he called the neutrino, Italian for "little neutron." He wrote a paper and submitted it to the British journal *Nature* in December 1933, but it was turned down as too speculative. The next year, it was published in two installments in the German journal *Zeitschrift für Physik* (which translates roughly as "Physics Times"), and it is generally regarded as the greatest work of one of the greatest physicists of the 20th century. The theory described beta decay as the transformation of a neutron into a proton by the emission of an electron and a neutrino.

Fermi's theory relied on a second previously unknown force, this one responsible for holding the neutron together. That force would cause the reverse of beta decay—the formation of a neutron from a proton, an electron, and a neutrino—when those particles came close enough together to recombine. He realized that such recombination always had to happen inside a nonradioactive nucleus. But within a radioactive nucleus, the electron and neutrino would sometimes escape. When they did, a proton would be left in place of a neutron, producing a daughter nucleus with less mass than the parent. The lost mass appeared as an equivalent amount of kinetic energy (according to Einstein's famous equation) that was carried off by the electron and neutrino. The neutrino was necessary, Fermi explained, because quantum mechanics required not only energy but also spin to be conserved. A neutron has spin $\frac{1}{2}$, as do both the elec-

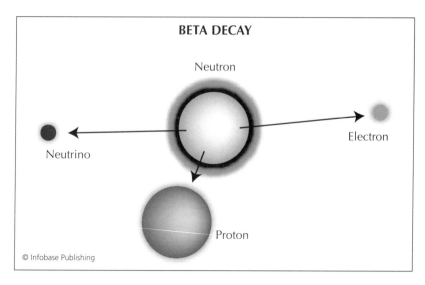

BETA DECAY

Neutron

Neutrino

Electron

Proton

© Infobase Publishing

Relying on the principles of conservation of energy and momentum and adding conservation of spin, Enrico Fermi attributed the missing energy in beta decay to a very tiny, electrically neutral particle that he named the "neutrino." Though neutrinos were not detected until the 1950s, indirect experimental evidence that they existed was strong.

tron and proton. Since the resulting particles had to have the same total spin as the neutron that decayed, another spin ½ particle had to be emitted. Consider the case where the decaying neutron had spin up. Then two of the three emitted particles would have spin up, while the third would have spin down, producing a net up spin of ½.

Fermi's proposed force was soon called the *weak nuclear force* because the force needed to hold the nucleus together was much stronger. At that point, no one had proposed a theory to explain the *strong nuclear force*, but physicists knew it had to be unusual compared to the well-understood electromagnetic and gravitational interactions. Gravitational, electric, and magnetic forces all decreased with distance according to an inverse-square relationship. If the separation between two interacting bodies doubles, the force between them drops by a factor of four (two squared). If their separation triples, the force decreases to one-ninth as much. Because electromagnetic and gravitational interactions between bodies are both inverse-square forces, the ratio between the two forces remains the same, no matter how close or far apart the two bodies are. For example, the electric repulsion between two protons always overwhelms their gravitational attraction.

Because nuclei hold together, the strong nuclear force is clearly much stronger than electromagnetic forces when protons and neutrons (which together are called *nucleons*) are within nuclear distances. But at larger distances, electromagnetic forces must be stronger than nuclear forces. Otherwise all the nucleons in the universe would be drawn together into one giant nucleus. So the strong nuclear force must drop off more rapidly with increasing distance than an inverse-square relationship. Among the theoretical physicists trying to develop a theory to explain the strong force was Hideki Yukawa (1907–81) of Kyoto, Japan. In 1935, he proposed that the strong force was the result of nucleons exchanging subatomic particles of a kind not yet detected. The particles had a mass about one-seventh of a nucleon, or about 250 times that of an electron. Yukawa's theory and its predicted particles were neither well known nor fully appreciated in Europe and America. As noted in the next section, that would soon change, thanks to some unexpected discoveries in cosmic-ray research.

New Subatomic Particles

With the detection of the neutron and strong evidence that neutrinos were also real, physicists realized that the subatomic world was more complicated than they had imagined. Could the discoveries of those two neutral particles be the beginning of a trend? Research into cosmic rays in the 1930s would show that the answer to that question was a resounding yes!

As noted in chapter 3, American physicist Carl Anderson at Caltech had begun his research into cosmic rays in 1930 as a student of the renowned professor Robert Millikan. Anderson soon emerged as one of the world's leading cosmic-ray researchers. Unlike the earlier scientists who detected cosmic rays high above the Earth's surface, Anderson built equipment to study them in a ground-based laboratory. Millikan had read about some interesting cloud chamber tracks in 1927–28 experiments by Dmitri Skobeltzyn in Leningrad, Soviet Union (now known by its original name of Saint Petersburg, Russia).

Skobeltzyn had been studying the interaction of gamma rays with electrons. He placed his cloud chamber in a strong magnetic field, which caused electrically charged particles to curve. Charged particles created ions as they passed through the chamber, and when the pressure was suddenly reduced, tiny droplets of water vapor condensed around the ions, revealing the path the particles had followed. The direction of curvature indicated whether they were positively or negatively charged, and the sharpness of the curvature allowed him to compute their momentum. The greater their momentum, the less they curved. Neutral particles did not create any ions, so they left no tracks. Besides noting the paths made by electrons, Skobeltzyn reported a few paths that were almost straight. Whatever was causing them was moving very fast. He speculated that the particles were electrons that had been struck by very high-energy cosmic gamma rays, but he was unable to say more than that.

Anderson's project was to build a cloud chamber that was able to study those high-energy particles. It would need much greater magnetic fields than Skobeltzyn's. With the help of some engineers, he designed and built a very powerful water-cooled electromagnet. His first results came in 1932, and they were remarkable. Physicists had assumed that cosmic rays were mainly electrons knocked out of atoms by gamma rays from

The first image of Carl D. Anderson's position track, which confirmed the existence of antiparticles (C. D. Anderson, courtesy AIP Emilio Segrè Visual Archives)

outer space, but Anderson detected equal numbers of positive and negative particles. At first, Millikan thought the positive particles were slow-moving protons. But slow-moving particles leave denser tracks than the ones Anderson was seeing. Anderson suggested that they were electrons moving upward rather than downward as they expected. The paths were visible, but there was nothing to tell the experimenters which way the particle had traveled. They needed better measurements to be sure.

Anderson modified his experimental setup by adding a lead plate to slow down the particles as they passed through. That way, he could tell whether they were moving upward or downward. The result showed that neither Anderson nor Millikan was entirely correct, nor was either entirely wrong. The particles were positive and moving downward as Millikan had said, but, as Anderson had thought, they were much smaller and fast moving. How small? Their mass turned out to be the same as electrons. They were *positrons*, the antimatter counterpart of electrons that Dirac's theory had predicted but that no one had expected to exist! For that discovery, Anderson shared the 1936 Nobel Prize in physics with

Victor Hess, who had confirmed the existence of cosmic rays by bravely riding to high altitudes in a hot-air balloon in 1912.

The year 1936 was memorable for Anderson in another way. He and his colleague Seth Neddermeyer were studying cosmic rays in their cloud chamber when they observed a new kind of particle with a mass between that of the electron and the proton. They called it the *mesotron* to signify its intermediate mass. Mesotrons came in both positive and negative varieties, and both had the same mass, which was close to the value Yukawa expected for the particles in his theory.

This discovery brought well-deserved attention to the Japanese theorist's work, but the more Anderson and others looked at mesotrons, the less the particles fit Yukawa's theory. If they were responsible for the nuclear force, they ought to have powerful interactions with nuclei, but no such interactions were seen. "Who ordered that?" American nuclear physicist Isidor I. Rabi famously asked when it became clear that mesotrons behaved like oversize electrons and positrons. That question remained open until 1947, when Yukawa's predicted particles were finally found (see the next chapter). The mesotron was renamed the *muon*, because scientists were calling Yukawa's strong-force particles *mesons*. Later the term *meson* was extended to include a whole family of subatomic particles, including Yukawa's, which were renamed *pions* or pi mesons. In 1949, Yukawa's work was recognized with the Nobel Prize in physics.

Particle Accelerators

By the early 1930s, physicists were no longer satisfied with the high-energy particles from radioactive decay and cosmic rays that nature had to offer. They wanted to create more energetic particles and more intense, controllable beams for their experiments. At the Cavendish Laboratory in 1932, John Cockcroft (1897–1967) and Ernest Walton (1903–95) built a machine that created a high-energy beam of protons that could collide with other atoms and break their nuclei apart. Although Cockcroft and Walton became the first to split the atom, a machine devised and built the previous year by Berkeley physics professor Ernest Orlando Lawrence (1901–58) soon eclipsed that achievement. Lawrence called his device the *cyclotron*, and many of the great particle accelerators in use today are based on Lawrence's original ideas.

By the end of the decade, a number of cyclotron laboratories had been built around the world, and the race was on to build bigger and more energetic machines. Lawrence, who in 1939 won the Nobel Prize in physics for his invention (12 years before Cockcroft and Walton shared the same award), secured the funding to build a machine that he expected to create a beam of alpha particles so energetic that they would free Yukawa's mesons from a nucleus. Because of World War II, his work was delayed. That was probably fortunate, because Lawrence was about to

Ernest Orlando Lawrence at the control table of an early cyclotron (AIP Emilio Segrè Visual Archives)

hit a technological obstacle that could not be overcome without advances made during the war.

The principle behind the cyclotron's operation is fairly simple to explain. It consists of a pancake-shaped vacuum chamber separated into two D-shaped regions. Particles are injected into the chamber near its center at one side of the gap. The assembly is surrounded by a powerful electromagnet that creates a vertical magnetic field in the chamber. An alternating electrical source creates an electric field across the gap. Thus the gap behaves as a battery that reverses its polarity at regular intervals.

Inside the cyclotron, the magnetic field causes the charged particles to follow circular paths. As they accelerate to higher speeds, they move in larger circles, but each circle takes the same amount of time. Taking advantage of that fact, Lawrence designed his machine so the frequency of the alternating current exactly matched the frequency of the charged particles' trips around the circle. An alpha particle that reached the positive side of the gap just as the electric field peaked would be accelerated across the gap and then go in a larger semicircle at higher speed around the other "dee." It would reach the gap again just as the electric field peaked in the opposite direction and accelerate across to the first side. If there were 1,000 volts across the gap, then after 1,000 crossings, it would be as if the alpha particle had been accelerated by 1 million (1,000 × 1,000) volts. The particle's energy would increase with each loop until the radius of its path

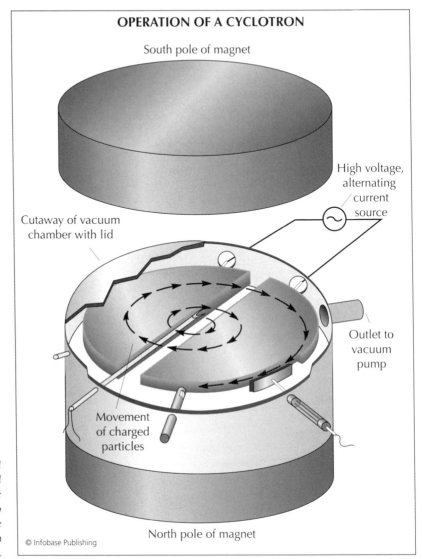

OPERATION OF A CYCLOTRON

South pole of magnet

High voltage, alternating current source

Cutaway of vacuum chamber with lid

Outlet to vacuum pump

Movement of charged particles

North pole of magnet

© Infobase Publishing

Cyclotrons produced controlled beams of high-energy charged particles by using large magnetic fields to force them to follow circular paths and large electric fields to accelerate them twice on every trip around.

was the same as the radius of the chamber. At that point, it would leave the cyclotron and head for its target.

To give a particle higher energy, either the cyclotron would have to be bigger or the magnetic field would have to be stronger. (A higher magnetic field produces a tighter curvature at the same speed.) Another factor limiting the energy that the machine could deliver was due to relativity. An energetic particle's mass begins to increase notably as its speed becomes a significant fraction of the speed of light. At that point, much of the energy that the particle gains crossing the gap goes into increased mass instead of increased speed, and the particle takes longer to complete a larger circle. The frequency of its circular motion no longer matches the alternating electric field. Each trip across the gap produces a smaller increase in energy than the one before it, and soon there is no increase at all. Until scientists were able to devise a way to synchronize the frequency of the alternating electric with the particle's motion, the energy the cyclotron could deliver was limited by relativity. For Lawrence to build the powerful cyclotron he envisioned in 1939, he would need a new generation of accelerator technology, which became known as *synchrocyclotrons* when they were finally built after the war.

Artificial Radioactivity and Nuclear Fission

Physicists typically build their careers around either experimental or theoretical work, but Enrico Fermi was adept in both. Having developed a theory that explained the phenomenon of beta decay, he turned to experimental work to illuminate the physical forces at work within the nucleus.

Recent reports from the Joliot-Curie lab in Paris had piqued his curiosity. They had been bombarding various elements with energetic alpha particles, and they created radioactive isotopes that had never before been seen. Fermi thought about what it took for that the process to work. Fermi realized that when alpha particles approach target nuclei, they experience very large repulsive electric forces. Unless they were heading for a near head-on collision, the alphas would probably be deflected away before they got close enough to cause nuclear transformations. The process had to be very inefficient. Since the idea was to probe inside nuclei with subatomic bullets, he decided that he would eliminate the electrical repulsion by using a beam of neutrons.

A systematic scientist, Fermi started with hydrogen (actually water) and worked his way up the periodic table. He had nothing to show for his work and was nearly ready to give up after testing nitrogen, atomic number 7, but he decided to try one more. He skipped number 8, oxygen, since nothing had shown up in his experiments sending neutron beams into water, and he moved on to number 9, fluorine. This time, the neutrons combined with a normal fluorine nucleus to produce a radioactive isotope. With that promising result under their belts, Fermi and his colleagues began extensive research into the interaction of neutron beams with various nuclei.

They soon had some peculiar results to explain. When bombarding silver, they observed more intense radioactivity when the target was on a wooden laboratory bench rather than a marble one. Fermi's first thought was to put a wedge-shaped piece of lead between the source of the beam and the target. But something was troubling him, and he insisted that the lead had to be carefully machined. Then, without waiting for the lead to come back from the machine shop, Fermi acted on what he described to an interviewer as an impulse. He "immediately took some old piece of

Enrico Fermi, whose brilliance in both theoretical and experimental physics led to the understanding of beta decay and the first controlled nuclear reaction (NARA, courtesy AIP Emilio Segrè Visual Archives)

paraffin and placed it where the lead was to have been." The result was a strong increase in radioactivity.

A few hours later, he had figured out what was happening. The neutrons in the original beam were moving so fast that they would most often zip by without being captured. Bouncing a neutron off a heavy nucleus first, as in lead or the atoms in the marble table, would make little difference. It would change direction, but its speed would remain essentially the same, like a ball bouncing off a wall. However, paraffin and wood contain many hydrogen atoms. A neutron that hits a hydrogen nucleus—a proton—would behave like a billiard ball that hits another.

It could easily transfer most of its energy to the proton, slowing down enough for the silver nucleus to capture it.

The paraffin or the wooden table acted as what nuclear scientists now call a moderator, transforming fast neutrons into slow ones. The phenomenon led to a new technique called *neutron activation analysis* that is still used today to determine the chemical and isotopic makeup of a substance. Fermi and his group laid the groundwork for that analytical method by studying the neutron bombardment of the entire periodic table of elements and measuring the radioactivity that resulted. When they bombarded uranium 238 nuclei (92 protons and 146 neutrons) with slow neutrons in 1934, the resulting radiation did not match anything they had seen before. In a 1935 publication, Fermi described three separate emissions, which he surmised were the result of decays from uranium 239 (92 protons, 147 neutrons, produced from the capture of a neutron by uranium 238) and its radioactive successors. He theorized that the first decay produced a beta particle and a new radioactive nucleus with 93 protons and 146 neutrons (later named neptunium). The second decay, also a beta, produced a nucleus with 94 protons and 145 neutrons (later named plutonium), which would then decay to uranium 235 by emitting an alpha particle.

Fermi's group was unable to do the chemical analysis necessary to demonstrate that they had indeed created nuclei of new elements. The new atoms would have to be separated from the much larger concentration of uranium, and that would be difficult because of their presumed rapid radioactive decay into a different element with different chemical properties. The three emissions had half-lives—the time in which half of the nuclei decay—of 15 seconds, 13 minutes, and 100 minutes. Still, the results were so striking that Fermi was awarded the Nobel Prize in physics in 1938 for the discovery of new radioactive elements. Ironically, although Fermi richly deserved the prize since the neutron bombardments had surely produced the nuclei he described, the radioactive emissions he measured came from unknown radioactive isotopes of familiar elements produced by a different nuclear process—fission—that was still unknown. When the half-lives of uranium 239, neptunium 239, and plutonium 239 were finally measured, they were found to be 23.5 minutes, 2.35 days, and 24,360 years, respectively.

Another irony is that a German chemist named Ida Noddack (1896–1978) had criticized Fermi's assumption that the radiation came from new elements above uranium in an article in the German journal *Zeitschrift fur angewandte Chemie* (Journal of Applied Chemistry). She argued that the uranium nuclei could have broken up into several large fragments instead. She did not have additional evidence to support her alternate hypothesis of *fission* (although she did not use that term), and her reputation had been tainted by an earlier incorrect claim to a significant discovery. Thus most people accepted Fermi's explanation, and the discovery of fission went to others, as noted below.

Fermi's research into *transuranic elements* stimulated a lot of research elsewhere, including in the Paris lab of Irène Joliot-Curie. She and her Yugoslavian colleague, Pavel Savitch, were interested in the chemistry of those elements, so in 1938, they applied techniques of chemical separation and analysis to the products of uranium that had been bombarded by neutrons. One of those radioactive products behaved chemically like the much lighter element lanthanum, atomic number 57, but it was obviously not the stable isotope lanthanum 139. If this radioactive isotope was really lanthanum, it appeared that uranium nuclei were splitting approximately in half. That peculiar result intrigued Lise Meitner, her longtime chemist colleague Otto Hahn (1879–1968), and a young analytical chemist coworker named Fritz Strassman (1902–80) in Berlin.

Because of the growing oppression of Jews in Germany, Meitner had already made arrangements to flee to Scandinavia, and she had to leave before Hahn and Strassman could repeat the experiment of Joliot-Curie and Savitch. At about the same time, Fermi and his Jewish wife, Laura (1907–77), were escaping anti-Semitic laws that the Italian government of Benito Mussolini (1883–1945) had adopted after allying itself with the German Third Reich. After Fermi accepted the Nobel Prize in Stockholm, he and his wife did not return to Rome. Instead, they sailed directly to New York City, where he had been offered a professorship at Columbia University.

Not long after Meitner left, Hahn and Strassman's experiment began to yield interesting results. They isolated isotopes of a radioactive element that they knew was not radium—the half-lives of the various decays were too short—but had to be a close chemical relative. Further analysis by Strassman revealed it to be barium, which sits just below lanthanum on the periodic table. How could that be? Hahn wrote his physicist colleague a letter that described his excitement and puzzlement about the results.

The letter reached Meitner in Sweden just before Christmas. She was pondering it when her favorite nephew and fellow physicist, Otto Frisch (1904–79), arrived on a holiday visit, eager to tell her about his work with Bohr in Copenhagen. She insisted he read the letter first. What could cause a uranium nucleus to split? Frisch had some thoughts, which they discussed on a walk in the snowy woods. Bohr had been doing some interesting work with a visiting young Russian theorist named George Gamow (1904–68) on the way a nucleus might be held together. They imagined it to behave like a liquid droplet that could elongate as the nucleons within it moved around. If it stretched enough, it might form two globules joined by a neck of fluid that held them together by surface tension produced by the strong nuclear force.

Frisch reasoned that an additional neutron might cause the nuclear droplet to stretch so much that it could break in two. Then, without the strong nuclear force to hold them together, the two pieces, both having large positive electric charges, would repel each other and head

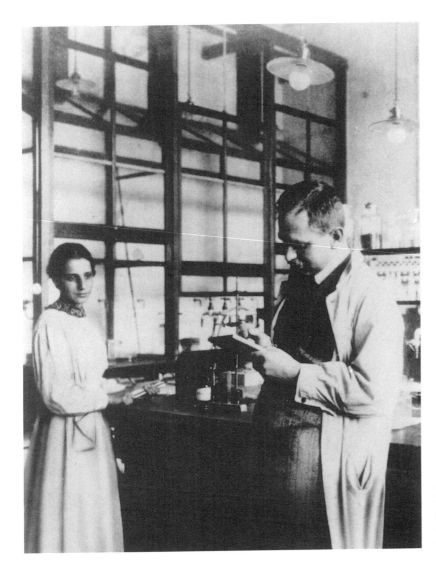

Lise Meitner and Otto Hahn, longtime collaborators and codiscoverers of nuclear fission, early in their careers (AIP Emilio Segrè Visual Archives)

in opposite directions with a huge amount of kinetic energy. That left another problem. Energy had to be conserved, so the increase in kinetic energy had to be accompanied by a decrease in energy of another form. The two physicists stopped walking, sat down against a tree trunk, took out some scraps of paper, and started to calculate. The Bohr and Gamow droplet model could indeed break into two smaller nuclei with some extra neutrons left over. When they computed the total mass of the resulting pieces, it turned out to be less than the mass of the original nucleus. And when that missing mass was multiplied by the square of the speed of light according to Einstein's famous formula, the result accounted for the gain in kinetic energy.

Once Meitner and Frisch published their result and named the process nuclear fission, it did not take long for scientists and military experts to recognize the possible applications of their work. If a neutron emitted in the fission of one nucleus struck a second nucleus, it could induce that one to break apart also. A single fission event could trigger a *chain reaction*, releasing an unimaginable amount of energy. With the world on the brink of a major war, science had revealed a technique that might lead to a fearsome bomb.

Other Developments in 1930s Physics

Though subatomic phenomena dominated physics in the 1930s, very interesting work was taking place in other subfields of the science. Astrophysics was a particular hotbed of activity. In 1931, Indian-born British mathematician and astrophysicist Subrahmanyan Chandrasekhar (1910–95) developed theories that described the life cycle of stars and predicted the existence of *black holes* decades before they were discovered. (He won the Nobel Prize in physics in 1983.) In a similar leap of insight in 1934, two European-born astronomers working in California, Fritz Zwicky (1898–1974) from Switzerland and Walter Baade (1893–1960) from Germany, predicted super-dense stars made completely of neutrons. Few scientists paid attention until 1967, when the first *pulsar* was discovered. Some people interpreted the pulsar's regular fluctuation in intensity as a cosmic message from intelligent beings, but it turned out to be the first evidence of the existence of *neutron stars.* Another astrophysical advance came out of Cornell University, where in 1939 Hans Bethe (1906–2005) developed a theory that explained the nuclear processes that took place in the interior of normal stars as they passed through the various stages of their lives.

Bethe, whose mother was Jewish, had fled his native Germany earlier in the decade. While still in Europe, along with Fermi, Dirac, and many other prominent theoretical physicists, he had been grappling with a major issue. They wondered how the theoretical foundations of electromagnetism as established by Maxwell could be adapted to the modern relativistic and quantum understandings of the physical world. Their work was significant, and it ultimately contributed to a successful theory of *quantum electrodynamics* (*QED*) in the 1940s. But their theoretical approaches in the 1930s always got caught on mathematical snags. That work therefore earns only this brief mention rather than a detailed explanation in this book.

Physics also contributed to significant developments in other fields during the 1930s. Chemist Linus Pauling (1901–94), who won Nobel prizes in chemistry in 1954 and peace in 1962, continued important work he had begun in the late 1920s on insights from quantum mechanics that led to a fuller understanding of chemical bonds. One type of bond occurs when one atom gives up its valence electrons, the ones outside the closed shells, to complete the outermost shell of another atom. That results in an *ionic bond*—electrically bound ions with filled electronic shells. *Covalent bonds* result from atoms' sharing of valence electrons to complete their electronic shells. In 1935, geologist Charles Richter (1900–85) developed his famous scale for measuring the intensity of earthquakes. And German engineers built the first successful jet plane in 1939.

The emergence of quantum physics also led to important developments in condensed matter physics in the late 1920s and the 1930s, both theoretical and technological. By then, quantum theory was well established at the atomic level, so several research groups in Europe and the United States sought ways to apply its mathematical techniques to electrons in crystals: repeating three-dimensional arrangements of atoms. Most solids are crystalline. Thus that work had broad application to understanding the physics of the solid state. In single atoms, such as hydrogen, quantum theory predicts certain allowed energy levels. In crystals, each atom has its own energy levels for electrons in the closed shells. For the remaining electrons, instead of a distinct set of allowed energy levels, there are two allowed energy bands with a gap between them. The lower-energy band is the called the *valence band*, and its electrons occupy quantum states that belong to individual atoms. The other is the *conduction band*, and its energy states belong to the crystal as a whole. In metals, the valence band does not have enough allowed quantum states to accommodate all the crystal's outer electrons (those beyond the closed shells). Some of those go into the conduction band. They belong to no atom in particular and thus move freely, carrying electricity and energy with them. That is why metals are good conductors of electricity and heat. Insulators and semiconductors have room for all the outer electrons in the valence band. Their electricity- and heat-conducting properties depend on the number of unfilled quantum states in the valence band and the size of the energy gap between the two bands.

In technology, probably the most significant quantum application was the first electron microscope, built in 1931 in Berlin, Germany, by Ernst Ruska (1906–88), who won the Nobel Prize in physics in 1986, and Max Knoll (1897–1969). The imaging power of a microscope is limited by the wavelength of the energy it uses to illuminate the sample being studied. The wavelength of visible light is thousands of times as big as atoms and molecules, so an optical microscope can reveal very little about the internal crystalline arrangements of the atoms in solids. But high-energy electrons, according to de Broglie's formula, have much shorter wavelengths and thus offer the potential to make images of crystal structures and to study the behavior of crystal defects and imperfections. In later decades, as its technology improved, the electron microscope became not only a laboratory device but also a very important industrial tool for the creation of high-technology materials and devices.

Another interesting condensed-matter phenomenon was first observed in 1937 and 1938 by Russian physicist Pyotr Kapitsa (1894–1984), who won the Nobel Prize in physics in 1978. He reported the odd property

Scientist of the Decade: Lise Meitner (1878–1968)

If professional accomplishments alone were the criteria for choosing a featured scientist, the choice for the 1930s would be Enrico Fermi. But the work of science can affect and be affected dramatically by social, political, and historical factors. And among the top physicists of the 1930s, there is no one whose life better illustrates the influence of the times in which she worked than Lise Meitner.

Meitner's story is not of the 1930s alone. In fact, by the time she and Otto Frisch developed the first theory of nuclear fission in 1938, she had passed her 60th birthday and had built a notable career in physics. And although the persecution she faced as a person of Jewish ancestry was part of a much larger horror that should never be minimized, it was not the only time in her life that she had to overcome discrimination to succeed. She was born female at a time, November 7, 1878, and in a place, Vienna, Austria, where the traditional expectations for women were enforced by societal norms and sometimes in the law.

Lise was the third of eight children born to lawyer Philipp Meitner and his wife, Hedwig. As in most educated, liberal, middle-class Jewish families of the time, they identified primarily as Austrians and were proud of the rich cultural heritage that Vienna had to offer. Lise was exposed to learning and the arts. Her older sister, Auguste ("Gusti"), was a musical prodigy and became a composer and concert pianist. Lise also loved music, but her interest in mathematics and physics was compelling, even as early as age eight. Thus even though her public school education ended at age 14, as it did for all girls, Lise aimed for a university education. She read widely—the family joked about her always carrying a book—and with the help of a tutor she passed the entrance exams for the University of Vienna in 1901 at the age when many of her male counterparts were graduating.

Fortunately, Lise had the opportunity to study physics with the legendary professor Ludwig Boltzmann (1844–1906), who "gave her a vision of physics as a battle for the ultimate truth, a vision she never lost," according to her nephew and fellow physicist, Otto Frisch. She also learned from fellow students—especially Paul Ehrenfest (1880–1933), who became a noted theoretical physicist in his own right. Ehrenfest was impressed with Meitner's detailed notes from Boltzmann's lectures, and they often studied together. Meitner's writings suggest that Ehrenfest's interests in her may have gone beyond physics, but she was shy and naive and kept her focus on their studies. By 1905, she was not only proficient in theoretical physics, but she had also completed an original laboratory research project. She was the second woman awarded a doctorate at the university, and her diploma carried the highest possible honors, summa cum laude.

The world of academic science was not particularly welcoming to women at that time, but Meitner loved her subject too much to let that stand in her way. She saw physics as more than scholarship and sought out mentors and colleagues who would relate to her on a human level. That was certainly the case when she left Vienna for Berlin to study with Max Planck. To Meitner, Planck seemed dubious about women as professional scientists, but on the personal level, he was warm and welcoming. His twin daughters became her good friends, and she often enjoyed musical evenings at their home with their father on the piano and, on occasion, Einstein playing the violin.

Often the other guests included Otto Hahn, a young chemist who had recently studied with Rutherford in Montreal. In contrast to Meitner's natural reserve, Hahn was outgoing. She enjoyed his tenor voice and his friendship and thus eagerly agreed to join him in studying radioactive substances. Her strength in physics was a natural complement to his expertise in chemical separation, and he offered her a doorway to academic research. It was a basement door to an unpaid job (she lived on a modest allowance from her family), but it was a rare opportunity for a woman.

Hahn worked in the University of Berlin Chemistry Institute, directed by 1902 Nobel Prize–winning chemist Emil Fischer (1852–1919). Fischer did not allow women in the institute, in part because he considered their hairstyles a fire hazard, but Hahn persuaded him to convert a former car-

penter's shop with an outside entrance into a workspace for Meitner. She was not allowed anywhere else in the institute and had to use a restroom in a nearby restaurant. When colleagues saw her with Hahn, their greeting was "Guten Tag, Herr Hahn," as if she were nonexistent, and, given the social norms of the day, Hahn did nothing to correct them. But their friendship and collaboration flourished, though for the first 16 years they always addressed each other as Herr Hahn and Fräulein Meitner.

Gradually, German universities became more welcoming for women. In 1909, women were accepted as students, and Meitner was allowed inside the other laboratories of institute, which had at last installed a ladies' room. In 1912, Hahn earned a promotion and the leadership of a radioactivity research group in the Kaiser Wilhelm Institute of Chemistry, and he brought Meitner along as an unpaid guest physicist. At the same time, Planck offered her a paid position as his assistant to grade papers.

A few years later, Fischer gave Meitner the same title as Hahn but with a much smaller salary. In 1917, he gave Meitner her own physics section and raised her salary to match Hahn's with the exception of a marriage allowance. And in 1919, Meitner became probably the first woman in Germany to carry the title "professor." During the 1920s, her laboratory became renowned for its work in beta decay. But, as described in this chapter, her most significant work (fission) was to come years later, just as her laboratory collaboration with Hahn was forcibly ended.

For the first eight years of the Nazi government's existence, Meitner had been protected by her Austrian citizenship. That changed when the Nazis took over the Austrian government in 1938. At that point, even though she had converted to Protestantism 30 years earlier, she was subject to the Nazi government's restrictions on Jews. She even lost her passport, which made arranging an escape particularly difficult. With the help of a colleague who bribed a Dutch border guard, and thanks to Hahn's gift of an inherited diamond ring to ease her finances, she was able to spend a few months in Holland. Not long before the Nazis overran that country, she left for a less than ideal post in Stockholm. It was there that she received the momentous letter from Hahn that led her and Frisch to describe nuclear fission.

Lise Meitner, a pioneer for women in science, visits with Bryn Mawr College students late in her life. (AIP Emilio Segrè Visual Archives)

She was invited to join the United States's wartime nuclear program, but she refused to have anything to do with building a bomb. Because of that, she was the only significant nuclear physicist that the press could interview after the atomic bomb exploded over Hiroshima. Some reporters even wrote (incorrectly) that she had taken the secrets of the bomb with her when she left Germany. That was particularly ironic because Hahn alone had been awarded the Nobel Prize in chemistry in 1944 for the discovery of nuclear fission. In what must have seemed to Meitner a painful reminder of the early days of her career, Hahn usually spoke as if the discovery was his alone.

Still, Meitner maintained her friendship with Hahn as long as they both lived. She died on October 27, 1968, a few days before her 90th birthday, and was buried in a country churchyard near Cambridge, England, where she had retired eight years earlier to be near her nephew Otto Frisch. She did not live to see the naming of synthetic element number 109 Meitnerium in her honor. At about the same time, element number 105 was officially named Dubnium after the city of Dubna, where it was discovered. For many years, it had been unofficially called Hahnium.

of liquid helium known as *superfluidity*. Just as a superconducting material loses all resistance to the flow of electricity through it at very low temperatures, liquid helium loses all viscosity—its resistance to flow. Thus the force of surface tension causes it to crawl up and over the wall of a container or through the tiniest hole. Theorists eventually explained both superfluidity and superconductivity as the result of quantum effects at the atomic level that manifest themselves on a much larger scale. Superconductivity will be discussed further in chapters 6 and 9.

Further Reading

Books

Bortz, Fred. *The Neutrino*. New York: Rosen Publishing, 2004. An easy-to-read history of the neutrino and its significance.

———. *The Neutron*. New York: Rosen Publishing, 2004. An easy-to-read history of the neutron and its applications.

Cassidy, David. *Uncertainty: The Life and Science of Werner Heisenberg*. New York: W. H. Freeman, 1991. An interesting personal history of Heisenberg's life and science, with the theme of uncertainty in both.

Cathcart, Brian. *The Fly in the Cathedral: How a Group of Cambridge Scientists Won the International Race to Split the Atom*. New York: Farrar, Straus and Giroux, 2004. A fascinating story of Cockroft and Walton's achievement, with insights into Rutherford's leadership and Chadwick's discovery of the neutron.

Chown, Marcus. *The Magic Furnace: The Search for the Origin of Atoms*. New York: Oxford University Press, 2001. A readable history of the quest to understand the composition of the universe, including a discussion of the work of Hans Bethe.

Close, Frank, Michael Marten, and Christine Sutton. *The Particle Odyssey: A Journey to the Heart of Matter*. New York: Oxford University Press, 2002. A detailed and colorfully illustrated overview of the discovery of subatomic particles.

Cornwell, John. *Hitler's Scientists: Science, War, and the Devil's Pact*. New York: Viking, 2003. Provides insight into the political forces that shaped research in physics and the lives of physicists in the 1930s and 1940s.

Cropper, William H. *Great Physicists: The Life and Times of Leading Physicists from Galileo to Hawking*. New York: Oxford University Press, 2001. The life and times of many great physicists, including Fermi, Meitner, and Chandrasekhar.

Fermi, Laura. *Atoms in the Family: My Life with Enrico Fermi*. Chicago: University of Chicago Press, 1954. A memoir by Fermi's wife, providing insights into the life of a fascinating man and scientist.

Frisch, Otto. *What Little I Remember*. Cambridge: Cambridge University Press, 1979. A very readable autobiography of Lisa Meitner's nephew and a great physicist in his own right.

Gribbin, John, with Mary Gribbin. *Stardust: Supernovae and Life; The Cosmic Connection.* New Haven, Conn.: Yale University Press, 2001. Covers similar material as Marcus Chown's *The Magic Furnace* (above), with a greater emphasis on science and a lesser emphasis on history.

Hahn, Otto. *Otto Hahn: My Life, The Autobiography of a Scientist.* Translated by Ernst Kaiser and Eithne Wilkins. New York: Herder and Herder, 1970.

Kragh, Helge. *Quantum Generations: A History of Physics in the Twentieth Century.* Princeton, N.J.: Princeton University Press, 1999. An in-depth history of 20th-century physics and physicists.

Lightman, Alan. *The Discoveries: Great Breakthroughs in 20th Century Science, Including the Original Papers.* New York: Pantheon, 2005. Includes Pauling's paper on the nature of chemical bonds, the landmark nuclear fission papers by Hahn and Strassman and by Meitner and Frisch, and commentaries on their significance.

Sime, Ruth Lewin. *Lise Meitner: A Life in Physics.* Berkeley: University of California Press, 1996. The definitive biography of Lise Meitner.

Suplee, Curt. *Physics in the 20th Century.* New York: Harry N. Abrams, 1999. A pictorial history of 20th-century physics.

Web Sites

American Institute of Physics, Center for History of Physics. Available online. URL: http://www.aip.org/history. Accessed March 27, 2006. Follow pull-down menu for a special online exhibit on Lawrence and the cyclotron, among other topics, or browse for a variety of written resources and images.

Nobelprize.org. Available online. URL: http://nobelprize.org. Accessed March 27, 2006. The official Web site of the Nobel Foundation contains brief biographies of Nobel Prize winners, summaries of their prize-winning work, and their acceptance speeches.

The Science Museum. Available online. URL: http://www.sciencemuseum.org.uk. Accessed March 27, 2006. A British online science education resource that includes useful exhibits on many topics discussed in this book.

The Science Shelf, Books for the World Year of Physics 2005. Available online. URL: http://www.scienceshelf.com/WorldYearofPhysics.htm. Accessed April 26, 2006. This page on the book review site of Fred Bortz has brief comments about a number of books published in recognition of the World Year of Physics, plus links to reviews of a number of other physics books for nonspecialist readers.

World Year of Physics 2005. Available online. URL: http://www.physics2005.org. Accessed March 27, 2006. An online resource developed in honor of the centennial of Albert Einstein's "Miracle Year."

5

1941–1950:
Physics in a Time of War

As the fifth decade of the 20th century began, the German military machine had taken over much of continental Europe, and the Japanese forces were asserting their dominance of Asia and the Pacific. Of the world's major powers, only the United States remained officially neutral, although its government clearly opposed German and Japanese expansionism. On December 8, 1941, the day after Japan attacked the American naval base at Pearl Harbor, Hawaii, the United States declared war on Japan, which naturally led to an alliance with England, France, and the Soviet Union against Germany and its allies. The conflict had become World War II, and it was about to transform not only the lives of physicists but also the culture of their science.

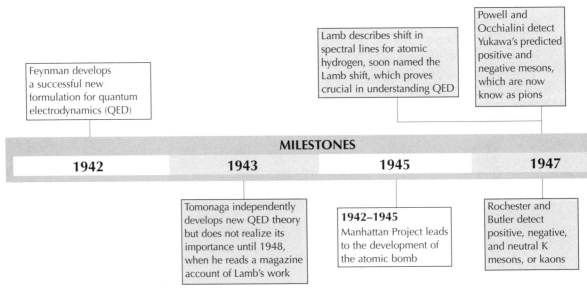

Feynman develops a successful new formulation for quantum electrodynamics (QED)

Lamb describes shift in spectral lines for atomic hydrogen, soon named the Lamb shift, which proves crucial in understanding QED

Powell and Occhialini detect Yukawa's predicted positive and negative mesons, which are now know as pions

MILESTONES

| 1942 | 1943 | 1945 | 1947 |

Tomonaga independently develops new QED theory but does not realize its importance until 1948, when he reads a magazine account of Lamb's work

1942–1945
Manhattan Project leads to the development of the atomic bomb

Rochester and Butler detect positive, negative, and neutral K mesons, or kaons

As described in the preceding chapter, the 1930s were years of transformation for international physics as many physicists fled Hitler's rising power. To those with Jewish roots or connections, it was literally a matter of life or death; others left because they were opposed to what the Nazis stood for, but the majority of non-Jewish German physicists remained. In the rest of Europe, physicists looked to the United States for its economic and scientific opportunities. Its major universities now had research programs that rivaled or surpassed the great European laboratories and centers of learning. New American industrial research and development programs were also beginning to emerge. The center of gravity for physics was moving westward across the Atlantic, and events of the 1940s would accelerate that movement of people and intellectual energy.

Wartime technological needs drove scientific research and reinforced an already emerging trend toward expensive, "big science" projects requiring large, coordinated teams of people to build massive devices such as cyclotrons and nuclear reactors. Even without the war, the freewheeling culture of the United States was better suited to that trend than the more tradition-bound European institutions. The marriage of physics and technology during the war led to an American dominance in both that lasted through the rest of the 20th century. By the late 1940s, the United States was the clear leader in nuclear technology, thanks to its wartime development of bombs based on nuclear fission (popularly known as atomic bombs). By the end of the decade, it had made considerable progress toward thermonuclear fusion devices, or hydrogen bombs,

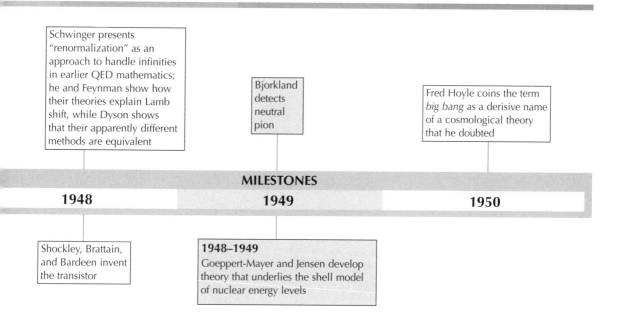

Schwinger presents "renormalization" as an approach to handle infinities in earlier QED mathematics; he and Feynman show how their theories explain Lamb shift, while Dyson shows that their apparently different methods are equivalent

Bjorkland detects neutral pion

Fred Hoyle coins the term *big bang* as a derisive name of a cosmological theory that he doubted

MILESTONES

1948   **1949**   **1950**

Shockley, Brattain, and Bardeen invent the transistor

1948–1949
Goeppert-Mayer and Jensen develop theory that underlies the shell model of nuclear energy levels

that would yield tens or hundreds of times as much energy as the first fission devices. Even those fields where German technology had dominated before or during the war, jet aircraft and rocketry, became American strongholds, thanks in part to the 1945 surrender of the leading Nazi rocket scientists, most of whom deliberately arranged to be captured by forces of the United States rather than its emerging major global competitor, the Soviet Union.

Another critical wartime technology was radar, with important developments in both the United States and England. Many historians consider that technology to have been far more important to the war effort than either rocketry or the bomb. American leadership there led to dominance in electronics in the decades to follow. But this book is a history of physics, not technology or politics. Thus while acknowledging the importance of politics and technology in providing direction to physics research in the period 1941–50, its focus remains on the science itself, including the emergence of a brash young physicist from Far Rockaway on the outskirts of New York City named Richard Feynman (1918–88), who not only contributed to the war effort but also laid the groundwork for a reinterpretation of electromagnetism according to the principles of quantum theory.

QED: Quantum Electrodynamics

For physicists, grasping the significance of the quantum universe did not come easily. Like Einstein's relativity in the early decades of the century, quantum theory was challenging their instincts and the fundamental premises of their science. By the beginning of the 1940s, however, the success of the new theory was undeniable. Physicists had to accept the strange but profound quantum view of the universe. They could no longer draw a sharp distinction between particles and waves. They had to accept inherent limits on the precision of physical measurements and on the mathematical predictability of the universe. As much as some would have preferred the familiar clockwork universe of the late 19th century, they understood that their science is not about making rules to dictate the behavior of the universe. Rather, it is about observing the universe and deducing the rules that govern its behavior.

One 19th-century theory had still not been fully reshaped to fit the new reality: electromagnetism. As noted in the preceding chapter, a number of prominent European physicists had made progress toward a theory of quantum electrodynamics, or QED, but none had been able to finish the job. QED was clearly in need of a groundbreaking idea. Such dramatic innovations in scientific thought almost always arise from the minds of the youngest scientists, since they are not yet bound by older concepts. That is certainly true of 20th-century theoretical physics. Einstein, Bohr, de Broglie, Pauli, Schrödinger, Heisenberg, Dirac, and many other pioneers of quantum physics were in their twenties when they did their most celebrated work. And in almost every case, their innovation was based on a new way of looking at well-known physical phenomena. So it was no surprise that an important breakthrough came in 1942 from the research of Richard Feynman, a 24-year-old physics graduate student at Princeton University.

Feynman provided a way around a troubling mathematical feature in previous attempts to describe electromagnetic effects in quantum terms. Maxwell's equations had successfully unified the theories of electricity, magnetism, and light, but those 19th-century formulas were based on the assumption that electrical charge and light energy were continuous quantities, meaning that they could be measured out in any amount like a liquid. Twentieth-century studies of subatomic particles and spectra had shown that assumption was not valid. Both electric charge and light energy come in quantized chunks, like grains of sand.

Physicists applying quantum mechanics and relativity to electromagnetism had been remarkably successful—but not perfect—in describing the properties and behavior of electrons. The trouble with their calculations lay not in the theories or equations but rather in the mathematical model describing the way electrical charge is distributed within the electron. The calculations include a mathematical expression for a quantity called the electron's self-energy, which results from the electron's charge interacting with its own electromagnetic field. The self-energy depends on the details of the model of the electron's charge distribution. Unfortunately, when the requirements of relativity are introduced into that model, the self-energy term is always infinity, which makes numerical calculation meaningless.

Feynman's insight was to create a new formulation of quantum mechanics. His method focused not on the Schrödinger and Dirac equations but rather on the different underlying processes that could lead to observed events. Consider, for example, an electron that moves from point A at one time to point B at another, changing its momentum in the process. That transition can result from many different interactions with photons. Feynman's insight was to find a way to add together all possible interactions, producing what physicists call the probability amplitude of the transition. This technique replaced quantum mechanical wave functions with sets of diagrams of particle interactions, yet yielded the same transition probabilities.

Elsewhere in Princeton, Albert Einstein was particularly pleased when he learned of the new approach from John Archibald Wheeler (1911–), Feynman's research adviser. Einstein had often criticized the quantum mechanical description of particles as wave functions, because it forced physicists to accept a degree of randomness in the laws of physics. "God does not play dice with the Universe," he would say. Feynman's approach produced the same degree of randomness in the results, but it resulted

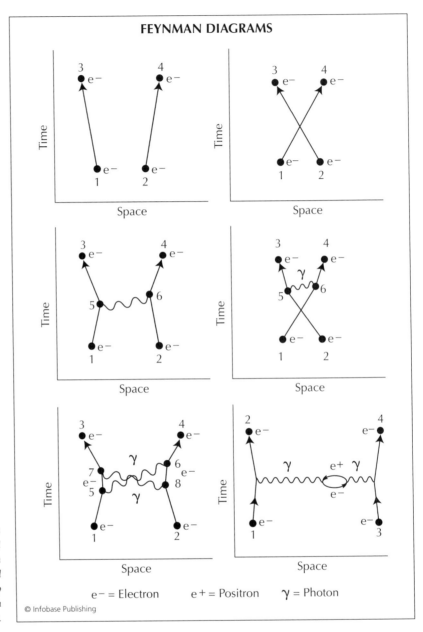

FEYNMAN DIAGRAMS

e− = Electron   e+ = Positron   γ = Photon

© Infobase Publishing

Richard Feynman's famous diagrams summarized all possible interactions between electrons and photons and enabled him to develop a full theory of quantum electrodynamics.

from a set of predictable interactions. Einstein told Wheeler, "I still cannot believe that God plays dice, but maybe I have earned the right to make mistakes."

Feynman's thesis did not produce a complete QED theory immediately, but it laid the groundwork for one that was completed later in the decade, after an interruption that diverted Feynman's attention to a more pressing matter: the development of the atomic bomb. After the war, Feynman became a professor at Cornell University, where he resumed work on QED. At an invitation-only conference at a resort on Shelter Island, New York, attended by 25 leading physicists during the summer of 1947, Willis Lamb (1913–   ) of Columbia University presented results of his very careful measurements of the spectrum of atomic hydrogen (different from molecular hydrogen, which is composed of two hydrogen atoms bonded together). His experiments revealed a minuscule splitting of spectral lines that was traced to a difference in energy between two different quantum states. This difference became known as the *Lamb shift* and led to the 1955 Nobel Prize in physics for Lamb. It forced physicists to reconsider quantum theory. Dirac's equation predicted that the energy of those two states should be exactly the same. Any difference, no matter how small, was hugely important to understanding the subatomic world.

Could the latest work on QED explain the Lamb shift? Feynman and other theorists at the conference, including another New Yorker of about Feynman's age named Julian Schwinger (1918–94), had some thinking to do. At an American Physical Society meeting the next year and at another invitational conference in Pennsylvania's Pocono Mountains, a mathematical explanation slowly emerged. At the Pocono conference, Schwinger, a professor at Columbia University, made a brilliant presentation full of advanced mathematics. Math was a language that everyone

Willis Lamb (left), Richard Feynman (seated, center), Julian Schwinger (right), and others discuss details of the hydrogen spectrum at Shelter Island Conference in the summer of 1947. (AIP Emilio Segrè Visual Archives)

in attendance understood, but the computations were so complex and detailed that few could follow him through to the end. Still, they recognized that his innovative approach, called *renormalization*, brilliantly hid the infinities of the self-energy calculations and allowed him to calculate the energy levels of atomic hydrogen. His result reproduced the Lamb shift. If only the mathematics were less complicated and more clearly connected with physical phenomena, Schwinger's approach to QED would gain widespread acceptance.

Feynman's presentation followed. His pictorial approach had the virtue of being straightforward and clearly tied to physical phenomena, but to the mathematical thinkers in the audience, it was as if he were speaking in a foreign tongue. He deduced the solutions directly from his diagrams without using equations. So although he, too, managed to come up with the Lamb shift from his theory, the attendees favored Schwinger's complicated but recognizable approach to Feynman's simpler but unfamiliar method. Everyone recognized that both Schwinger and Feynman had made significant progress, but few were satisfied that either had developed a complete working theory of QED. It took the insights of someone not in attendance at either conference to put the two theories together.

That person was the young Englishman Freeman Dyson (1923–   ), who in 1947 had come to the United States from Cambridge University to study with Bethe at Cornell. One of his Cambridge mentors described him as "the best mathematician in England," so it was no wonder that he was interested in tackling QED. After reading Wheeler's notes from Schwinger's and Feynman's presentations at the Pocono conference, he was eager to learn from both of them. He signed up for a summer seminar on QED that Schwinger was planning to offer at the University of Michigan. At Cornell, he took every opportunity he could to talk to Feynman, who had become a close friend as well as a teacher.

As summer began, Feynman invited Dyson to ride cross-country with him to Albuquerque, New Mexico. Feynman's objective was to pursue a girlfriend and to have a few adventures along the way. (For details, see the profile of Feynman on page 108). Dyson knew he could get in some touring, which was high on his agenda for his summer, and still have plenty of time to pick Feynman's brain about his diagrams and QED. He quickly agreed. From Albuquerque, he took a Greyhound bus to Ann Arbor, Michigan, for more sightseeing and Schwinger's seminar.

Both legs of the trip accomplished what Dyson had hoped for. With his brain filled with Feynman diagrams and Schwinger's equations of QED, he needed a vacation. He boarded a westbound Greyhound, spent some time in San Francisco and Berkeley, California, then headed back east again. He had not thought much about QED for two weeks, but suddenly, somewhere in Nebraska, insight struck. Feynman's pictures and Schwinger's equations came together in his mind. He realized that both approaches were built on the same ideas, and he saw a way to combine them into a mathematically precise theory of QED built on insights clear enough to represent in diagrammatic form. When Dyson presented his ideas at a meeting of the American Physical Society in January of the next year, 1949, he became a physics celebrity.

Schwinger, Feynman, and Dyson soon found themselves sharing the QED spotlight with another physicist, Sin-Itiro Tomonaga (1906–79) of Japan. While World War II had interrupted Feynman's work, Tomonaga was able to continue his work at Riken Kenkyusho, the Institute for Physical and Chemical Research in Tokyo. The director of Riken, Yoshio Nishina (1890–1951), who had studied in Europe at the height of the development of quantum mechanics, encouraged Tomonaga's work on QED and protected him from military service. The result was a series of papers in the Japanese journal whose name translates to "Progress in theoretical physics." Those publications laid out the same ideas for QED that Schwinger used as the basis of his detailed mathematical approach. That was in 1943, four years before Lamb's important discovery and five years before Schwinger's publication. Because of the war, Tomonaga's work remained unknown outside of Japan. He did not even recognize its importance until he read about Lamb's work in *Newsweek* magazine in 1948. At that point, he contacted J. Robert Oppenheimer (1904–67), who had led the scientific efforts of the U.S. atomic bomb project. Oppenheimer recommended that Tomonaga submit a summary to *Physical Review*, which brought his work to the attention of American scientists.

Tomonaga was asked to be a participant in the next invitational conference on QED in 1949, and in 1965, he shared the Nobel Prize in physics with Schwinger and Feynman. Because no more than three people can share a Nobel, Dyson, despite his major contributions to QED, was not included.

Nuclear Fission, "Big Science," and the Bomb

With the world at war, understanding and applying nuclear fission became a top priority for all combatants. Although the early studies indicated that a chain reaction was possible in theory, it was not clear how to cause one in practice. As this section recounts, a number of technological obstacles had to be overcome to build a bomb. From the perspective of history, science is a brash newcomer compared to technology. Technology is older than civilization itself. In contrast, the systematic practice of science began only a few hundred years ago. However, by the mid-20th century, science and technology were clearly interdependent. Engineers and technologists were applying scientific knowledge in their work, and many scientific quests required the engineering of complex equipment.

Like most major trends in history, it is difficult to place the beginning of "big science" precisely in time, but the development of the cyclotron in the late 1930s is surely an early example. If particle accelerators mark the birth of big science, then the development of the first nuclear bomb in the early to mid-1940s represents its adolescence, and the remainder of the 1940s and 1950s can be described as its young adulthood. The bomb project required a vast array of talents, plus skilled management to coordinate those talents. New knowledge had to be applied almost as quickly as it was developed, which meant that physics and physicists were central to the bomb-building enterprise on all sides of the global conflict.

In the United States, the atomic bomb project began before the country entered the war. In the summer of 1939, physicists Leo Szilard (1898–1964), Eugene Wigner (1902–95), and Edward Teller (1908–2003), all of whom had fled their native Hungary for the United States to escape the Nazi threat, drafted a letter that urged President Franklin D. Roosevelt (1882–1945) to begin a major effort to develop a bomb. They persuaded Einstein, who normally leaned toward pacifism, to sign it. A year later, a small organization called the Advisory Committee on Uranium, began to function. After the Pearl Harbor attack, the U.S. government quickly escalated its efforts. The highly classified Manhattan Project brought together many different research activities and focused them on building atomic bombs.

Research into chain reactions had already been under way in a number of laboratories. For a chain reaction to occur, an average of at least one neutron from every fission event would have to cause another fission. By the beginning of the 1940s, physicists knew that naturally occurring uranium could not sustain a chain reaction. Natural uranium consists mainly of two isotopes. The most common, comprising 99.27 percent of all the atoms, is designated ^{238}U, because its 92 protons and 146 neutrons give it an atomic mass of 238. Almost all the remaining atoms are ^{235}U. These two isotopes behave very much the same in chemical reactions, but their interactions with neutrons are quite different. Fission of a ^{238}U nucleus can occur, but it is so rare that a chain reaction is out of the question. Most of the time, when a neutron interacts with a ^{238}U nucleus, it just bounces off, and sometimes it is absorbed to create a short-lived ^{239}U nucleus. The ^{239}U nucleus quickly decays by emitting a beta particle to become a neptunium (^{239}Np), which in turn decays by emitting another beta particle to become plutonium, ^{239}Pu. Fission occurs much more frequently when a neutron hits a ^{235}U nucleus. That event yields two more or less equally sized smaller nuclei as well as about three extra neutrons that could potentially cause other fission events. However, Fermi's work had shown that fast neutrons, like those produced by fission, rarely interacted with uranium nuclei. Without a moderator to slow them down, most of them simply escaped into the outside world.

Once physicists understood the different behavior of the two main uranium isotopes, they realized that there were two routes to a uranium chain reaction. One was to make a nuclear reactor or "pile," an arrangement of

HOW TO CREATE A NUCLEAR CHAIN REACTION (1)

Before   After

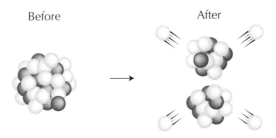

Large nucleus undergoes fission, breaking into two
smaller nuclei and a few fast-moving neutrons.

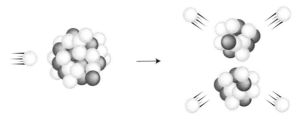

Each neutron can hit another nucleus and cause another fission.

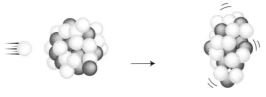

Or it can be absorbed to create a different isotope.

Or it can bounce off (or scatter) or miss
entirely and escape from the material.

*When a large nucleus undergoes
fission, it emits several neutrons,
which may or may not cause
other fission events, as shown
here.*

HOW TO CREATE A NUCLEAR CHAIN REACTION (2)

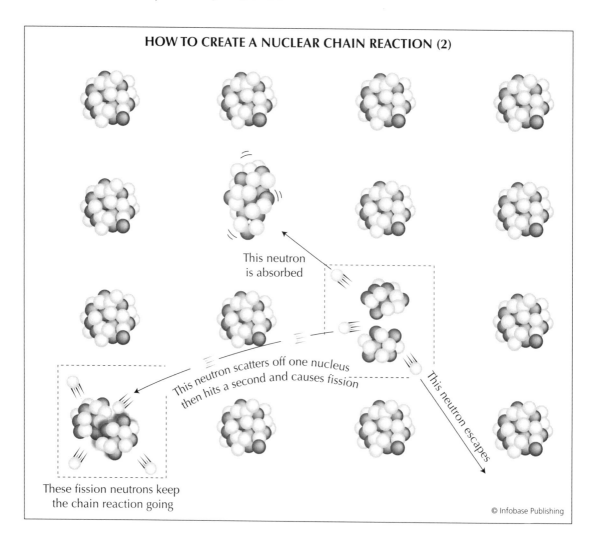

This neutron is absorbed

This neutron scatters off one nucleus then hits a second and causes fission

This neutron escapes

These fission neutrons keep the chain reaction going

© Infobase Publishing

A chain reaction occurs if an average of at least one neutron from each fission event causes another nucleus to undergo fission. If the average is exactly one, the process continues to release energy steadily, as in a nuclear power plant. If the average is greater than one, the number of fissions will grow very quickly and release an enormous amount of energy in a very short time—a bomb.

pieces of uranium and a moderator. Fast neutrons from the fissions in one piece of uranium would be slowed down by the moderator, then enter another piece of uranium where they would cause more fissions. Fission neutrons could be lost by escaping the pile or by being absorbed by other nuclei, such as ^{238}U, without causing fission. The key was to develop an arrangement in which a large enough fraction of neutrons produced in fission went on to cause another fission. This was the approach Fermi took at Columbia. The pile was much too large and complex to be developed as a weapon, but it was very valuable to make measurements that increased physicists' knowledge of the properties of uranium nuclei and the fission process. It also turned out to be a forerunner of the nuclear power industry, although the researchers' focus was on other applications at the time.

The other approach to a chain reaction possible was to separate "fissile" ^{235}U nuclei from natural uranium. Calculations showed that even without a moderator, fast neutrons in nearly pure ^{235}U had a good chance to cause another fission. The key was having a large enough piece of uranium so that a neutron was likely to encounter several ^{235}U nuclei before it reached the surface, where it could escape. The larger the piece of uranium, the more likely a neutron would be to cause a fission and the less likely it would be to escape. Physicists therefore spoke of a "critical mass" for a chain reaction to occur. For pure ^{235}U, the critical mass was only about 10 kilograms (roughly 22 pounds), small enough that it could easily be put it in a bomb. Plutonium 239 also underwent fission easily, but making it in sufficient amounts from ^{238}U required a controlled chain reaction in an atomic pile, followed by chemical separation. The Manhattan Project included research into both uranium and plutonium bombs.

The two uranium isotopes could not be separated chemically, so scientists and engineers developed a technique to separate them physically. It required a huge gaseous diffusion plant. The technique works because uranium reacts with fluorine to produce a gas called uranium hexafluoride, or UF_6. Just as gravity can separate the oil and vinegar in a salad dressing into layers, passing the UF_6 gas through a diffusion column separates the molecules containing the lighter ^{235}U isotope from those containing the heavier ^{238}U. (Current technology uses centrifuges instead of diffusion columns.) The separation is not nearly as complete as in salad dressing, because, unlike vinegar and oil, the gas molecules tend to stay mixed. Also, the fraction of ^{235}U molecules in natural uranium is very small to begin with. Thus achieving high purity of ^{235}U in the gas is a multistep process.

Once the war was under way, the U.S. government began the construction of a plant to make ^{235}U in Oak Ridge, Tennessee. Like all activities under the umbrella of the Manhattan Project, few people knew its exact purpose, though it was impossible to hide the existence of a project of that scale. The Manhattan Project also funded a major project at the University of Chicago under the leadership of Arthur Compton (1892–1962). The object there was to build a "critical assembly," an atomic pile capable of achieving a controlled chain reaction. Compton's previous work, as well as Fermi's at Columbia, were on subcritical piles. The Project consolidated the efforts of the two groups in Chicago, so Fermi reluctantly left Columbia in 1942 to pursue the next stage of his research. Later that year, in the so-called Metallurgical Laboratory in a squash court underneath the stands of the University of Chicago's football field, he made history with the world's first controlled nuclear chain reaction.

The most secretive part of the Manhattan Project took place in Los Alamos, New Mexico. That was where the bomb itself was being developed, with Oppenheimer taking the scientific lead. Bethe led the theoretical physics group, which soon included Feynman, who had just

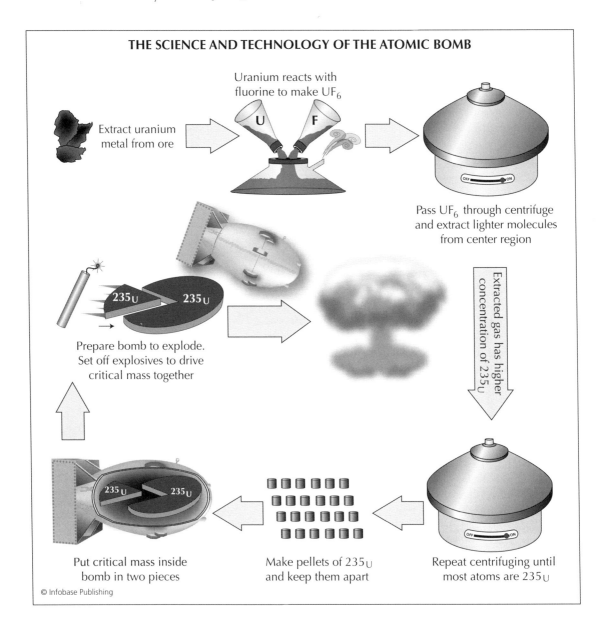

THE SCIENCE AND TECHNOLOGY OF THE ATOMIC BOMB

Uranium reacts with fluorine to make UF_6

U   F

Extract uranium metal from ore

Pass UF_6 through centrifuge and extract lighter molecules from center region

Extracted gas has higher concentration of 235_U

Prepare bomb to explode. Set off explosives to drive critical mass together

235_U 235_U

Put critical mass inside bomb in two pieces

235_U 235_U

Make pellets of 235_U and keep them apart

Repeat centrifuging until most atoms are 235_U

© Infobase Publishing

finished his breakthrough Ph.D. thesis. He was to become Bethe's colleague at Cornell after the war. Although the nuclear calculations were the newest physics to be used in building a bomb, other calculations were also important. How would the bomb be detonated? The device would have to contain a critical mass of uranium, but divided so that the chain reaction would not begin until the pieces came together. Then, when the chain reaction began, how would the pieces of uranium stay together? If the bomb blew itself apart too quickly, the chain reaction would stop before most of the energy was released. The solution was to use conventional explosives to drive the pieces of uranium together at high speed. Every change in the nuclear calculations would lead to changes in the engineering design of the bomb, including its shape, and that would change its trajectory once it was dropped. Teams of physicists using mechanical calculators predicted everything they needed to know about every possible design of the bomb. Some used newly developed electronic computers with the latest in vacuum tube technology, built especially for them. (The first commercial electronic computers did not appear until 1946.)

Finally, in the New Mexico desert on July 16, 1945, the first atomic bomb was tested successfully. The war in Europe had ended in the spring, but fighting was continuing in the Pacific. The leaders of the United States decided that the quickest way to end the war was to use the bomb. It took two attacks to persuade the Japanese to surrender: a uranium bomb that devastated Hiroshima on August 6 and a plutonium bomb that did the same to Nagasaki three days later.

The American nuclear program did not end after the war. Though the terrible human toll in Hiroshima and Nagasaki horrified many scientists and led them to advocate pacifist or antinuclear causes, others saw further developments of nuclear weapons as necessary for their country's leadership and survival in a hostile world. Teller, especially, became an articulate and passionate advocate of the next generation of nuclear weapons: the so-called hydrogen bomb. The source of that weapon's power would be nuclear fusion, which releases energy when smaller nuclei like hydrogen combine to form larger nuclei, like helium. That phenomenon powers the Sun and stars. Ironically, Bethe, one of the staunchest postwar antinuclear advocates, was the author of many important theoretical papers on fusion reactions, beginning while he was still in Germany in the 1930s.

(Opposite page) *Ordinary uranium cannot sustain a chain reaction because only a small fraction of the nuclei are fissionable ^{235}U. Most of the rest are slightly heavier ^{238}U. To make a bomb, scientists have to separate the two isotopes, a difficult multistage process that involves creation of uranium hexafluoride (UF_6) gas. Today's technology uses high-speed centrifuges to separate the heavier UF_6 molecules containing ^{238}U from the lighter UF_6 molecules containing ^{235}U. The Manhattan Project relied on much larger gaseous diffusion cells to accomplish the same thing. If a "critical mass" of the resulting enriched uranium is in one place, a chain reaction will start, but it is likely to blow itself to pieces before generating much energy. Making a bomb required a way to keep a critical mass together long enough for the chain reaction to involve most of the ^{235}U nuclei. Driving it together in an implosion with conventional explosives was the solution.*

The atomic bomb dropped on Nagasaki, Japan, on August 9, 1945, used plutonium as its fissionable material. (U.S. Department of Energy Office of History & Heritage Resources)

He was awarded the Nobel Prize in physics for his contributions to the theory of nuclear reactions in 1967. By then the hydrogen bomb was 15 years old, and the world was in the midst of a thermonuclear arms race.

Other countries also had secret nuclear programs during the war, but none of them was as large and sustained as the American program. The Japanese navy worked on a nuclear reactor to power its warships but soon backed away when the cost seemed too high and the benefits too uncertain. Nishina led a group studying ^{235}U separation at the University of Tokyo, but their progress was slow. The Soviet Union had a much smaller version of the Manhattan Project. Their "Laboratory No. 2," had 74 employees, including 25 scientists, in contrast to the 2,000 people working at Los Alamos. Although they were still far from having a bomb when the war ended, they continued their bomb-making efforts with both research and espionage. In the 1950s, their weapons program emerged as a significant rival to American nuclear superiority.

The failure of Germany's nuclear weapons program continues to fascinate historians. In the early years of the war, with Heisenberg's leadership and the work of many brilliant physicists and engineers, progress in Germany toward ^{235}U separation may have matched that in the United States and Britain. However, after 1942, the leaders of the German war machine turned their interest elsewhere, and Heisenberg focused the program on nuclear reactors instead. Had they known the extent of the American progress toward purifying ^{235}U, their choices might have been different. Captured after the war, many German scientists claimed to have failed deliberately because the device's destructive power was so fearsome, but that was most likely a face-saving explanation contrived to make them look good and to justify their actions.

The historical verdict is that the Third Reich was among the most evil governments ever to rule a nation, but the German nuclear scientists who worked for that government have been judged more charitably. Most of them, Heisenberg included, were never members of the Nazi party or supporters of its ideology. They saw themselves as loyal citizens using their considerable talents in their country's cause. In that sense, their motivations were not very different from most of the Manhattan Project physicists who succeeded where the Germans did not. Still, even if they did not know about the Nazi death camps, they were aware of their government's brutal laws and actions against Jews and other people deemed to be inferior or defective. Sixty years later, people still debate about what the scientists should have done under those circumstances. And people still wonder what the world would be like if the race to build the bomb had turned out the other way around.

Cosmic Rays and Subatomic Particles

Feynman's approach to QED had an interesting element in common with Yukawa's theory of the strong nuclear force. Both recognized that the quantum uncertainty principle put the law of conservation of energy in a new light. In Feynman's theory, photons or other particles could flicker into and out of existence. As long as the product of the lifetime and the energy (or mass) of those "virtual" particles is less than Planck's constant, their existence does not violate the uncertainty principle. Energy may not be conserved for an instant, but the uncertainty principle states that there is no way to detect that. As shown in the Feynman diagram illustration on page 94, these virtual events must be included in QED computations. In his theory of the strong force, Yukawa applied a similar line of thinking. He realized that confining a particle to a nucleus imposes a very small uncertainty in its position. That yields a correspondingly large uncertainty in its momentum—and thus its energy or mass. That was how he determined the mass of the theoretical mesons that are exchanged in the strong nuclear interactions between nucleons.

In Yukawa's theory, those mesons are like Feynman's virtual photons. They exist and then disappear so fast that it is impossible to measure any increase in nuclear mass. However, if the nucleus undergoes a sufficiently energetic collision, some of that energy could shake a meson loose where it could be detected. Events of that sort might take place in cyclotrons or at the upper limits of Earth's atmosphere where high-speed particles from space were generating cosmic rays. Particle-detection techniques were constantly improving, including new photographic emulsions that were sensitive to the ions produced by electrons and other subatomic particles passing through. When the film was developed, the paths of particles were revealed as dark tracks. In 1947, physicists Cecil Powell

Hideki Yukawa, developer of the theory of the strong interaction, with his wife, Niels Bohr (left), and J. Robert Oppenheimer, scientific leader of the Manhattan Project. (Niels Bohr Archive; AIP Emilio Segrè Visual Archives)

(1903–69) and Giuseppe Occhialini (1907–93) from Britain's Bristol University took some photographic plates with an advanced emulsion to a cosmic-ray laboratory high in the French Pyrenees Mountains and made a stunning discovery. They saw short tracks from particles of a previously unknown type. Their masses were somewhat larger than the mesotron, the oversize electron discovered by Anderson and Neddermeyer in 1937 (see the preceding chapter). Where a track from one of those particles ended, another track began in another direction. Powell and Occhialini recognized the new track and concluded that the first particle had decayed into two pieces: a mesotron and an electrically neutral particle that left no trail. It quickly became clear that the original particle was the meson predicted by Yukawa's theory, which was expected to decay into a mesotron and a neutrino.

As the Bristol Group was discovering Yukawa's meson, George Rochester (1908–2001) and Clifford Butler (1922–99) at Manchester University were puzzling over two odd cloud chamber observations, one from the previous October 15 and one from May 23. Ultimately, these were recognized as particles with slightly more than half the mass of a proton. The term *meson*, meaning a particle with mass was intermediate between an electron and a proton, suddenly covered more territory than anticipated. The particles found by Rochester and Butler, like those detected by Powell and Occhialini, responded to the strong nuclear force. The mesotron did not. It was time to clarify terminology. Eventually, the mesotron became known as a muon, and the name meson was given to a class of particles including the renamed pions (or pi mesons), found by the Bristol scientists, and the *kaons* (K mesons), found by the Manchester group.

The kaon observations found particles not only with positive and negative charges but also a slightly heavier neutral kaon. Powell and Occhiliani did not find neutral pions, even though Yukawa's theory predicted their existence. That hole in the theory was filled in 1949, when R. Bjorkland and colleagues detected the neutral pion in Berkeley's newest cyclotron. It was no wonder that the particle proved so elusive. Not only was it neutral, which meant that it could only be found as a result of its decay, but it also lived only a hundred-millionth as long as its charged pion siblings.

Clearly, the new accelerators and detection techniques had set the stage for more particle discoveries. Those discoveries would continue for the remainder of the century, and they would lead to theories about the nature of matter that would be every bit as challenging as quantum mechanics had been.

Other Fields in Physics in the 1940s

While technology was focusing on the application of unstable (radioactive or fissile) nuclei, many physicists were more interested in stable ones. In particular, they were curious about why certain elements were more abundant and had more naturally occurring isotopes than others. Nature appeared to favor certain numbers of protons and neutrons over others. During the 1930s, a few physicists had suggested that protons and neutrons in nuclei might fill shells of quantum states just as electrons did, but they had no strong theory to explain why 2, 8, 20, 50, 82, and 126 were *magical numbers*, a term probably coined by Wigner. The first solid theory came independently from two researchers in 1948–49, Polish-born German physicist Maria Goeppert-Mayer (1906–72), who had immigrated to the United States in 1930, and German physicist Hans Jensen (1907–73) and two colleagues. Their theories were based on quantum numbers and wave functions rather than the liquid-drop model that had proven so successful for explaining fission. In 1963, Wigner, Goeppert-Mayer, and Jensen shared the Nobel Prize in physics for their theories of the structure of the atomic nucleus.

One of the motivations for Goeppert-Mayer was to understand what phenomena underlay the relative abundance of the elements in the universe. Her work proved to be particularly useful to Gamow and his student Ralph Alpher (1921–   ) in calculating the ratio of helium to hydrogen in their model of the early universe. They proposed that the cosmos began with a giant explosion and has been gradually expanding and cooling ever since. In 1950, British astronomer Fred Hoyle (1915–2001), who had developed an alternative proposal for the origin of atoms called the steady-state hypothesis, derisively named Gamow's concept the "big bang." The name stuck, and a tug-of-war between the two cosmological ideas that would go on for decades was under way.

Radioactivity began to take on an important role in other scientific fields in the 1940s. The best-known example is the use of the radioactive isotope carbon 14 to date once-living objects found at archaeological sites. The isotope has a relatively short half-life (5,730 years) and would not exist at all on Earth if it were not constantly being replenished by cosmic rays interacting with nuclei of atmospheric gases. Once an organism dies, it no longer takes in fresh carbon dioxide from the air. Thus the ratio of ^{14}C atoms to the more common ^{12}C gradually decreases in formerly living matter and serves as a way to date an archaeological site.

Major advances in the technology of flight continued after the war, as engineers applied physics to create the first supersonic aircraft and the first commercial jet planes. But probably the most significant technological development of the late 1940s was not widely recognized at the time. In 1948, physicists William Shockley (1910–89), Walter H. Brattain (1902–87), and John Bardeen (1908–91) of Bell Laboratories in New Jersey invented a *semiconducting* device known as the *transistor*. Only eight years later, with a revolution in miniaturization and advances in electronics well under way, the public was not surprised to learn that the trio had been awarded the Nobel Prize in physics. This work is discussed in more detail in the next chapter.

Scientist of the Decade: Richard Feynman (1918–1988)

Richard Feynman will always be known as the genius who reenvisioned the electromagnetic force as a quantum phenomenon and who replaced complex equations with simple diagrams. But he will also be recalled as a "curious character," which is how he described himself in the subtitles of his best-selling autobiographical memoirs, *Surely You're Joking, Mr. Feynman,* published in 1985, and *What Do You Care What Other People Think,* published only months before his death in 1988. Feynman was not merely a person who marched to the beat of a different drummer, as individualists are often said to do. He *was* that different drummer.

To say that Feynman was born and raised in New York City is true, but misleading. He grew up in the middle-class village of Far Rockaway on the city's outer limits on the south shore of Long Island. His father, Melville Feynman, probably would have studied science if he had been able to afford college. Instead, he earned the family's living from a variety of business ventures that never quite produced the success he had hoped for. Melville read to Richard from the *Encyclopaedia Brittanica,* explaining things as they went along. Richard inherited Melville's adventurous curiosity and knack for explaining things. In the 1960s, at the height of his career as a physics professor at the California Institute of Technology (Caltech), he took on the task of teaching the introductory physics courses. His lectures quickly became famous for their clarity and lively presentation. They were filmed and distributed throughout the world, and they became the basis of a classic 1963 three-volume text called *The Feynman Lectures on Physics.* Today scientists nearing retirement remember those books from their student days, as much for the picture of the author playing the bongos as for the content.

If Melville can be credited for the clarity of those lectures, then Feynman's mother, Lucille,

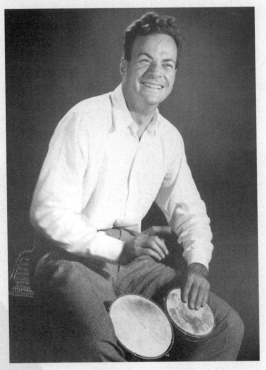

Richard Feynman, known for his free spirit as well as his creativity, playing bongo drums (Tom Harvey, courtesy Brookhaven National Laboratory)

deserves recognition for the style. Feynman described her in *What Do You Care What Other People Think?* "My mother didn't know anything about science, [but] she had a great influence on me as well. In particular, she had a wonderful sense of humor, and I learned from her that the highest forms of understanding we can achieve are laughter and human compassion."

Feynman's brilliance became apparent at an early age. By the time he was in high school, he taught himself calculus and was earning money by repairing radios in the neighborhood. In his senior year, he stood out as by far the best student in an honors physics class. His quick mind for schoolwork allowed him plenty of time for studying what may have been his greatest interest: girls, especially the popular and artistic Arline Greenbaum, whom he met when they were both 13.

In the fall of 1935, Feynman enrolled as a freshman physics major at the Massachusetts Institute of Technology (MIT). In his sophomore year, he enrolled in an advanced theoretical physics course normally taken by seniors and graduate students and quickly stood out. In his senior thesis, he developed an ingenious quantum mechanical technique that he published in the major physics journal *Physical Review* and that became a standard mathematical tool for physical chemists. He then went on to Princeton University for graduate school and produced the remarkable doctoral thesis described in this chapter.

Meanwhile, Arline's health became fragile. Despite a diagnosis of tuberculosis of the lymphatic system—a slow death sentence—the couple decided to marry. They eloped in June of 1942 and drove west to New Mexico after Feynman finished his doctorate. Arline lived in a sanitorium in Albuquerque, while her husband worked at Los Alamos and visited her on weekends. She died in the spring of 1945.

At Los Alamos, Feynman was noted for his brilliant analyses, his willingness to argue with anyone—including Hans Bethe, the leader of the theoretical physics group—and his exploits as a self-appointed guardian of security. He used his safe-cracking skills to get past the protection of others' secret results, leaving notes behind to tell them how he did it. After the war, he joined Bethe on the faculty at Cornell University in Ithaca, New York. After a few years, he got fed up with snowy weather there. Though he regretted leaving Bethe, he accepted a position with the California Institute of Technology (Caltech) in Pasadena in 1951.

Among Caltech's attractions was its proximity to the Sunset Strip. In *Surely You're Joking,* he wrote about "the nightclubs and the bars and the action." Caltech allowed him to start with a yearlong sabbatical in Rio de Janeiro, a city he had wanted to return to ever since a six-week visit in 1949. He lectured in the mornings and spent his afternoons and evenings meeting friendly women at Rio's famous beaches and bars. Recognizing the early signs of alcoholism, he soon gave up drinking, but he continued going to bars. One day, he took a young woman to the Egyptology section of the museum and shared some interesting facts that he had learned from Mary Louise Bell, an old girlfriend from Ithaca who had relocated near Pasadena. Impulsively, he proposed to her by mail. They were married the next June (1952) and divorced in 1956.

Feynman's third marriage, to Gweneth Howarth, lasted the rest of his life. He noticed a girl in a polka-dot bikini on a beach at Lake Geneva and was immediately attracted. They married in 1960 and had two children and as normal a family life as a character as curious as Richard Feynman could manage. He died after a long battle with cancer in 1988, but not until he had one last public triumph. He was asked to join the commission investigating the 1986 explosion of the space shuttle *Challenger*. Though he was already desperately ill, Gweneth encouraged him to accept. The commission needed someone like him to poke around off the beaten track. The most memorable moment of those hearings took place when Feynman demonstrated that a critical O-ring lost its flexibility at low temperatures. He dipped a piece of rubber into a glass of ice water and showed how stiff it became. From that moment forward, no one could doubt that the *Challenger* tragedy was due to its launching on a rare Florida day when the temperatures had dropped below freezing. Richard Feynman, that famously different drummer, had set the cadence for the rest of the investigation.

Further Reading

Books

Close, Frank, Michael Marten, and Christine Sutton. *The Particle Odyssey: A Journey to the Heart of Matter.* New York: Oxford University Press, 2002. A detailed and colorfully illustrated overview of the discovery of subatomic particles.

Cornwell, John. *Hitler's Scientists: Science, War, and the Devil's Pact.* New York: Viking, 2003. Provides insight into the political forces that shaped research in physics and the lives of physicists in the 1930s and 1940s.

Cropper, William H. *Great Physicists: The Life and Times of Leading Physicists from Galileo to Hawking.* New York: Oxford University Press, 2001. The life and times of many great physicists, including Feynman.

Feynman, Michelle. *Perfectly Reasonable Deviations from the Beaten Path: The Letters of Richard P. Feynman.* New York: Basic Books, 2005. A collection of Feynman's correspondence, selected and edited by his daughter.

Feynman, Richard. *The Feynman Lectures on Physics.* 3 vols. Reprint, Boston: Addison-Wesley Longman, 1970. A classic set of lectures that captures Feynman's unique approach and teaching style.

————. *QED: The Strange Theory of Light and Matter.* Princeton, N.J.: Princeton University Press, 1986. Based on a series of lectures at UCLA in which Feynman explained quantum electrodynamics to a broad audience.

————(as told to Ralph Leighton). *Surely You're Joking, Mr. Feynman: Adventures of a Curious Character.* New York: Norton, 1985. The first of two popular memoirs.

———— (————). *What Do You Care What Other People Think? Further Adventures of a Curious Character.* New York: Norton, 1988. Feynman's second memoir published just months before his death.

Gleick, James. *Genius: The Life and Science of Richard Feynman.* New York: Pantheon, 1992. One of two definitive Feynman biographies.

Kragh, Helge. *Quantum Generations: A History of Physics in the Twentieth Century.* Princeton, N.J.: Princeton University Press, 1999. An in-depth history of 20th-century physics and physicists.

Leighton, Ralph, ed. *Classic Feynman: All the Adventures of a Curious Character,* by Richard Feynman. New York: Norton, 2005. A compilation of Feynman's two memoirs in chronological order, with a foreword by Freeman Dyson.

Mehra, Jagdish. *The Beat of a Different Drum: The Life and Science of Richard Feynman.* Oxford: Oxford University Press, 1994. One of two definitive Feynman biographies.

Rhodes, Richard. *The Making of the Atomic Bomb.* New York: Simon & Schuster, 1986. A history of the Manhattan Project.

Suplee, Curt. *Physics in the 20th Century.* New York: Harry N. Abrams, 1999. A pictorial history of 20th-century physics.

Web Sites

American Institute of Physics, Center for History of Physics. Available online. URL: http://www.aip.org/history. Accessed March 27, 2006. Follow pull-down menu for special online exhibits or browse for a variety of written resources and images.

Feynman Online. Available online. URL: http://www.feynman.com. Accessed April 3, 2006. A tribute to Richard Feynman with many useful links to all aspects of his life and science, including streaming video of four lectures on QED in New Zealand in 1979.

Nobelprize.org. Available online. URL: http://nobelprize.org. Accessed March 27, 2006. The official Web site of the Nobel Foundation contains brief biographies of Nobel Prize winners, summaries of their prize-winning work, and their acceptance speeches.

The Science Museum. Available online. URL: http://www.sciencemuseum. org.uk. Accessed March 27, 2006. A British online science education resource that includes useful exhibits on many topics discussed in this book.

The Science Shelf, Books for the World Year of Physics 2005. Available online. URL: http://www.scienceshelf.com/WorldYearofPhysics.htm. Accessed April 26, 2006. This page on the book review site of Fred Bortz has brief comments about a number of books published in recognition of the World Year of Physics, plus links to reviews of a number of other physics books for nonspecialist readers.

World Year of Physics 2005. Available online. URL: http://www.physics2005.org. Accessed March 27, 2006. An online resource developed in honor of the centennial of Albert Einstein's "Miracle Year."

6

1951–1960:
Physics and the Rise of New Technologies

At the midpoint of the 20th century, physicists found themselves at a crossroads both as scientists and citizens. Their science had played a central role in ending World War II, but now many of the developers of the atomic bomb became politically active in opposition to nuclear weapons research. They warned of a new kind of war that could destroy civilization itself.

Others took the viewpoint that stopping weapons research was a mistake. No country could prevent its adversaries from developing more

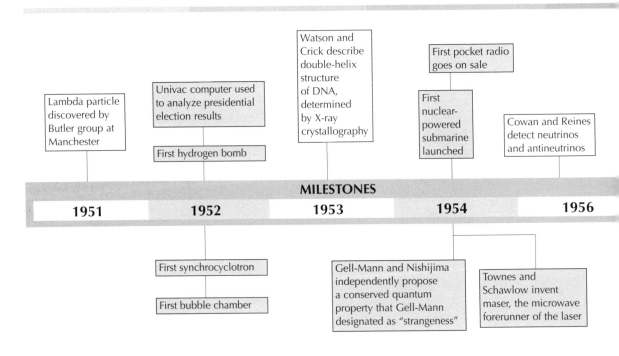

MILESTONES

| 1951 | 1952 | 1953 | 1954 | 1956 |

Lambda particle discovered by Butler group at Manchester

Univac computer used to analyze presidential election results

First hydrogen bomb

Watson and Crick describe double-helix structure of DNA, determined by X-ray crystallography

First nuclear-powered submarine launched

First pocket radio goes on sale

Cowan and Reines detect neutrinos and antineutrinos

First synchrocyclotron

First bubble chamber

Gell-Mann and Nishijima independently propose a conserved quantum property that Gell-Mann designated as "strangeness"

Townes and Schawlow invent maser, the microwave forerunner of the laser

powerful weapons systems. Thus nuclear weapons research was necessary for self-preservation. In the postwar world, new alliances, led by the United States and the Soviet Union, were intensely engaged in a different kind of competition. The battleground of this so-called cold war was ideology, capitalism against Communism. Each side was now pouring its resources into technologies that would demonstrate the superiority of its political system. They were racing to develop hydrogen bombs—thermonuclear devices that, like the Sun, produced energy from nuclear fusion reactions—and missiles that could deliver those bombs from half a world away.

Whether or not they were politically active after the war ended, most physicists were eager to return to their prewar research interests. Some pursued basic science, but others preferred investigations with technological applications. During the 1950s, physics research produced its share of surprises for both scientists and the public at large. As this chapter will discuss, particle accelerators and new detectors led to the discovery of a host of previously unimagined subatomic particles. But from the historical and cultural perspective, the most notable physics-related development of the decade was in solid-state electronics, particularly the transistor. It began a revolution in communication and computers that continues 50 years later.

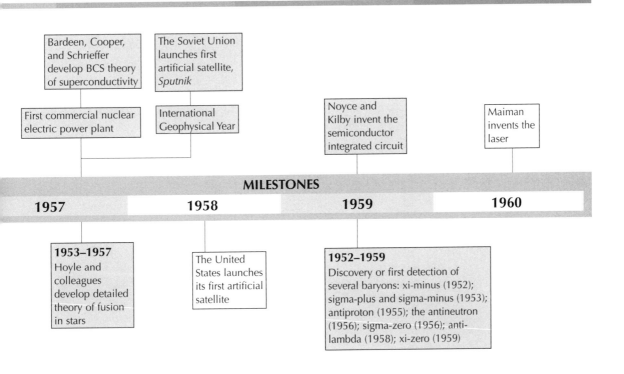

For solid-state physicists, the 1950s turned out to be a remarkable decade indeed. Not only did the transistor bring public attention to applications of their field, but a theoretical breakthrough also solved the mystery of superconductivity 46 years after the phenomenon was discovered. Both produced Nobel Prizes in physics—in 1956 for the transistor and in 1972 for superconductivity. Both prizes were shared by teams of three researchers. And the theoretical genius behind both achievements was John Bardeen, who became the first (and so far only) person to win two Nobel Prizes in the same field.

Solid-State Physics and Technology

Physicists and engineers foresaw the transistor's impact immediately when it was invented in 1948 at Bell Laboratories, but it was not until the middle of the 1950s that it entered people's everyday lives. For that reason, and because the 1940s were dominated by the war and quantum electrodynamics, the discussion of the research that led to the transistor has been deferred to this chapter.

At the beginning of the 1950s, few people outside of science and the electronics industry had heard of the transistor. Those familiar with the technology understood that transistors would begin to replace vacuum tubes in all types of electronic devices. Vacuum-tube radios were about the size of a modern toaster oven, and televisions were in boxes several feet long and at least two feet high and deep. Computers were as large as living rooms. They all were filled with vacuum tubes with glowing filaments that periodically burned out like lightbulbs.

That began to change in November 1954, when the Regency company began selling the TR-1 pocket radio with transistors instead of vacuum tubes for $49.95, about as much as the average worker earned in a week. Within a few years, manufacturers learned how to make transistors for a much lower cost. Soon transistor radios were so common that by the early 1960s, the word *transistor* had become almost synonymous with "pocket radio." People spoke of listening to their "transistors." Ten years after that, vacuum tubes were no longer being manufactured, except for use in specialized equipment.

In the late 1950s, most people were aware that transistors were replacing vacuum tubes in television sets, but fewer knew about a much more significant change in solid-state technology. With transistors replacing vacuum tubes, computers quickly required less power and maintenance, ran much faster, and had much more capability. The digital revolution had begun.

As noted, William Shockley, Walter Brattain, and John Bardeen shared the 1956 Nobel Prize in physics for inventing the transistor when they were at Bell Laboratories. But by the time they went to Stockholm to receive their awards, they were no longer a team. Bardeen had become a professor at the University of Illinois, and the trip interrupted his work with two students, Leon Cooper (1930–   ) and J. Robert Schrieffer

Inventors of the transistor (left to right) John Bardeen, William Shockley, and Walter Brattain in the laboratory (Lucent Technologies' Bell Telephone Laboratories, courtesy AIP Emilio Segrè Visual Archives)

(1931–   ), when they were on the verge of cracking one of the oldest and most important problems in solid-state physics, the mechanism underlying superconductivity.

Bardeen always sought projects that were both theoretically challenging and practically important. Among the most intriguing to him were so-called *many-body problems*, and no subfield of physics demanded more creative many-body analysis than solid state. Probably more than any other science, physics depends on mathematical models to represent and describe natural phenomena. Physicists often begin by noticing mathematical relationships in a set of measurements. Then they look for fundamental physical principles to explain them.

Planetary motion is a prime example. Johannes Kepler had noted three mathematical relationships or "laws" that applied to the orbits of the planets. The physical explanation came decades later from Sir Isaac Newton. His laws of motion and gravity produced Kepler's formulas as a consequence. Newton's laws produce Kepler's exact equations only in a special case, namely the interaction of two bodies such as the Sun and one planet. The real solar system has more than one planet, and the full computation of their motions is more complex. Each planet influences the others, and the resulting orbits deviate slightly from Kepler's prediction. Because the planets are much smaller than the Sun, those deviations are small and were not noticed until more precise measurement tools became available. Thus two-body, rather than many-body, analysis was sufficient at first.

A similar situation arose in quantum physics. Physicists had noticed mathematical patterns in the hydrogen spectrum (such as the Balmer series of spectral lines). Early quantum theory treated the hydrogen atom as a two-body system (a proton and an electron), and calculations produced an exceptionally good match for the observed spectrum. But to go beyond hydrogen to larger atoms, quantum mechanics needed to describe the states of many electrons. The computations became increasingly complex.

When faced with complexity, physicists often look for approximations. In this case, for each electron in a multi-electron atom, they averaged out the electrical repulsions from all the others and treated that as a *perturbation*—a minor correction—to the electrical attraction of the nucleus. In other words, they replaced the many-body calculation by a set of two-body calculations, one for each electron interacting with a modified nucleus. That made the mathematics manageable and produced not quite exact—but exceptionally useful—results. It worked because an electron in an atom experiences one dominating force from the nucleus and many much smaller forces from other electrons.

Many-body mathematics becomes much more difficult when there is not a single dominant force. For example, certain electrons in a solid interact with more than one nucleus, so computing their quantum states and energy levels requires innovative many-body calculations. That analysis results in three different types of electron wave functions. The first type is for electrons bound to a single atom, such as those in closed shells. Their wave functions and corresponding energy levels can be computed from two-body mathematical models involving only the electron and its nucleus. The wave function for such an electron is concentrated around its orbit in the atom to which it belongs.

Electrons involved in chemical bonds have the second type of wave functions. Those wave functions can be computed from mathematical models involving a small number of bodies—the electrons involved in the bonding plus the nuclei of the atoms they bind together. The resulting wave functions are concentrated in the region of the bonds, as described in the sidebar "Electron Energy Levels and Wave Functions in Solids" on page 118. Those electrons have energy levels in the valence band, which was described in chapter 4. That sidebar also describes the third type of electron wave function, which corresponds to energy levels in the conduction band (also described in chapter 4). Conduction electrons belong to all the atoms equally. Thus their wave functions rise and fall like waves on a limitless ocean, with the pattern of wave crests and troughs matching the crystal pattern of atoms in the solid.

As physicists sought to understand the properties of solids, it became clear that many phenomena—among them the conduction of heat and electricity; the reflection, transmission, and absorption of light; and the material's magnetic behavior—were related to electrons. The Pauli exclusion principle dictates that each electron has a unique quantum state and corresponding energy level, either within a closed shell of an atom, as part of a chemical bond with its energy level in the valence band or as a free electron with energy level in the conduction band.

Electrical Conductors, Insulators, and Semiconductors

To understand the history of semiconductor electronics, it is first necessary to understand the electrical properties of solids. That means this book must make a temporary but necessary diversion from the history of physics to the science itself.

Solids fall into three different classifications according to the way that they conduct electricity: conductors, insulators, and semiconductors. Conductors are usually metallic, and they allow electricity to pass through them easily. On the atomic level, they have electrons in their conduction band. Conduction electrons move through the conductor at random, occasionally bouncing off atoms and changing direction speed and direction. When the conductor is connected to a source of electrical pressure (voltage), such as a battery or generator, the electrons' motion is no longer completely random. Though they still move irregularly, the conduction electrons generally flow away from the negatively charged terminal (the cathode) and toward the positive terminal (the anode) of the voltage source. As fast as those electrons enter the anode, other electrons flow into the conductor from the cathode to replace them.

Except for the special case of superconductivity, the electrons lose some energy as they bounce their way through the material from the cathode to the anode. That phenomenon is responsible for electrical resistance. The resistance of an electrically conducting material usually increases as it gets warmer. The atoms of a solid are always vibrating around their "home" or equilibrium position. When the material is hotter, its atoms vibrate more rapidly, which makes an electron's collisions with those atoms more disruptive to its motion. When the temperature is higher, an electron travels a longer, jerkier path on the way to the anode, which means it meets more electrical resistance.

Many-body quantum mechanical calculations for solids always yield a valence band and a conduction band with a gap between them. The size of that gap dictates whether a material is a good insulator. Insulators do not conduct electricity, but no material is a perfect insulator. As temperatures rise, the average energy of the electrons in each atom increases. Some electrons do not stay in the lowest set of energy levels. In insulators, the valence band has plenty of available higher-energy states to accommodate the increase in thermal energy. To jump out of the valence band into the conduction band, the electrons would need so much energy that it almost never happens. Thus most electrons in insulators remain bound to single atoms. Almost all the rest serve as bonding electrons

Electron Energy Levels and Wave Functions in Solids

This is a simplified discussion of some of the mathematics that physicists developed to treat the many-body interactions that electrons experience in solids. It begins with the two-body interaction between an electron and its nucleus.

Mathematically, physicists represent that interaction as a three-dimensional graph of the electron's potential energy, which increases as the electron moves outward from the nucleus, but the illustrations here show one dimension only. The result is the top of illustration (a), a "potential well" with the nucleus in the middle. Horizontal lines in the well represent the allowed quantum mechanical energy levels, which get closer together as the electron gets farther from the nucleus. That decreasing spacing between energy levels means that there is an unlimited (infinite) number of quantum states for the electron in its atom.

The bottom of illustration A) is a representation of the electron wave function for one particular quantum state and its corresponding energy level. It peaks sharply at a distance from the nucleus corresponding to the orbital radius for that quantum state, signifying that the probability of finding the electron along that path is high, and the probability of finding it elsewhere is very low.

In solids, the atoms are so close together that an atom's outermost electrons may experience an electrical attraction to a neighboring nucleus that is as strong as to its own. In that case, it no longer can be said to belong to a particular atom. It may belong to two (or a few) atoms. Those atoms are then bound together either covalently or ionically, as described in chapter 4.

Illustration B) shows what happens when physicists apply the mathematics of quantum mechanics to two atoms that share electrons. The atoms' potential wells overlap and produce a double-dip well with a peak in the middle that is lower than the outside. That cuts off the upper portion of the original two wells where they overlap and leaves behind a small, finite number of allowed single-atom energy states. Because of the Pauli principle, no two electrons can have the same quantum state. In many two-atom cases, the number of single-atom states is less than the number of elec-

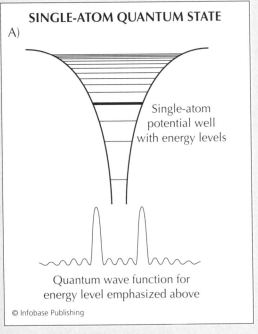

SINGLE-ATOM QUANTUM STATE

A)

Single-atom potential well with energy levels

Quantum wave function for energy level emphasized above

© Infobase Publishing

The upper part of this drawing envisions a single atom as an extremely deep potential well with the nucleus at the center. The walls of the well represent the amount of potential energy an electron would have at that distance from the center. The lines represent electron energy levels, one of which is emphasized. The lower part of the drawing represents the wave function of an electron occupying the emphasized energy level. The wave function peaks sharply at a distance equal to the radius of the orbit for that energy level. That means the electron has a very high probability of being found at that distance from the nucleus, though other distances are possible.

trons in the atoms. That means some electrons must occupy a new set of energy levels belonging to both atoms. Those levels make up the valence band discussed in chapter 4. Their wave functions do not have a sharp peak in an orbital region around one atom or the other; rather, they extend across the region between them where the bond forms. That means a binding electron is just as likely to be near one atom or the other and also has a high probability of being between them.

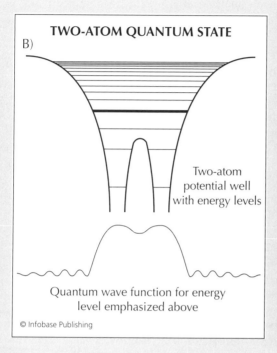

TWO-ATOM QUANTUM STATE

B)

Two-atom
potential well
with energy levels

Quantum wave function for energy
level emphasized above

© Infobase Publishing

If two atoms are close enough together for their potential wells to overlap, the result is a double-dip well with some low-energy levels for states in which the electron belongs to one atom plus higher-energy valence band levels in which it is shared by two atoms in a covalent bond. The wave function for a valance-band energy level has a broad peak, showing that the electron is most likely to be found in the region between the atoms.

Illustration C) shows the next step, when the entire solid body is considered. Now even the outer walls of the two-body potential wells are lowered. This reduces the valence band to a finite number of quantum states. In certain materials such as metals, the number of single-atom states plus the number of valence band states is less than the total number of electrons. Some electrons must belong neither to any atom nor to any bond between atoms but rather to all the atoms. Their energy levels are in the conduction band, and they flow freely throughout the material. Reflecting the probability that a conduction electron can be found anywhere in the material, its wave function rises and falls in a pattern that matches the crystalline arrangement of the atoms.

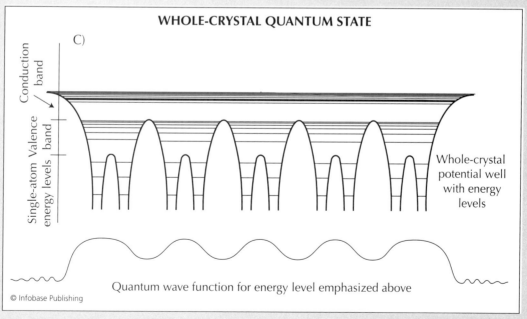

WHOLE-CRYSTAL QUANTUM STATE

C)

Conduction band

Single-atom Valence band
energy levels

Whole-crystal
potential well
with energy
levels

Quantum wave function for energy level emphasized above

© Infobase Publishing

In a crystal, besides the single-atom and two-atom energy levels, there is a higher set of energy levels belonging to all the atoms. This is the conduction band, and the wave functions of its electrons have a series of low, broad peaks, meaning that they can be found near any atom in the crystal.

between atoms—which means their energy is in the valence band—so they are not free to flow. That means insulators block the flow of electric current almost completely. Another way to put it is that the resistance of an insulator is extremely high.

In semiconductors, the valence band electron energy levels are nearly full, and the gap between the valence and conduction bands is small. As the temperature of a semiconductor rises, some electrons gain enough energy to jump out of the valence band into the conduction band. Thus the electrical resistance of a semiconductor is high but not extremely high, making it neither a good conductor nor a good insulator. A semiconductor's resistance decreases (or its conductivity increases) as its temperature rises, which is opposite to the behavior of a conductor.

The most important property of a semiconductor for electronics is the way its electrical conductivity can be manipulated. The most commonly used semiconductor is the element silicon, which has four valence electrons per atom. Pure silicon forms covalently bonded crystals in which every silicon atom shares one of its valence electrons with each of four neighbors. That arrangement gives each atom in the crystal a closed shell of eight electrons. However, because those electrons are shared among several atoms, that closed shell is not bound as tightly as it would be if all eight electrons belonged to one atom. The valence band is filled, and the gap between it and the conduction band is not very large. Thus even at room temperature, there is enough heat energy to shake loose a few valence electrons into the conduction band.

Since electrons carry a negative electric charge, every silicon atom that loses an electron to the conduction band is left with an excess of positive charge. The electron in the conduction band has, in effect, created a positively charged *hole* associated with a silicon atom. That hole can attract an electron from a neighboring atom. When that happens, the hole has moved to the neighbor. Because of the heat energy in the crystal, electron-hole pairs are created at a steady rate. The number of pairs would grow steadily except that a conduction electron created in one place will sometimes meet a hole someplace else and fill it. That is called an *annihilation* event because it makes both the electron and hole disappear. When the electron-hole annihilation rate is equal to the electron-hole creation rate, the number of each type of charge levels off, and both types move freely through the crystal in equal numbers.

If the terminals of a battery are connected to opposite sides of a crystal of silicon, electrons flow toward and into the anode, while holes flow toward the cathode where they are filled by electrons from the battery. The flow of current is much smaller than it would be if the battery terminals were connected across a metal wire, but the silicon is clearly not behaving like an insulator.

So far, except for a brief mention of crystal defects in chapter 4, this book has been treating crystals as if they are perfectly repeating arrangements of atoms. In fact, the most important technological

ELECTRICAL CONDUCTIVITY IN A SEMICONDUCTOR

© Infobase Publishing

The presence of impurity atoms can influence whether a semiconductor has an excess of electrons (n-type) or holes (p-type).

applications of semiconductors result from intentionally introducing impurities into an otherwise nearly perfect crystal of a semiconducting material. Suppose a little bit of phosphorus—silicon's neighbor in the periodic table with one more proton and one more electron per atom—is added to silicon. The phosphorus atoms replace silicon atoms in the crystal arrangement. They share four of their five valence electrons with neighboring silicon, and the fifth electron ends up in the conduction band without creating a hole. Because of the electrons in the conduction band, the impure silicon is a better conductor, but the current is only due to the flow of negative particles. For that reason, it is called an *n-type semiconductor.*

On the other hand, suppose the added impurity is silicon's other neighbor, aluminum, which lacks one proton and one electron compared to silicon. When an aluminum atom replaces a silicon atom, it only has three valence electrons to share, and the crystal ends up a *p-type semiconductor* with a surplus of positively charged holes. Again, its ability to conduct electricity is enhanced, but this time, it is the holes that carry the current.

Joining a *p*-type semiconductor to an *n*-type semiconductor creates a device called a *diode.* If the anode of a battery is connected to the *p*-type side, and the cathode is connected to the *n*-type side, the voltage drives

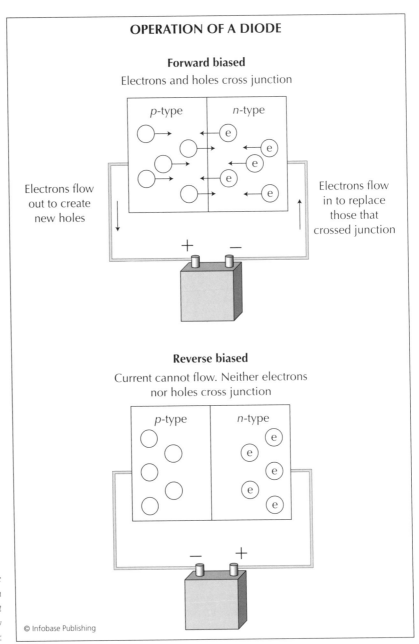

OPERATION OF A DIODE

Forward biased
Electrons and holes cross junction

p-type   *n*-type

Electrons flow
out to create
new holes

Electrons flow
in to replace
those that
crossed junction

+   −

Reverse biased
Current cannot flow. Neither electrons
nor holes cross junction

p-type   *n*-type

−   +

© Infobase Publishing

The junction between an n-type and a p-type semiconductor can function as a diode, a device that allows electrical current to flow in one direction but not the other.

both the holes in the *p*-type side and the electrons in the *n*-type side toward the junction, where they meet and annihilate each other. The anode attracts electrons and creates new holes in the *p*-type side, while the cathode sends new electrons into the *n*-type side. The result is a steady current. The diode is said to be forward biased.

But if the battery is reversed, the voltage draws the *n*-type side's electrons toward the anode and the *p*-type side's holes toward the cathode. This time, opposite charges build up on the outside of the diode and neutralize the battery's voltage. There are no charges to move through the junction, and so no current flows, and the diode is said to be reverse biased. The diode is thus a one-way valve for electricity. It is useful for transforming alternating current into direct current.

Transistors are semiconductor devices that act as amplifiers or controllable electrical switches. They now take many forms, but one of the first types made—and the easiest to explain—is like two diodes back-to-back, forming a three-layer sandwich of *n*-type and *p*-type semiconductors. The diagram shows the operation of an *n-p-n* transistor, where electrons may flow from the cathode into one *n*-type region called the emitter, through a *p*-type region called the base, to a second *n*-type region called the collector, and then into the anode. (Holes may flow in the opposite

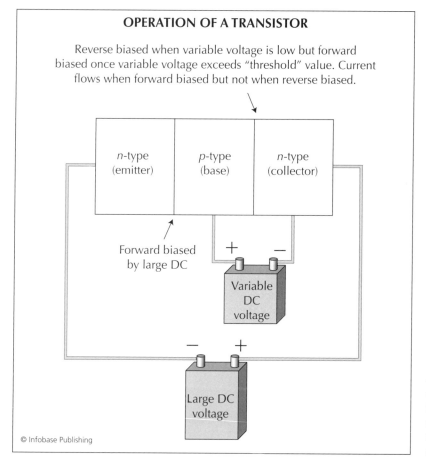

OPERATION OF A TRANSISTOR

Reverse biased when variable voltage is low but forward biased once variable voltage exceeds "threshold" value. Current flows when forward biased but not when reverse biased.

n-type (emitter)

p-type (base)

n-type (collector)

Forward biased by large DC

+ −

Variable DC voltage

− +

Large DC voltage

© Infobase Publishing

A transistor is a semiconductor device in which a small change in applied voltage can control a large change in current flow, making it useful as an amplifier or a controllable on-off switch.

direction.) Whether and how much current flows depends on a small variable voltage (opposite to the main voltage) placed across the base-collector junction. Without that voltage, the base-collector junction would block the current like a reverse-biased diode; but if that voltage is large enough, the junction is forward biased, and the electrons pass through.

In other words, there is a threshold base-collector voltage at which a change in transistor current occurs. If the threshold is sharp, changing the voltage acts like a switch to turn the transistor on and off. If the threshold is more gradual, then the transistor can be an amplifier, which responds to a small change in voltage with a large change in its current across the threshold region.

In the late 1940s, many physicists were working out the many-body quantum theory of the solid state, especially as it applied to semiconductors. At Bell Laboratories, John Bardeen emerged as a leader because he also understood the practical engineering issues of creating semiconducting electronic devices. It is one thing to talk about controlling the impurities in a piece of silicon and quite another to create a *p-n-p* or *n-p-n* sandwich with the desired properties. It took a blend of mathematical insights, laboratory skills, and technological inclination to actually fabricate a transistor. As noted in the previous chapter, the team of William Shockley, Walter H. Brattain, and Bardeen were the first to accomplish that feat, and it earned them the Nobel Prize in physics for 1956.

Superconductivity

In 1951, John Bardeen left Bell Labs to become a professor of electrical engineering at the University of Illinois. There he decided to tackle one of the most challenging outstanding problems in solid-state physics: superconductivity.

As described in chapter 2, the phenomenon was discovered in 1911 and soon led to a Nobel Prize for Heike Kamerlingh Onnes, but 40 years later, no one had come up with an explanation for it. Even as physicists began to understand how quantum mechanics and the crystalline arrangements of atoms and molecules in solids could produce electrical conductivity, they could not come up with a mechanism for an electron to travel through a conductor without any loss of energy. Inevitably, the electron would experience collisions with the atoms of the solid, and each collision would result in an exchange of energy. Using statistical mechanics, physicists calculated that the average effect of those collisions was a small decrease in the electron's energy that can be measured as electrical resistance. The lost energy would show up as heat in the solid.

The calculations predicted that cooling the solid would decrease its resistance. A graph showing how resistance changed with temperature should be a straight line that would reach zero at the unattainable temperature of absolute zero. That decreasing trend is in fact what Kammerlingh Onnes saw until his wires were cooled to a certain critical

*John Bardeen (left), Leon
Cooper (center), and John
Robert Schrieffer (right) at
the Nobel Prize ceremony
recognizing their development
of the BCS theory of
superconductivity* (AIP Emilio
Segrè Visual Archives)

temperature where the resistance abruptly dropped to zero. The electrons were still colliding with the atoms of the solid, but they bounced
off with no loss of energy. Bardeen was not alone in thinking that quantum mechanics might hold the explanation for this phenomenon. As a
professor, he supervised a number of graduate students, assigning them
research problems that would lead to insight into the quantum mechanical properties of solids.

One such property related to vibrations in the crystal lattice. Physicists
created mathematical models that represented crystals as a lattice of
atoms or molecules joined together by springs. If one molecule started
oscillating—jiggling back and forth, the springs would transmit the
vibration to its neighbors. Soon the whole crystal would be vibrating.
The analysis predicted that only certain modes and intensities of vibrations could be sustained. Just as quantum mechanics related the energy
of photons to transitions between allowed electron states with quantum
numbers, the new analysis predicted that vibrational energy also came
in packets corresponding to transitions between allowed states of lattice
oscillation. Physicists called the packets of vibrational energy *phonons*,
since they correspond to sound waves passing through the crystal.

Bardeen, Cooper, and Schrieffer thought that superconductivity might
result from electrons creating and absorbing phonons when they collided
with atoms. Instead of exchanging energy with a single atom in a collision, what would happen if electrons exchanged energy with the lattice as
a whole? They struggled with a number of ideas until Schrieffer made a

breakthrough—a different way to look at the electron wave function—and showed it to Cooper. Cooper agreed that Schrieffer's idea would work, and he added an important feature to it. Imagine that a pair of electrons with the same set of quantum numbers except for opposite spins were traveling through the lattice together. One would interact with the lattice to create a phonon, which the other would then absorb. They would both be bouncing along, interacting with the lattice but with no loss of energy as long as they remained paired up and exchanging phonons. Thermal activity in the crystal would tend to disrupt the "Cooper pairs," but just as water freezes into ice below a certain temperature, the rate of pair formation would exceed the rate of disruption when things got cold enough. That explained the critical temperature. Further calculations showed that Schrieffer's wave equation and Cooper's pairs explained other properties of superconducting materials as well.

As soon as the Bardeen, Cooper, and Schrieffer (BCS) theory of superconductivity appeared in print in 1957, there was little doubt that it was of Nobel Prize caliber. No one had ever been awarded two Nobels in the same field, but denying Bardeen would also mean denying Cooper and Schrieffer. The BCS threesome was honored with the award in 1972.

Nuclear Physics and Technology

Though solid-state physics dominated the scientific spotlight in the 1950s, nuclear physics continued to get more than its share of attention. As the cold war competition intensified, two distinct areas of nuclear technology were transforming national defense and the generation of electrical energy.

As noted in the preceding chapter, the 1940s ended with a clear American lead in the development of thermonuclear weapons. In 1952, the United States successfully detonated the first hydrogen bomb, which used a fission bomb as a trigger for an explosive nuclear fusion reaction. The Soviet Union quickly challenged American superiority and began detonating its own thermonuclear weapons. By 1960, it was clear that both nations had the capacity to destroy each other.

While nuclear fusion was being exploited for destructive purposes, physicists and engineers were developing beneficial uses for nuclear fission. As the Fermi reactor had first demonstrated, it was possible not only to produce a nuclear chain reaction but also to control and sustain it. It was only a matter of engineering to create plants that generated electricity from the energy of a controlled fission reactor. In 1954, the submarine USS *Nautilus* became the first ship powered by a nuclear generator, and in 1957, the first commercial nuclear electric power plant began operation in Shippingport, Pennsylvania, 25 miles from Pittsburgh.

While some physicists and engineers were learning how to apply nuclear fission and fusion, others were setting out to understand those phenomena better. Among them was British Astronomer Fred Hoyle. As noted in the preceding chapter, Hoyle was dubious of the Gamow-Alpher description that space, time, and the universe originated in a massive explosion of matter and energy, followed by an expansion and cooling that has continued ever since. He derided that model as the "big bang" and contrasted it with his own "steady-state" theory in which matter and energy is constantly created, keeping the concentration of matter of the universe constant even as it expands.

But no matter whether the universe is expanding in the aftermath of a cosmic explosion or because of the slow but steady creation of new matter, physicists agreed that the chemical elements beyond hydrogen and helium originated in the nuclear fusion reactions that power the stars. Between 1953 and 1957, Hoyle and his colleagues worked on a detailed theory of stellar fusion, including changes in the composition of stars and the reactions within them as they age. In the October 1957 issue of *Reviews of Modern Physics*, Hoyle, nuclear physicist William A. ("Willy") Fowler (1911–95) from Caltech, and the British husband-wife team of Geoffrey (1925–   ) and Margaret Burbidge (1919–   ) from Cambridge University published a landmark article that calculated how much of each isotope, from hydrogen through uranium, would be expected to exist in stars based on their life histories. Their calculated results matched the best measurements remarkably well, and Fowler shared the 1983 Nobel Prize in physics with Chandrasekhar for this work.

The Subatomic Particle "Zoo"

The 1950s also marked an explosive growth in the study of subatomic particles. In 1952, a new type of accelerator was invented and built. Called the synchrocyclotron or synchrotron, it compensated for relativistic limitations in the original cyclotron design noted in the preceding chapter. As such, it was able to mimic the production of cosmic-ray particles in the upper atmosphere.

In the same year, Donald A. Glaser (1926–   ) of the University of Michigan invented a new and more sensitive kind of particle detector called the bubble chamber. The combination of new accelerators to reach higher energy and improved detectors to measure the paths of short-lived subatomic particles—they often would decay into other particles—led to the discovery of several new particles whose existence was as puzzling as the "Who ordered that?" muon. Scientists named each new particle and cataloged its mass, charge, spin, lifetime, and its interactions with or transformation into other particles.

With the exception of the neutrino and antineutrino (see below), all the newly discovered particles of the 1950s were at least as massive as protons and neutrons. Physicists call those particles *baryons*, from the Greek word for heavy. The first new baryon to be discovered, in 1951 by the Butler cosmic ray group at Manchester (who had previously found the kaon), was an electrically neutral particle about 20 percent heavier than a neutron. They named it the lambda because of the tracks that revealed its existence in a cloud chamber. The uppercase version of that Greek letter looks like an inverted "V." Because it is uncharged, the lambda itself leaves no visible track in a cloud chamber, but it decays into a pair of charged particles that leave a distinctive lambda-shaped record of their passage.

In order of discovery, the other baryons discovered in the sixth decade of the century were the xi-minus (1952), the sigma-plus and sigma-minus (1953), the antiproton (expected but not detected until 1955), the anti-neutron (also expected but undetected until 1956), the sigma-zero (1956), the anti-lambda (1958), and the xi-zero (1959). No new middleweight mesons were detected in the 1950s, but in 1956, Clyde Cowan (1919–74) and Frederick Reines (1918–98) of Los Alamos National Laboratory detected the long-predicted but elusive neutrino and antineutrino in a nuclear reactor. These two new members of the lightweight *lepton* family joined the electron, positron, muon, and anti-muon.

The Cowan-Reines discoveries were soon more properly called electron-neutrinos and electron-antineutrinos. The reason for adding *electron* to their names is the discovery that radioactive beta decay—in which a neutron transforms into a proton, an electron (the beta particle), and an electron-antineutrino—is just one example of particle transformation governed by the weak nuclear force. Bubble chambers and synchrotrons not only made it possible for physicists to discover new baryons but also to study the various interactions and transformations that those particles underwent. They discovered that the larger baryons decay similarly to neutrons in beta decay, but they produce a muon and a muon-neutrino (or muon-antineutrino) instead of an electron and its neutrino. There was now an answer to the question of who ordered the muon, but it carried with it the prediction of a new undetected kind of neutrino.

Physicists were soon faced with an array of particles with properties that varied as much as species in a zoo. It reminded them of the situation in chemistry before the discovery of the periodic table of the elements. They hoped a modern Mendeleyev would arise in the 1960s to discover an orderly scheme for arranging the members of the "particle zoo" and for a new Pauli to find the principle on which that order was based. Murray Gell-Mann (1929–   ) would turn out to be both.

Gell-Mann first came to wide attention for a fruitful discovery in 1954, when he was a young professor at the University of Chicago. Japanese physicist Kazuhiko Nishijima (1926–   ) independently came up with the same idea at about the same time. Each proposed a new quantum number to describe interactions among those recently discovered strange particles: the kaon in the meson family, and the lambda, xi, and sigma in the baryon group. With a typical physicist's sense of humor, Gell-Mann called that number *strangeness*. Though Gell-Mann and Nishijima were unsure of the physical property that new quantum number represented, they were certain it was important because it was conserved in interactions involving the strong nuclear force: No matter what transformations took place, the total strangeness of the particles involved was the same afterward as it was before. Conservation laws always signify something of deep physical significance. As discussed in the next chapter, Gell-Mann's ability to see orderliness among the particles in the zoo not only brought an understanding of strangeness but also redefined what physicists considered a fundamental particle of matter.

Other Developments in 1950s Physics and Technology

Despite the political hostility of the cold war, the sixth decade of the 20th century was marked by remarkable international efforts, which, if not entirely cooperative, had more of the flavor of an athletic competition than a battle. The best example was the International Geophysical Year (IGY) of 1957, which not only produced evidence that Alfred Wegener's theory of continental drift was correct but also provided a mechanism for it called plate tectonics. The modern understanding of Earth as a multilayered planet, with its thin, rocky crust fractured into plates that slowly drift on a thick, hot, semisolid mantle, emerged from a variety of IGY projects.

The IGY competition also had military implications, especially in the race to orbit the world's first artificial satellite, which was won by the Soviet Union when it launched *Sputnik I* on October 4, 1957. The United States did not match that feat until January 31, 1958. By the end of the decade, the two nations were vying to be the first to place a human into orbit and return him safely.

In other physics-related developments, between 1951 and 1953 Rosalind Franklin (1920–58) of King's College in London used X-ray crystallography to investigate the structure of the deoxyribonucleic acid (DNA) molecule, which was known to carry genetic information in the nuclei of living cells. She was well on the way to deducing the famous double-helix structure of DNA when Francis Crick (1916–2004) and James Watson (1928–   ) of Cambridge University published their results in *Nature* on April 25, 1953. Many historians claim she would have been first if not for a very contentious relationship with her King's College colleague, Maurice Wilkins (1916–   ). Watson, Crick, and Wilkins shared the 1962 Nobel Prize in medicine or physiology for their accomplishments. Franklin may well have been more deserving than Wilkins, but she died of ovarian cancer in 1958. The prize is only given to living people and is never shared more than three ways.

The decade also saw several physics-related technological achievements. These include the first laser, invented in 1960 by Theodore Maiman (1927–   ). The word *laser* is an acronym for *light amplification by stimulated emission of radiation*. Albert Einstein first described the phenomenon of stimulated emission theoretically in 1917, but it was not

Scientist of the Decade: John Bardeen (1908–1991)

During the first half of the 20th century, physics was dominated by breakthrough ideas: relativity, which blended space and time, matter and energy; quantum mechanics, which blurred the distinction between waves and particles and replaced predictability with uncertainty; and nuclear physics, which led to the atomic bomb. These transformative discoveries, combined with the public persona and influence of Einstein, made the word *physicist* synonymous with eccentric genius to most people. The physicist's public image was this: brilliant but narrow, speaking in equations or working with giant "atom smashers," and far too wrapped up in work to have a normal life.

But just as the 1950s moved physics beyond theoretical breakthroughs to practical concerns, the decade also brought a different kind of individual to prominence in the field. This chapter's featured scientist, John Bardeen, pursued practical and technological applications with a down-to-earth midwest-American work ethic and way of life. He was not, as people would say, "an Einstein." Rather, he was an example of what the authors of his biography called *True Genius*, a quiet, innovative brilliance that brought out the best in his colleagues. He was a golf-playing family man whose work on the quantum mechanics of solids unleashed the semiconductor revolution and revealed the underlying mechanism of superconductivity.

John Bardeen was born in Madison, Wisconsin, on May 23, 1908, to parents who were firm believers in the value of an education. His father, Charles Bardeen (1871–1935), was the founder of the medical school at the University of Wisconsin and its first dean. His mother, Althea Harmer Bardeen (1875–1920), had been a teacher at a progressive experimental

John Bardeen, shown here with grandson Chuck in 1968, valued nothing more than family, though golf may have been a close second. He famously remarked that his two Nobel Prizes were probably better than his one hole-in-one on a favorite golf course. (The Bardeen Family Archives)

school established by John Dewey (1859–1952), who is generally regarded as one of the greatest educational reformers of the late 19th and early 20th century. Together Charles and Althea recognized and nurtured John's exceptional abilities, especially in mathematics. Althea died when John was only 11 years old, but he was already well launched. He finished his required courses at University High School by age 13 and began his studies at the University of Wisconsin at age 15.

Because he had difficulty selecting a major, considering physics and mathematics before settling on electrical engineering, John took five years to earn a bachelor's degree in 1928. He was able to apply some of his additional cred-

achieved in practice until brothers-in-law Charles Townes (1915–) and Arthur Schawlow (1921–99) of Columbia University invented the maser, the microwave equivalent of the laser, in 1954. Townes shared the Nobel Prize in physics in 1964 for that and other work related to the develop-its toward a master's degree, so he stayed on at Wisconsin to complete it. His thesis topic was on the use of electrical techniques to detect oil deposits. After completing his thesis at Wisconsin, he applied to the graduate program at Trinity College of Cambridge University but was turned down, so he stayed another year taking courses. Over the seven years he spent at Wisconsin, he studied with a number of notable physicists, including Werner Heisenberg, Paul Dirac, and Arnold Sommerfeld.

In 1930, John accepted a position at the Gulf Oil Company's research laboratories in Pittsburgh, Pennsylvania, working on new techniques to find oil. After three years, he was ready to go back to graduate school. This time, he applied and was accepted to a doctoral program in mathematics at Princeton University. Soon he was working with some of the world's best theoretical physicists on the many-body mathematics of electrons in solids. As he completed the work in the spring of 1935, he learned that it had caught the attention of the prestigious Harvard Society of Fellows. They invited him for an interview and offered him a three-year research fellowship in physics to begin that fall. John was able to share the good news with his father, Charles, who was then desperately ill. John returned to Madison in May, and his father died on June 12. Following the funeral, John returned to Princeton, finished writing his thesis, and submitted it for his professor's approval.

The years at Harvard set John on course for a remarkable professional career that would include the Nobel Prize–winning research at Bell Laboratories and the University of Illinois, described in detail in this chapter. But the story of his life would be incomplete without mentioning his wife, Jane (1907–97), with whom he had three children.

The night before he left Pittsburgh in 1933, John was invited to a dinner party at the home of a Gulf colleague, whose wife had a friend named Jane Maxwell, whom she thought John would enjoy meeting. By the end of the evening, the hostess could tell her matchmaking had been a success. In John, Jane saw a handsome, athletic man with a gentle smile. He was thoughtful, witty, and confident with a brilliance that shone through his quiet demeanor. John was equally impressed. On the long drive to New Jersey the next day, he could not stop thinking about the articulate and attractive biologist. He decided that a Christmas trip back to Pittsburgh would be a very good idea. Because of their separation and their careers, their relationship progressed more slowly than Jane would have liked, but they were eventually married in 1937 and enjoyed a warm family life until John's death on January 30, 1991.

Throughout his life, John Bardeen always found time for recreation. As an undergraduate student at Wisconsin, he earned letters on the swim team although he was younger than most of his teammates. He loved bowling and billiards, but his friends and family remember most fondly his avid golfing. Not long after receiving his first Nobel Prize, he achieved another of his lifelong goals, a hole in one on the university golf course. "He thought that was almost as good as the Nobel," his student and colleague Bob Schrieffer observed. Years later, after winning his second Nobel Prize, John told a friend, "Well, perhaps *two* Nobels are worth more than one hole in one." The fact that such stories surface any time people remember John Bardeen demonstrates that this *True Genius* left a legacy not only of accomplishment in physics but also an example of how to live a balanced life of genuine humility and humanity.

ment of masers and lasers, while Schawlow shared the 1981 Nobel Prize in physics for his work related to laser spectroscopy.

In 1959, Robert Noyce (1927–90) of Fairchild Semiconductors and Jack S. Kilby (1923–2005) of Texas Instruments Corporation invented the integrated circuit, commonly known as the microchip, in which a large number of transistors and their connecting circuitry are created on a single piece of silicon (or other semiconducting material). Kilby was awarded a share of the 2000 Nobel Prize in physics for that accomplishment, which is largely responsible for the remarkable computer and communication technologies of the present day.

Further Reading

Books

Chown, Marcus. *The Magic Furnace: The Search for the Origin of Atoms*. New York: Oxford University Press, 2001. A readable history of the quest to understand the composition of the universe, including a discussion of the work of Fred Hoyle and his colleagues.

Close, Frank, Michael Marten, and Christine Sutton. *The Particle Odyssey: A Journey to the Heart of Matter*. New York: Oxford University Press, 2002. A detailed and colorfully illustrated overview of the discovery of subatomic particles.

Cropper, William H. *Great Physicists: The Life and Times of Leading Physicists from Galileo to Hawking*. New York: Oxford University Press, 2001. The life and times of many great physicists, including Gell-Mann.

Gribbin, John with Mary Gribbin. *Stardust: Supernovae and Life; The Cosmic Connection*. New Haven, Conn.: Yale University Press, 2001. Covers similar material as Marcus Chown's *The Magic Furnace* (above), with a greater emphasis on science and a lesser emphasis on history.

Hoddeson, Lillian, and Vicki Daitsch. *True Genius: the Life and Science of John Bardeen*. Washington, D.C.: Joseph Henry Press, 2002. The definitive biography of John Bardeen, including considerable detail about his scientific work.

Kragh, Helge. *Quantum Generations: A History of Physics in the Twentieth Century*. Princeton, N.J.: Princeton University Press, 1999. An in-depth history of 20th-century physics and physicists.

Lightman, Alan. *The Discoveries: Great Breakthroughs in 20th Century Science, Including the Original Papers*. New York: Pantheon, 2005. Includes DNA papers by Watson, Crick, and Franklin plus commentaries on their significance.

Suplee, Curt. *Physics in the 20th Century*. New York: Harry N. Abrams, 1999. A pictorial history of 20th-century physics.

Web Sites

American Institute of Physics, Center for History of Physics. Available online. URL: http://www.aip.org/history. Accessed March 27, 2006. Follow pull-down menu for special online exhibits or browse for a variety of written resources and images.

Feynman Online. Available online. URL: http://www.feynman.com.
    Accessed April 3, 2006. A tribute to Richard Feynman with many useful
    links to all aspects of his life and science, including streaming video of
    four lectures on QED in New Zealand in 1979.

National Inventors Hall of Fame. Available online. URL: http://www.
    invent.org. Accessed April 18, 2006. Search Web site by name of inven-
    tor or invention.

Nobelprize.org. Available online. URL: http://nobelprize.org. Accessed
    March 27, 2006. The official Web site of Nobel Foundation contains
    brief biographies of Nobel Prize winners, summaries of their prize-win-
    ning work, and their acceptance speeches.

Reyer, Steve. 1954–2004: The TR-1's Golden Anniversary. Available online.
    URL: http://people.msoe.edu/~reyer/regency. Accessed September 19,
    2005. Describes the world's first transistor radio.

The Science Museum. Available online. URL: http://www.sciencemu-
    seum.org.uk. Accessed March 27, 2006. A British online science
    education resource that includes useful exhibits on Atomic Firsts;
    Life, the Universe, and the Electron; Marie Curie and the History of
    Radioactivity; and many other topics discussed in this book.

The Science Shelf, Books for the World Year of Physics 2005. Available
    online. URL: http://www.scienceshelf.com/WorldYearofPhysics.htm.
    Accessed April 26, 2006. This page on the book review site of Fred
    Bortz has brief comments about a number of books published in recog-
    nition of the World Year of Physics, plus links to reviews of a number of
    other physics books for nonspecialist readers.

World Year of Physics 2005. Available online. URL: http://www.phys-
    ics2005.org. Accessed March 27, 2006. An online resource developed in
    honor of the centennial of Albert Einstein's "Miracle Year."

7

1961–1970:
Explorations

Though the Apollo program and the first landing of humans on the Moon will always be recognized as the greatest scientific and technological accomplishments of the 1960s, physicists pursued a broader agenda. Their work, both theoretical and experimental, ranged from the subatomic to the cosmic. By the end of the decade, the big bang hypothesis for the origin of the universe was gaining wide acceptance, thanks in large part to further calculations by Fred Hoyle and his colleagues but also to odd signals detected by a radio telescope that were first attributed to pigeon droppings on its large dish antenna.

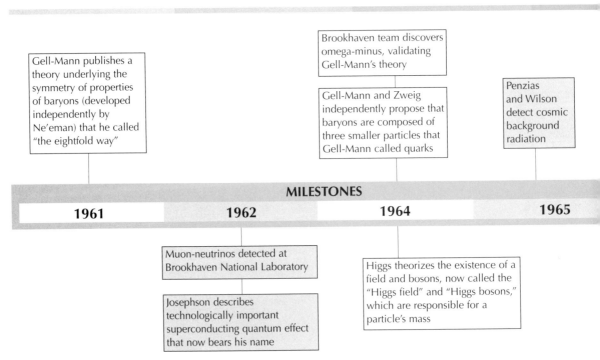

Brookhaven team discovers omega-minus, validating Gell-Mann's theory

Gell-Mann publishes a theory underlying the symmetry of properties of baryons (developed independently by Ne'eman) that he called "the eightfold way"

Gell-Mann and Zweig independently propose that baryons are composed of three smaller particles that Gell-Mann called quarks

Penzias and Wilson detect cosmic background radiation

MILESTONES

| 1961 | 1962 | 1964 | 1965 |

Muon-neutrinos detected at Brookhaven National Laboratory

Josephson describes technologically important superconducting quantum effect that now bears his name

Higgs theorizes the existence of a field and bosons, now called the "Higgs field" and "Higgs bosons," which are responsible for a particle's mass

Meanwhile, this chapter's featured scientist, Murray Gell-Mann, proposed an underlying organization of the subatomic particle "zoo" based on a mathematical symmetry, which led him to propose an entirely new class of sub-nuclear particles called *quarks* and a corresponding new description of the mechanism underlying the strong nuclear force. Other physicists were refining the understanding of the weak nuclear force, laying the groundwork for a theory that would unify it with electromagnetism in the 1970s. Still others were probing deeper into quantum phenomena in solids and their application in electronics.

Thus the 1960s was truly a decade of explorations in physics. Discoveries came from deep within atoms and from the limits of the universe, from research made possible by new technologies and space missions, and from innovative theories that provided new perspectives on nature's inner workings.

Fundamental Particles and Forces

Probably the most remarkable trend of 1960s physics was the redefining of what particles and forces were considered fundamental. Since Newton's times, physicists had understood that large bodies were drawn together by gravity, a force that acted on the bodies' mass.

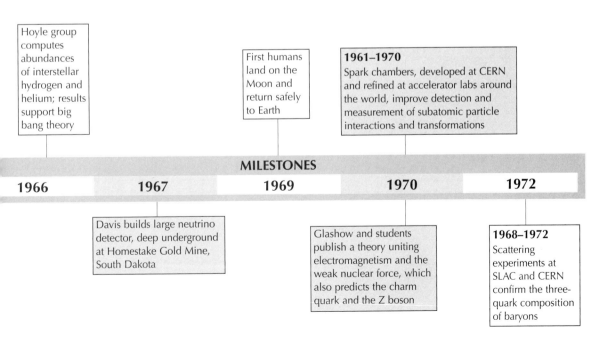

Hoyle group computes abundances of interstellar hydrogen and helium; results support big bang theory

First humans land on the Moon and return safely to Earth

1961–1970
Spark chambers, developed at CERN and refined at accelerator labs around the world, improve detection and measurement of subatomic particle interactions and transformations

MILESTONES

1966   1967   1969   1970   1972

Davis builds large neutrino detector, deep underground at Homestake Gold Mine, South Dakota

Glashow and students publish a theory uniting electromagnetism and the weak nuclear force, which also predicts the charm quark and the Z boson

1968–1972
Scattering experiments at SLAC and CERN confirm the three-quark composition of baryons

Understanding gravity enabled them to understand the dynamics of the solar system. In the 19th century, they began to understand electromagnetic forces. By the early 20th century, they understood that atoms and their component particles carry electric charge and magnetism and that the electric force acts on the charge of electrons and nuclei to hold them together in atoms. It also binds atoms together into molecules and, with its companion magnetic force, is the basis of light energy. As physicists began to understand radioactivity, they recognized two forces that acted within the nucleus, but they could not immediately identify the physical properties corresponding to mass and electric charge on which those forces operated. They also asked this question: Were those four forces—gravity, electromagnetism, and the strong and weak nuclear interactions—all that nature had to offer, and should they be considered fundamental? Work in the 1960s would put physicists on the track to surprising answers to that question, which are described later in this section and in chapter 8.

Similar questions were emerging about the subatomic world. In the 19th century, physicists and chemists thought of atoms as the fundamental building blocks of matter. Then in the last years of that century, the discoveries of radioactivity and the electron, the first-known subatomic particle, called that definition of fundamental into question. Research in the first third of the 20th century soon removed all doubt: With the discovery of the atomic nucleus and its component particles, the proton and the neutron, physicists showed that there were entities more fundamental than atoms. Besides the proton, neutron, and electron, by the mid-1930s physicists were confident that the neutrino was also part of the roster of subatomic particles, though it was not detected experimentally until 1956.

By the 1960s, because of the growing list of subatomic particles, many of which did not seem to belong in atoms, a new question rose to prominence. Which of those particles should be considered fundamental, and which are composed of even smaller particles? Yukawa's theory of the strong force gave pions a place inside nuclei. But where did muons, kaons, and the strange particles discovered in the 1950s fit into the atomic scheme? One of many physicists who began to realize that "subatomic" was not synonymous with "fundamental" was Murray Gell-Mann of Caltech. Just as Mendeleyev had done in developing the periodic table of the elements a century earlier, Gell-Mann and others began to look for patterns in the properties of the particles in the subatomic "zoo." If they could find a pattern, perhaps they could figure out the basis for it, just as the properties of protons, neutrons, and electrons in atoms eventually explained the patterns Mendeleyev had found among the properties of the chemical elements.

A favorite approach for physicists is looking for mathematical symmetries. These involve mathematical operations performed on a system that produce a state that looks the same after the operation as it did before. For example, in describing the quantum properties of crystalline materials, physicists invoke translational symmetry, or the symmetry of motion in a particular direction. (The more familiar usage of the word *translate* derives from applying the Latin word for "to move across" to language rather than space.) They describe the crystal as an infinite repetition of unit cells in three dimensions. When they apply the equations of quantum physics, the resulting wave function at any point in one unit cell must be the same as at the equivalent point in any other. That is translational symmetry, and its application in the quantum mechanics of solids led to such productive ideas as the valence and conduction bands for electrons and the energy gaps between them.

Another familiar symmetry is rotational symmetry. Again, crystals provide a useful way to understand this phenomenon. Rotational symmetry requires an axis of symmetry about which the crystal is rotated. If the unit cells are cubic boxes, then rotating the crystal a quarter-circle around an axis through the edge of a cell produces an arrangement that is exactly the same as the starting point. That is called fourfold rotational symmetry. If the unit cells are rectangular solids but not cubes, the pattern repeats after a half-circle rotation—twofold symmetry.

Another type of symmetry is reflection symmetry—like a mirror image. That is not as simple as it seems, because rotations do not reflect the same way as linear motion. People define the four major compass points on Earth so that east is in the direction of sunrise, and the clockwise sequence of directions is north-east-south-west. That is considered a right-handed arrangement because if the fingers of the right hand are curled in the direction of the planet's rotation, then the thumb points north. Another way to think of that is to imagine looking down from space at the pole of a planet that is rotating counterclockwise. The pole in view must be the north one. The mirror image planet would rotate clockwise, which means that either the pole in view is the south one or the north-east-south-west sequence of directions is counterclockwise, a left-handed world. The drawing on page 139 shows the opposite handedness of planet Earth and its mirror image.

At the quantum level, the spin of a particle is not an actual rotation, but it behaves mathematically as if it is. When the spin quantum number was introduced into the quantum equations describing electrons in atoms, the result was the famous Pauli exclusion principle! That demonstrates how important symmetry is in physics.

Mathematical symmetry applies not only to geometry but also to any physical quantity that can be represented on a graph. Gell-Mann was among the first physicists to apply the ideas of symmetry to subatomic particles. He placed the protons, neutrons, and other baryons on a graph with the strangeness quantum number on the vertical axis

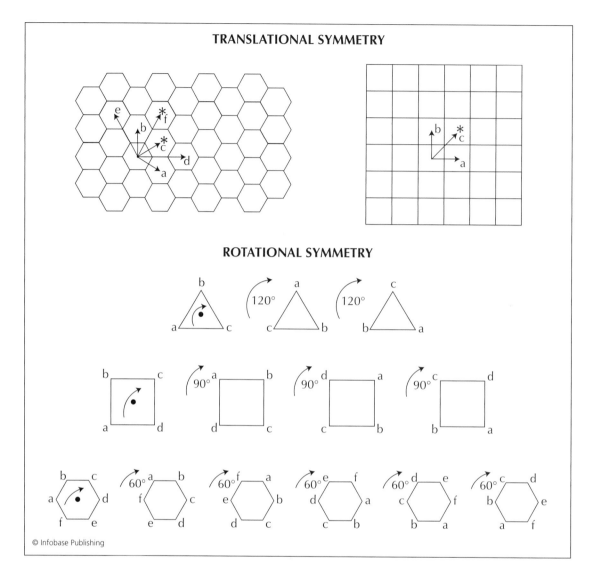

TRANSLATIONAL SYMMETRY

ROTATIONAL SYMMETRY

© Infobase Publishing

Physicists look for symmetry in nature, such as the translational (movement) and rotational symmetry of crystal structures, and use it in their mathematical descriptions of natural phenomena.

and another quantum number called *isospin* on the horizontal axis. The name isospin reflects the way the property behaves when subjected to a mathematical reflection; namely, in the same way as rotation or a pair of magnetic poles. With respect to the strong nuclear force (which does not act on mass or electric charge), protons and neutrons are the same particles with opposite isospin quantum number (-½ for neutrons, +½ for protons). The result, as shown in the diagram on page 141, was a diagram with a kind of symmetry called SU(2). SU stands for "special unitary," which combines rotational and reflection symmetry. The number 2 means that the rotational symmetry is twofold. If the particles on the diagram are rotated through a half-circle and

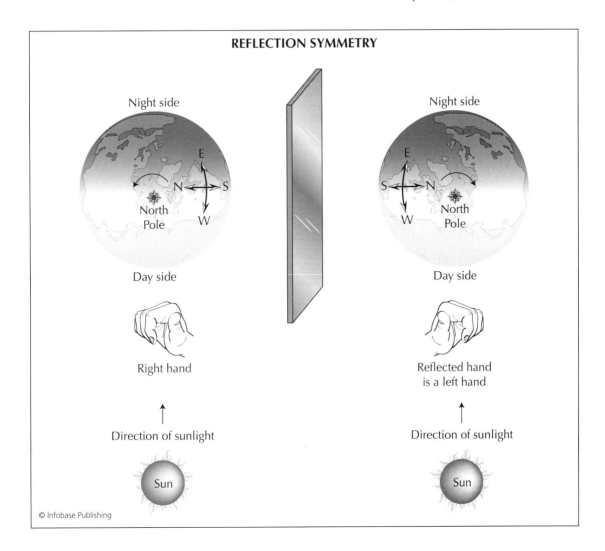

REFLECTION SYMMETRY

Night side

Day side

Right hand

Direction of sunlight

Sun

Night side

Day side

Reflected hand
is a left hand

Direction of sunlight

Sun

© Infobase Publishing

then the isospin is replaced with its mirror image (for example, protons become neutrons and vice versa), the result is exactly the same as the original picture.

In other words, the SU(2) symmetry enabled Gell-Mann to organize subatomic particles into groups of eight—or octets—such as the one in the diagram: The proton and neutron have strangeness 0 and isospin ½ (which allows for the proton, quantum state +½, and the neutron, quantum state -½); the neutral lambda with strangeness 1 and isospin 0; the sigma with strangeness -1 and isospin 1 (which allows for the three quantum states -1, 0, and +1 corresponding to the negative, neutral and positive sigmas); and the xi with strangeness -2 and isospin ½ (which allows for quantum states of +/-½, corresponding to the negative and

Reflection produces a different kind of symmetry reversing right- and left-handedness in phenomena like rotation.

On the Other Hand . . .

Besides rotation, a number of other physical phenomena have handedness. For instance, the equations relating the direction of the north pole of an electromagnet to the direction of current flow use a right-hand rule. It could just as well have turned out to be a left-hand rule if the Earth's magnetic field pointed in the opposite direction, since that is what defines the poles of a magnet. Likewise, physicists define the direction of current as if positive charges are flowing. That definition was set long before they knew that the current in metals was due to the flow of negatively charged electrons. Reversing that definition would turn the right-hand rule into a left-hand rule. The mathematics relating electric current to magnetic poles is right-handed because of arbitrary human definitions—the direction of north, the sign of electric charge, the direction of current flow. The important fact of nature is this: The mathematical relationship between electric current and magnetic poles is the same as that between a planet's rotation and the direction of its north pole.

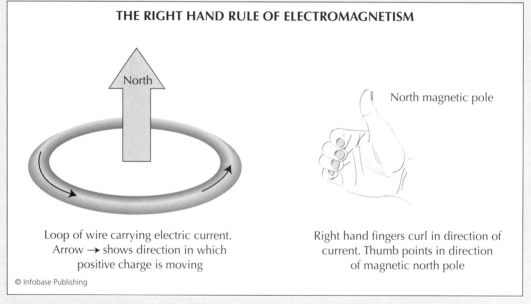

THE RIGHT HAND RULE OF ELECTROMAGNETISM

North

Loop of wire carrying electric current. Arrow → shows direction in which positive charge is moving

North magnetic pole

Right hand fingers curl in direction of current. Thumb points in direction of magnetic north pole

© Infobase Publishing

The equations relating electric and magnetic fields follow a right-hand rule.

neutral xi's). When he published his theory in 1961, he called it the *eightfold way*, borrowing a term from Buddhism. (Note: The negative sign of the strangeness results from an arbitrary choice Gell-Mann made when he first defined the term. It is included here for accuracy, even though it might distract some readers.)

Gell-Mann asserted that the SU(2) symmetry of the octets was only the beginning of the story. It was actually part of a higher degree of sym-

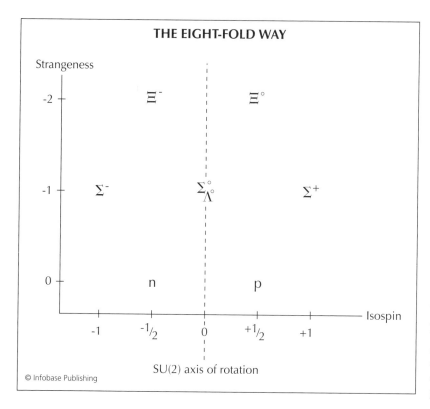

THE EIGHT-FOLD WAY

Strangeness

-2   Ξ⁻   Ξ°

-1   Σ⁻   Σ°   Σ⁺
                   Λ°

0   n   p

                                        Isospin

        -1   -¹/₂   0   +¹/₂   +1

SU(2) axis of rotation

© Infobase Publishing

Murray Gell-Mann recognized a conserved property he called strangeness among the properties of the "zoo" of subatomic particles that were being discovered. With strangeness on one axis of a graph and isospin (a property related to the weak interaction) on the other, he recognized a mathematical symmetry known as SU(2) among sets of eight particles.

metry designated SU(3), like the center layer of a three-layer cake. The outer layers would permit the isospin to be as large as 3/2 and thus could accommodate a grouping of 10 particles—a decuplet—as shown in the diagram on page 142. An Israeli military officer named Yuval Ne'eman (1925–2006), on leave to study physics in London, also proposed SU(3) symmetry at about the same time.

Physicists had glimpsed the four delta particles in that diagram and considered them to be "resonances" or excited states of the proton and neutron. Their existence is what led Gell-Mann and Ne'eman to look at SU(3) rather than SU(2). The theory gave particle accelerator physicists an idea of where to look for other resonances, which they quickly found and gave them new designations by adding an asterisk to the sigma and xi particles in the SU(2) diagram. Only the omega minus particle remained elusive because of its presumed large mass (Gell-Mann's theory predicted it would be almost 1,800 times as massive as the proton), which required collisions of very high energies to produce. When a team of researchers at Brookhaven National Laboratory announced its discovery in 1964, with its mass nearly exactly what Gell-Mann had predicted, it was clear that SU(3) symmetry was a useful way to bring order to the particle zoo.

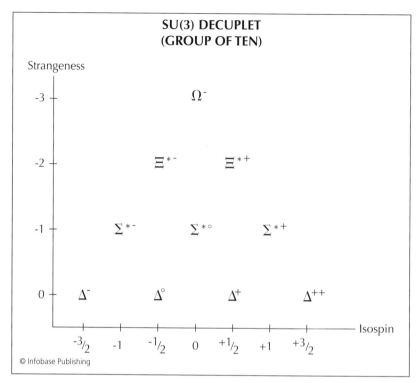

SU(3) DECUPLET (GROUP OF TEN)

© Infobase Publishing

Gell-Mann and Yuval Ne'eman soon realized that the observed SU(2) symmetry was actually part of a higher level of symmetry called SU(3). The eight particles were like the center layer of a three-layer cake, with groupings of 10 (decuplets) particles making up the outer layers.

The Flavorful Quark and the Strong "Color" Force

As noted above and illustrated in the SU(2) diagram, the number 2 describes a twofold rotational symmetry. But neglecting the labels (*p*, *n*, lambda, sigma, xi), the octet of particles in that diagram form a hexagon and thus could also have threefold, or even sixfold rotational, symmetry. So why not SU(6)? The 10-particle grouping in the SU(3) diagram provides the answer. They form a triangle, which has to be rotated through a third of a circle before it gets back to the same alignment. A sixth of a circle is not enough.

This may seem like so much mathematical game playing, except that subatomic particles just happen to fit into such a pattern. The next challenge for physicists was to understand the physical basis for that pattern. Discovering SU(3) was a great accomplishment, akin to Mendeleyev's devising the periodic table of the elements, but just like Mendeleyev's work, it represented only the first step to full understanding. The reason for the periodic arrangement of the elements did not become clear until the discovery of protons, neutrons, electrons, and quantum mechanics. Atoms and even nuclei turned out not to be fundamental. Might the same be true of baryons, including protons and neutrons? The answer turned out to be "yes," and Gell-Mann's great insight was to see that the baryons' SU(3) symmetry resulted from baryons being composed of three particles each. Gell-Mann's fellow Caltech theorist George Zweig (1937–   ) developed the same idea independently at the same time while working at the European reactor center CERN (an acronym for the center's French name, Conseil Européen pour la Recherche Nucléaire; European Council for Nuclear Research) in Geneva, Switzerland.

Building on that idea, Gell-Mann developed a full theory of the strong force. His ideas were so original that he had to develop a whole new vocabulary to go with the mathematics. He chose language that was memorable for its humor as well as its physical significance. For the component particles, he decided on the name quark. Zweig called them aces, but Gell-Mann's designation prevailed. As Gell-Mann explains in his book *The Quark and the Jaguar*, he came up with the sound—kwork— first. He borrowed the spelling from a line in *Finnegans Wake* by the Irish novelist James Joyce, "Three quarks for Muster Mark," and then came up with an excuse not to have it rhyme with "Mark." To distinguish the three quarks, physicists soon spoke of their different *flavors*,—up, down, and strange. The theory required up quarks (u) to carry an electric charge of 2/3 of a proton (+2/3), while the down (d) and strange (s) quarks had 1/3 of the charge of an electron (-1/3). It described the composition of protons as "uud" and neutrons as "ddu." A particle's strangeness quantum number depended on how many strange quarks were contained in the particle. The lambda, for example, had a composition of uds, which explained its strangeness of 1 and electric charge of 0.

A major problem with the theory was that no experiments had ever detected a particle with anything other than a whole number times the charge on a proton or electron—no halves, thirds, or other fractions. Could it be that quarks were bound together in such a way that they could never be separated? Another issue was how to describe the strong nuclear force if protons and neutrons (in fact all baryons) were composite particles instead of single particles. Did Yukawa's very successful theory need to be changed? Taking the second question first, the answer lies in the nature of mesons. Mesons, unlike baryons, are composed of only two quarks, or more specifically, a quark paired with an antiquark. For instance, a neutral pion is either an up paired with an anti-up or a down paired with an anti-down. A positive pion is up plus anti-down, and a negative pion is down plus anti-up.

In Yukawa's formulation, the strong force that holds a nucleus together results from protons and neutrons exchanging virtual pions—particles that flicker into existence and violate the law of conservation of energy but last only for such short a time that the uncertainty principle permits it. A proton might accept a negative pion that is emitted by a neutron, turning the proton into a neutron and the neutron into a proton. In Gell-Mann's new formulation, the negative pion is viewed as a pair of quarks, a down and an anti-up. The ddu neutron includes a down but not an

Gell-Mann developed a new theory of the strong interaction based on the observed SU(3) symmetry. The theory states that protons, neutrons, and other baryons are composed of three quarks, and they interact by exchanging virtual mesons, which are composed of a quark and an antiquark.

anti-up. However, the uncertainty principle permits an up/anti-up pair to come into existence from nothingness if its lifetime is short enough. The up antiquark joins with a down quark to form a negative pion and leaves its up quark partner behind in the former ddu neutron. The net result is that the ddu loses a "d" and adds a "u," making it a uud—a proton. The negative pion is a virtual particle, so it takes only an instant (a time too short to measure) to join with the original proton. The pion's up antiquark annihilates one of the proton's up quarks, and the down quark from the pion remains. The result is that the uud proton has become a ddu neutron.

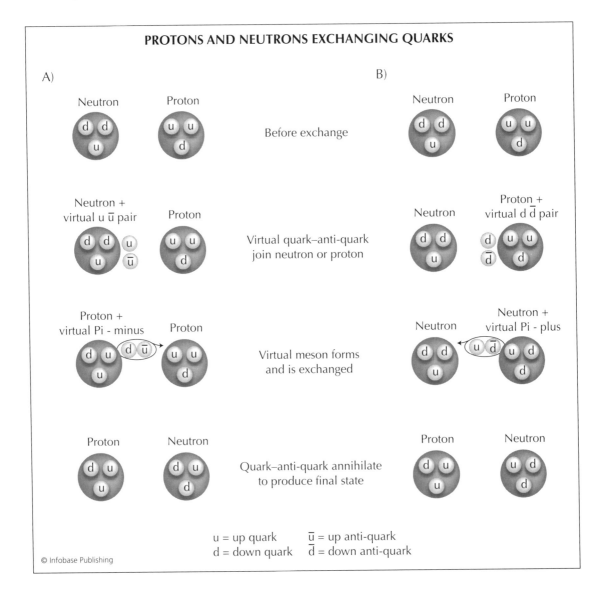

PROTONS AND NEUTRONS EXCHANGING QUARKS

Similar exchanges occur with virtual positive pions emitted by protons and absorbed by neutrons or virtual neutral pions exchanged between pairs of protons or pairs of neutrons. If a collision supplies enough energy, a pion no longer has to be virtual and can be shaken loose from a nucleus. When that happens to a neutral pion, its quark and its antiquark quickly annihilate each other, and the result is a pair of gamma rays or an electron and positron zooming off at high speeds in opposite directions. Charged pions have a quark and antiquark of two different flavors (one up, one down), so they do not annihilate each other. The pion lasts about 26 nanoseconds, held together by the weak nuclear force, before decaying into muons and muon-neutrinos (which were first detected at Brookhaven National Laboratory in 1962). As short as that seems, it is about 300 million times the lifetime of neutral pions and long enough for the fast-moving charged pions to leave easily recognizable tracks in detection chambers.

The most significant part of the theory is its explanation for how quarks are bound together and why that binding is so tight that no one had ever detected a particle with a fractional electric charge. Unlike gravity and electromagnetic forces, which act on properties of matter that can be measured for everyday objects—mass and electric charge—nuclear forces act on a property that exists only in quarks. Physicists had no name for that property, but it apparently came in three varieties, so Gell-Mann called it *color* and designated the varieties red, green, and blue, like the glow of sets of three dots that produce a color television image. His theory stated that each flavor of quark could come in any of the three colors. The antiquarks came in anti-colors. When three quarks of different colors came together as if to form white, they exhibited an enormous attraction for one another, forming a baryon. Likewise, if a quark of a particular color came together with an antiquark of the same anti-color, their bond was intense, creating a meson. Unlike gravity and electromagnetic forces, which decrease as the particles move apart, the color force behaved more like a coil spring, pulling quarks together with increasing intensity the farther apart they were. That is the reason bound quarks were inseparable.

That theory proved so successful that Gell-Mann was awarded the 1969 Nobel Prize in physics "for his contributions and discoveries concerning the classification of elementary particles and their interactions." The citation did not mention quarks, because at the time, no one had any firm evidence they really existed. Like photons and antimatter when they were first proposed, quarks seemed to be useful mathematical constructions whether or not they represented an actual physical entity. But unlike Planck and Dirac, or perhaps learning from their experiences, Gell-Mann was confident that quarks were more than figments of his equations.

Other physicists agreed and went looking for them. Beginning in 1968 at the Stanford Linear Accelerator Center (SLAC), investigators followed a path similar to the one Rutherford used to discover the nucleus. They directed a beam of high-energy electrons at protons and looked at the

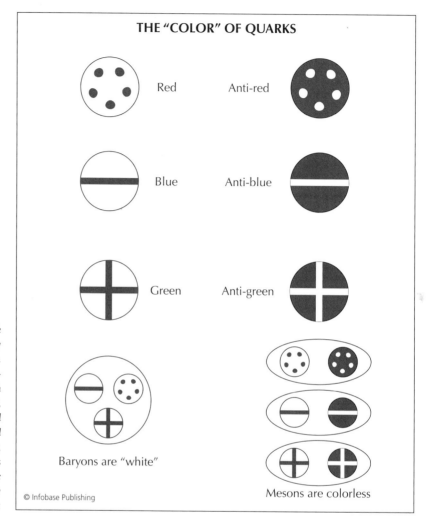

THE "COLOR" OF QUARKS

Red   Anti-red

Blue   Anti-blue

Green   Anti-green

Baryons are "white"

Mesons are colorless

© Infobase Publishing

An important part of the quark theory is an explanation of why quarks do not exist individually. They have a property that Gell-Mann called "color," which takes on three values—red, blue, and green—and they bind together to form white. Instead of weakening like gravity, the color force increases as the quarks separate from one another, which explains why they are always bound together.

scattering patterns. The experiments were extremely difficult to carry out because the electrons needed to be accelerated to such high speeds that their wavelengths were smaller than protons. (Electrons in atoms have wavelengths comparable to the size of their orbits, about 100,000 times as large as a proton.) Furthermore, as in the Rutherford experiment, most of the electrons would pass through without hitting a nucleus. Physicists at CERN did similar experiments using neutrinos. By 1972, the results of the experiments were clear. The electron and neutrino scattering from protons was not uniform. Careful comparisons of the results demonstrated that protons appeared to be lumpy in just the way quark theory predicted, containing three particles with fractional electric charges.

Charm and the Electroweak Force

A strong theme in the history of physics might be called simplification through unification. In the century leading up to the 1960s, the most prominent examples of that theme were the periodic table of the elements, Maxwell's theory of electromagnetism, Einstein's theory of relativity, and quantum mechanics. Gell-Mann's quark theory continued the trend begun with the periodic table. The periodic table brought order to the growing list of elements, and quark theory tamed the unruly subatomic zoo. Maxwell's equations unified the previously separate though clearly related forces of electricity and magnetism and, as a bonus, showed that light was an electromagnetic phenomenon. Einstein theory of relativity demonstrated that space and time, which humans perceive as quite different entities, were really different aspects of a single spacetime. Likewise, his work unified mass and energy. Quantum mechanics removed the differences between particles and waves, though humans perceive the two quite differently.

Because relativity and quantum mechanics challenge the everyday way of viewing nature, many people might call them complications, but physicists recognized them as part of the trend toward mathematical simplification. The 20th-century discovery of the two nuclear forces—strong and weak—seemed to go toward complication. Still, most physicists believed that the fundamental forces could be unified, and some of them set out to find a mathematical scheme to do that. In the early 1960s, Sheldon Glashow (1932–), a young professor at Stanford and then the University of California, began a quest to unify electromagnetism and the weak nuclear force. He moved to Harvard University in 1966, where he continued that work with professor Steven Weinberg (1933–). At the same time, at London's Imperial College, Pakistani-born professor Abdus Salam (1926–96) was attacking the problem independently.

In 1969, John Iliopoulos and Luciano Maiani came to Harvard and joined Glashow in his research. By 1970, they had developed a theory of the "electroweak" force that combined the weak nuclear force and

The physicists who unified electromagnetism and the weak nuclear force. Left to right: Abdus Salam, Steven Weinberg, Sheldon Glashow (All three photos courtesy AIP Emilio Segrè Visual Archives)

electromagnetism. Like many new theories, it provided some surprises. Among the most notable was the prediction of a fourth flavor of quark, which Glashow called charm. By the time Glashow, Salam, and Weinberg shared the 1979 Nobel Prize in physics, particles containing charm quarks had been discovered. The next chapter relates the remarkable—even charming—story of the discovery of the first such particle in two laboratories on opposite sides of the Pacific Ocean.

Gauge Bosons, the Higgs Field, and the Origin of Mass

As Gell-Mann was pondering whether protons and neutrons were fundamental particles, Peter Higgs (1929–) of Edinburgh University in Scotland was wondering why those and most other particles have mass while photons do not. In 1964, he proposed that the universe was filled with a third type of force field besides electromagnetism and gravitation. Particles acquire their mass through their interaction with that field, which physicists call the Higgs field after the man who proposed it.

The Higgs field also led to the prediction of a new particle, or perhaps a set of new particles, called Higgs *bosons*. The reason for that prediction is that the other fundamental forces all have associated carrier particles, which physicists call *gauge bosons*. In quantum electrodynamics (QED), electromagnetic forces result from the exchange of photons. The theory of the weak force relied on a pair of W particles, one positive and one negative, as carriers. The electroweak theory added a neutral Z to the theoretical scheme. And the theory called *quantum chromodynamics* (QCD), which describes the strong force in a way similar to QED, relies on gauge bosons with the whimsical name of *gluons*. As the next two chapters will describe, gluons, Ws, and Zs have all been detected experimentally. Higgs particles have not yet been found, probably because no accelerator has yet been able to achieve sufficient energy to shake them loose from the Higgs field. Many physicists expect that discovery to come, but until then, the Higgs particle remains nothing more than a mathematical notion.

New Particle Detectors

Although theoretical work dominated the 1960s news about the effort to understand subatomic particles, the decade also had some very significant developments in particle detection techniques. In particular, physicists developed two very different devices to detect subatomic events. The first was the spark chamber, designed by physicists at CERN and refined throughout the decade. Other particle accelerator facilities soon followed with their own spark chambers. Bubble chamber photographs revealed subatomic tracks, but experimenters had to take large numbers of photographs at intervals of about one second—the time it took to recycle the chamber for a new observation—in hopes of finding evidence of rare and very brief events. In most cases, the event would happen when the chamber was recycling and would thus escape detection. Spark chambers have much shorter recycling times than bubble chambers. Their main components are pairs of electrified metal plates with a gas confined between them. When a detector senses that a particle of interest has passed through, it sends a signal to electrify the plates and trigger a discharge (and a camera) so quickly that the ionization pattern left behind in the gas has not faded. Sparks follow the ionized pathways, and photographs reveal the interactions that took place. Thus spark chambers gave physicists a technique to catch many more events of interest.

The value of the spark chamber was immediately apparent, but another research project with a new detector seemed a bit unusual, and its scientific return seemed less obvious. In 1967, deep underground in the Homestake Gold Mine in South Dakota, Raymond Davis, Jr. (1914–2006), of Brookhaven National Laboratory built a neutrino detector whose most conspicuous element was a 100,000-gallon tank of dry-cleaning fluid. The reason for the cleaning fluid was its large concentration of chlorine atoms. The nucleus of a particular isotope of chlorine will, on rare occasions (but more commonly than most other nuclei), capture a neutrino. The capture transforms one of its neutrons into a proton—a reverse fission event. The nucleus itself becomes an isotope of argon.

The reason for the detector's subterranean placement was to shield it from cosmic rays. The rocks and soil above the detector will stop practically anything else, but neutrinos pass through readily because a reverse fission event requires a nearly direct hit on a neutron within a nucleus. Davis viewed his device as a detector of neutrinos from the Sun, which emits vast numbers of them as a result of the nuclear fusion events that produce its energy. Other stars emit neutrinos, too, but they are so far away that their neutrinos are too rare to be of concern. Most neutrinos pass through Earth without interacting at all, so it takes a large tank to detect even a few events. The Homestake neutrino detector was the second Davis had built. He had built a smaller one in an Ohio limestone mine in 1961. That one demonstrated that neutrinos could be detected, but Davis knew he needed a larger device to yield significant results.

The major reason for detecting solar neutrinos was to test the theory of the various fusion reactions that power stars. That theory predicts the number of neutrinos expected to pass through the Earth each second. From that number, physicists could calculate the amount of argon expected in the cleaning fluid after a long exposure. The detector's experimental results produced a surprise: The number of solar neutrinos detected was much less than expected. Other, larger neutrino detectors were built, most notably the Kamiokande and later the Super-Kamiokande of the International Center for Elementary Particle Physics, University of Tokyo, Japan, under the leadership of Professor Masatoshi Koshiba

(1926–   ). These detectors confirmed the deficiency and produced a more precise estimate that two-thirds of the predicted solar neutrinos were not being seen. Either the theory of solar fusion was wrong, or the neutrinos were not being captured as expected, or the detectors were not detecting the capture events. The "missing neutrino" problem was not resolved until 2001 (see chapter 11), and the solution gave physicists confidence that they had identified the full set of fundamental particles. The next year, Davis and Koshiba were awarded shares of the 2002 Nobel Prize in physics "for pioneering contributions to astrophysics, in particular for the detection of cosmic neutrinos."

Cosmological Evidence for the Big Bang

While many physicists were working in the subatomic realm, others' work took them to the other extreme—the entire universe. Cosmology was on its way to becoming a major area of inquiry for physicists, a trend that would continue throughout the 20th century and into the present.

At Caltech, research fellow Robert Wagoner (1938–) worked with Willy Fowler and Fred Hoyle, using techniques (described in the previous chapter) that Hoyle, Fowler, and the Burbidges found so successful in computing the abundance of isotopes in stars. This time they applied the theory to the big bang and to Hoyle's steady-state model, calculating the expected abundances of hydrogen, deuterium, and helium in the regions between the stars. In 1966, they published their results. Their computed numbers for the big bang model matched the observed interstellar gases quite well—much better than the predictions of Hoyle's steady-state model.

Hoyle did not dispute the calculations, but he still found the big bang theory hard to accept. For the rest of his long working life, he would seize on new data that suggested apparent flaws in that theory and would propose modifications to it or to his steady-state approach. Despite his out-of-the-mainstream ideas about the big bang, cosmologists even today continue to hold Hoyle and his work in high esteem. They are busily collecting and analyzing new data with new instruments, and the results have enough loose ends that Hoyle's ideas cannot yet be ruled out completely.

In the preceding year, 1965, two Bell Laboratories scientists, Arno Penzias (1933–) and Robert Wilson (1936–), announced a very different kind of observation that supported the big bang model. They were preparing a microwave dish antenna, previously part of an early satellite communications system, for use as a radio telescope. In whatever direction they looked, they were surprised to detect a strong signal at a wavelength of about seven centimeters (2.8 inches). At first, they suspected that they were detecting electronic noise from the instrument itself, even though it was supposed to be very sensitive and thus nearly noise-free. They even went so far as to check for and clean up pigeon droppings on the antenna, but the signal remained.

Arno Penzias (left), Robert Wilson, and the radiotelescope that detected the cosmic background radiation (AIP Emilio Segrè Visual Archives)

Eventually, they ruled out all sources other than actual radiation from outer space. Furthermore, they found that its intensity was the same in all directions and its wavelength matched what would be expected from the distant remnants of the big bang, if such an event had actually taken place.

By 1978, when Penzias and Wilson divided a half-share of the Nobel Prize in physics, other radio astronomers had discovered slight variations in this cosmic background radiation, which provided hints of the early evolution of the universe. As larger and more sensitive radio telescopes become available, 21st-century radio astronomers continue to search the cosmic background for echoes of the ancient explosion that led to the current state of the universe.

Scientist of the Decade: Murray Gell-Mann (1929–   )

From early childhood, Murray Gell-Mann dazzled everyone with his brilliance. At age three, he was multiplying large numbers together in his head. At age seven, he won a spelling bee against students five years older. Most adults did not know what to do with him. How does a parent raise such a child? And how do teachers guide the learning of a student who grasps new ideas instantly and jumps three steps ahead of the others in his class?

Murray's father was a frustrated intellectual. Born Isidore Gellmann in Vienna, Austria, he had begun to study philosophy and mathematics there when his parents, who had immigrated to the Lower East Side of Manhattan in New York City, needed his help. In New York, he took the less Jewish-sounding name of Arthur and added a hyphen to make his last name more distinctive. He quickly mastered English and decided that his ability with languages would be his ticket to success. He founded the Arthur Gell-Mann School to teach other immigrants English. It was a good idea, but Arthur was an overbearing and rigid teacher. His students needed to learn basic vocabulary and sentence structure to adapt to American life, but he insisted on teaching a long list of grammatical rules and terminology as well. The school did not survive the Great Depression. In 1932, Arthur took the best job he could find, as a bank guard. He kept his mind active by studying Einstein's relativity, but he retreated from his family and everyday life. Meanwhile his wife, Pauline, began sinking into mental illness. Refusing to deal with her difficulties, she escaped into a trouble-free dreamworld. She was unnaturally cheerful, even when everything was going wrong around her.

Young Murray soon learned to turn to his brother, Ben, instead of his parents. Ben, nearly 10 years older than Murray, was also an avid learner, and the two boys became great companions. Exploring New York City's museums and parks became their favorite activity and discov-

Murray Gell-Mann, recognized that a property he called "strangeness" was conserved in interactions due to the strong nuclear force. That property led him to a mathematical symmetry among the properties of baryons and then to propose that baryons and mesons were composite particles made of quarks. (AIP Emilio Segrè Visual Archives)

ery their favorite pastime. Murray needed formal education too, but he was clearly out of place in a regular school. His classroom teachers did not know what to do for him. Fortunately, his piano teacher took eight-year-old Murray to meet the headmaster of Columbia Grammar, an exclusive private school on Manhattan's Upper West Side. The headmaster recognized the boy's gifts and arranged for a full scholarship. Even his distracted parents realized that this was exactly what their son needed, and they moved to an apartment building in the same block as the school. This was not the only time that Arthur played an important role in guiding his son's education. Arthur encouraged Murray's mathematical interests and discouraged him from majoring in archaeology or linguistics in college. But Arthur's demanding perfectionism eventually became a burden to Murray in his college years.

At Columbia Grammar, Murray's classmates and even his teachers could not keep up with him. As far as he was concerned, he learned nothing there. More likely, the school staff gave Murray what he needed to teach himself, and then they got out of his way. At the very least, Columbia Grammar gave him the opportunity to get into an Ivy League college. At the age of 15, Murray entered Yale University on a full scholarship, even though the school at that time had a strict 10 percent quota for Jewish students. Despite being at least three years younger than his classmates, most of whom struggled to grasp new material, Murray breezed through his coursework, even in advanced mathematics and physics. Then he hit a roadblock when it came time to write his senior thesis. He would not ask his adviser for help, because he knew that he could never write anything good enough for his language-loving father.

Without a senior thesis, his applications for graduate school were rejected at Yale and every other Ivy League college except Harvard, which did not offer a scholarship. He reluctantly accepted an offer from MIT, the Massachusetts Institute of Technology. It had and still has one of the best graduate physics programs in the United States, but it was not an Ivy League school. He put it this way: "A little reflection convinced me that I could try MIT, and then commit suicide later if I wanted to, but not the other way around."

MIT's programs suited him well, and he completed his Ph.D. there at age 21, though his writer's block delayed his thesis for six months. Along the way, he learned that a theory is of little value if it disagrees with observational or experimental evidence and that he should strive for mathematical simplicity in his theories wherever possible. It was that philosophy that later led him to quarks, the eightfold way, and the Nobel Prize. He managed to put together and deliver a lecture when he received the Nobel Prize, but writer's block struck again, and he never submitted a written version for the Nobel archives.

Murray Gell-Mann has always had broad interests, both in his science and his personal life. While working at the Princeton University Institute for Advanced Studies in the early 1950s, he met a young Englishwoman, Margaret Dow, who was an assistant to an archaeologist there. Murray still loved archaeology, even though his father had discouraged him from studying it in college. And his experiences in New York's parks made him an ardent bird-watcher, a passion that Margaret shared. On one memorable trip together, they traveled to an island off the coast of Scotland to look for puffins. They saw only one, but it was enough. After they were married in 1955, the puffin became their personal good-luck charm.

The marriage humanized Murray Gell-Mann. Before he met Margaret, he was brilliant and self-centered with little in his life but his work. Her death from cancer in 1981 left him devastated, and it came at the same time that he was struggling to keep intact his relationship with his daughter, who had gotten involved in extremist political causes. After a few years, he also ran into difficulties with his relationship with his son.

Murray Gell-Mann remarried in 1992 while in the midst of yet another difficult writing task, an autobiography. He missed a deadline, and even with the help of his wife, Marcia Southwick, he was unable to produce a satisfactory manuscript. The publisher dropped the project. Fortunately, a new publisher and additional editorial help enabled him to finish *The Quark and the Jaguar,* the story of his life and his science, which he subtitled *Adventures in the Simple and the Complex,* in 1994. He is now reconciled with his children and spends most of his time in a lavish home in Santa Fe, New Mexico, filled with collections of art, cultural artifacts, and books.

The growing evidence for the big bang led Andrei Sakharov (1921–89), a physicist from the Soviet Union (now Russia), to develop a theory that connected cosmology to the subatomic world. Nothing in quantum theory or other subatomic theories favors either matter or antimatter. Yet the present universe has a large excess of matter rather than an even mixture of matter and antimatter. For such a situation to evolve, Sakharov realized that certain symmetries and conservation laws must have broken down under the extreme conditions of the big bang. Experimental evidence later demonstrated that this idea was correct. Outside of physics, Sakharov is better known for his leadership in two different areas. He led the Soviet efforts to develop a hydrogen (thermonuclear) bomb in the 1950s, but by the 1960s, he became increasingly concerned with the moral issues of that work and the serious biological effects that result from testing thermonuclear devices, not to mention a thermonuclear war. He spoke out and published articles on those issues, which resulted in his losing his security clearance and research privileges in military laboratories. Later, he added human rights to his list of political concerns. In 1975, scorned by his government but praised by most of the rest of the world, Sakharov was awarded the Nobel Prize for peace.

Other Developments in 1960s Physics and Technology

When the 1960s began, no human had ever been launched into Earth's orbit. By the end of that decade, humans had orbited and walked on the Moon. Physicists were involved in nearly every aspect of those missions, but the work was primarily engineering and technology and is therefore not a focus of this book. The further reading list at the end of this chapter includes several excellent histories of space exploration that cover the accomplishments of the 1960s in detail. Those accomplishments include not only human exploration of the Moon and the Earth but also a number of probes sent to other planets.

Space exploration was not the only technological area that experienced astounding progress during the 1960s. Solid-state electronics advanced rapidly as more transistors and other circuit elements could be packed into integrated circuits. Each advance in technology led to the ability to perform more sophisticated mathematical operations in less time using less energy. By 1970, computers had become essential not only for engineering and science but also for most modern business and financial work. Personal computing and the Internet would not emerge for another decade or so, but experts were already envisioning those advances. Paragraphs similar to this one could be included in the remaining chapters of this book, but they would not be particularly enlightening: This book is not intended as a technological history and thus lacks the details needed for a full accounting of the developments in electronics. Instead, the focus here is on the major contributions that physicists have brought to electronics.

One such contribution came in 1962 from a 22-year-old Welsh-born graduate student at England's Cambridge University. Brian Josephson (1940–   ) realized that quantum mechanics permitted electrons to form Cooper pairs (see preceding chapter) across a thin insulating gap between two superconducting layers. He predicted phenomena now known as Josephson effects that were extremely sensitive to changes in magnetic fields and described how those effects might be exploited in small electronic structures that were naturally called Josephson junctions. The next year, Bell Laboratories scientists had fabricated the first Josephson junctions, and in 1964, researchers at Ford Research Lab invented and built the first superconducting quantum interference device (SQUID), which enabled them to measure changes in magnetic fields much smaller than ever before. Today SQUIDs are used to make many of the most sensitive measurements in science and technology, and engineers are looking ahead to a new generation of quantum computers that rely on Josephson junctions in their operation. Brian Josephson's work earned him a share of the Nobel Prize in physics in 1973.

Further Reading

Books

Chown, Marcus. *The Magic Furnace: The Search for the Origin of Atoms*. New York: Oxford University Press, 2001. A readable history of the quest to understand the composition of the universe, including a discussion of the work of Fred Hoyle and his colleagues.

Close, Frank, Michael Marten, and Christine Sutton. *The Particle Odyssey: A Journey to the Heart of Matter*. New York: Oxford University Press, 2002. A detailed and colorfully illustrated overview of the discovery of subatomic particles.

Cropper, William H. *Great Physicists: The Life and Times of Leading Physicists from Galileo to Hawking*. New York: Oxford University Press, 2001. The life and times of many great physicists, including Gell-Mann.

Gell-Mann, Murray. *The Quark and the Jaguar: Adventures in the Simple and the Complex*. New York: W. H. Freeman, 1994. The story of the eightfold way and quarks in Murray Gell-Mann's own words.

Gribbin, John with Mary Gribbin. *Stardust: Supernovae and Life; The Cosmic Connection*. New Haven, Conn.: Yale University Press, 2001. Covers similar material as Marcus Chown's *The Magic Furnace* (above), with a greater emphasis on science and a lesser emphasis on history.

Johnson, George. *Strange Beauty: Murray Gell-Mann and the Revolution in Twentieth-Century Physics*. New York: Random House, 1999. A definitive and readable biography of Murray Gell-Mann and an explanation of his major scientific ideas.

Kragh, Helge. *Quantum Generations: A History of Physics in the Twentieth Century*. Princeton, N.J.: Princeton University Press, 1999. An in-depth history of 20th-century physics and physicists.

Lightman, Alan. *The Discoveries: Great Breakthroughs in 20th Century Science, Including the Original Papers.* New York: Pantheon, 2005. Includes the 1965 paper by Penzias and Wilson plus a theoretical paper explaining the cosmic background, a 1967 paper by Weinberg describing the unification of the electroweak force, and a 1969 paper by a Brookhaven Group describing the first experimental evidence of quarks, plus commentaries on their significance.

Suplee, Curt. *Physics in the 20th Century.* New York: Harry N. Abrams, 1999. A pictorial history of 20th-century physics.

Web Sites

American Institute of Physics, Center for History of Physics. Available online. URL: http://www.aip.org/history. Accessed March 27, 2006. Follow pull-down menu for special online exhibits or browse for a variety of written resources and images.

Feynman Online. Available online. URL: http://www.feynman.com. Accessed April 3, 2006. A tribute to Richard Feynman with many useful links to all aspects of his life and science, including streaming video of four lectures on QED in New Zealand in 1979.

National Inventors Hall of Fame. Available online. URL: http://www.invent.org. Accessed April 18, 2006. Search Web site by name of inventor or invention.

Nobelprize.org. Available online. URL: http://nobelprize.org. Accessed March 27, 2006. The official site of the Nobel Foundation contains brief biographies of Nobel Prize winners, summaries of their prize-winning work, and their acceptance speeches.

The Science Museum. Available online. URL: http://www.sciencemuseum.org.uk. Accessed March 27, 2006. A British online science education resource that includes useful exhibits on Atomic Firsts; Life, the Universe, and the Electron; Marie Curie and the History of Radioactivity; and many other topics discussed in this book.

The Science Shelf, Books for the World Year of Physics 2005. Available online. URL: http://www.scienceshelf.com/WorldYearofPhysics.htm. Accessed April 26, 2006. This page on the book review site of Fred Bortz has brief comments about a number of books published in recognition of the World Year of Physics, plus links to reviews of a number of other physics books for non-specialist readers.

World Year of Physics 2005. Available online. URL: http://www.physics2005.org. Accessed March 27, 2006. An online resource developed in honor of the centennial of Albert Einstein's "Miracle Year."

8

1971–1980:
A New Synthesis Begins

During the first seven decades of the 20th century, physicists had seen a radical transformation of their science. Newton's laws, Maxwell's equations, and atomic theory no longer told the whole story of matter and energy. Now relativity and quantum mechanics lay at the core of physical theory; atoms were known to be composed of even smaller particles, some of which interacted through previously unknown weak and strong nuclear forces; and physicists had found a host of other particles that were smaller than nuclei but were not part of any known substance. Gell-Mann's eightfold way brought order to the subatomic realm, but some physicists still thought quarks were nothing more than useful mathematical devices. Even the prediction of a fourth quark flavor (charm) in 1970, which made possible the unification of electromagnetism and the weak nuclear force, did not win over all the skeptics. Thus at the beginning of the eighth decade of the 20th century, research in subatomic particles was intense. But by the end of that decade, quarks had been observed in a variety of baryons, and there was evidence of a fifth quark flavor and strong suspicions of a sixth.

From a historical perspective, all the major elements of what came to be called the *standard model of particle physics* were in place by the late 1970s. But at that time, physicists still wondered if their science was heading for an ice-cream store full of quark flavors, like the earlier particle zoo. That possibility remained open until the early years of the 21st century, when physicists found firm evidence that there were no more than the same six quarks they had known or suspected for 25 years. Looking back, it is fair to say that the 1970s marked a transition period: a time of consolidating and applying new ideas, the beginning of a period of synthesis. Innovations in physics continued after that, of course, but most new developments were applications rather than theoretical breakthroughs.

This chapter is also transitional. The remainder of this book will have more emphasis on applications of physics than on transformative ideas. For that reason, the physicist of the decade of the 1970s is a man who straddled the divide between basic research and applications, Luis Alvarez (1911–88) of the Lawrence Berkeley Laboratory of the University of California. Alvarez won the Nobel Prize in physics in 1968 for innovations in bubble chamber technology that led to the discovery of numerous subatomic particles, but he is probably best remembered for transforming scientific understanding of mass extinctions on Earth. In 1980, he and his team of researchers reported evidence that a mountain-size asteroid crashed into the planet 65 million years ago. Such an impact would set off a chain of events that would wipe out many species. It seemed like a wild idea when first proposed, but it is now widely accepted as the most plausible explanation for the end of the age of the dinosaurs.

Quarks from Bottom to Top

As noted in the preceding chapter, by 1972 physicists had observed quarks indirectly. Quarks could not be separated from one another, but a series of electron-scattering experiments at the Stanford Linear Accelerator Center (SLAC) in California and neutrino-scattering experiments at CERN in Switzerland revealed the internal structure of protons, neutrons, and strange baryons. All of those particles were like lumpy bags holding three separate entities, just as Gell-Mann's theory predicted.

So up, down, and strange quarks took their place among the fundamental constituents of matter along with electrons, neutrinos, and the other leptons. The search was on for charm. On the morning of November 11,

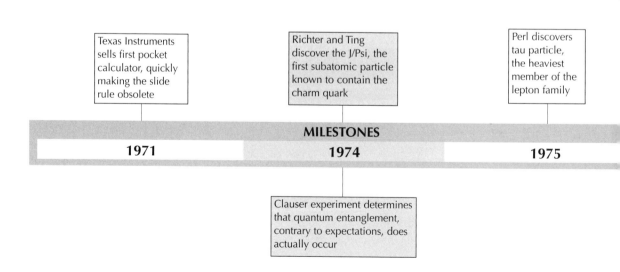

Texas Instruments sells first pocket calculator, quickly making the slide rule obsolete

Richter and Ting discover the J/Psi, the first subatomic particle known to contain the charm quark

Perl discovers tau particle, the heaviest member of the lepton family

MILESTONES

1971   **1974**   **1975**

Clauser experiment determines that quantum entanglement, contrary to expectations, does actually occur

1974, at a regularly scheduled advisory committee meeting at SLAC, two physicists began to realize they had found it. Samuel Chao Chung Ting (1936–) of Brookhaven National Laboratory on Long Island, New York, met Burton Richter (1931–) of SLAC and announced, "Burt, I have some interesting physics to tell you about."

Richter replied in kind. "Sam," he said, "I have some interesting physics to tell *you* about." In different experiments on opposite sides of North America, the two men had each found evidence of the same new particle. Richter's research team had been designating it by the Greek letter psi, while Ting chose J, which resembles the Chinese character for Ting. They quickly settled on the somewhat awkward designation of J/psi, the name by which the particle is still known. Richter and Ting knew that it had a mass more than three times that of a proton and typically decayed into other particles after about a hundred billionth of a billionth of a second. As short as that time seems, it is about 1,000 times as long as they would have expected for such a heavy resonance, or excited state, of another known particle (like the delta, sigma-star, and xi-star resonances described in the preceding chapter). That is what made it so interesting. If it was not an excited state, it must be a new particle in its own right, and it must have a property that delays its decay.

After several months of additional experimenting and theorizing, physicists came to a consensus. The J/psi's unknown property must be charm, and the particle is a meson made up a charmed quark and a charmed antiquark. The Nobel Prize committee did not delay in recognizing this achievement. Richter and Ting shared the physics award for 1976.

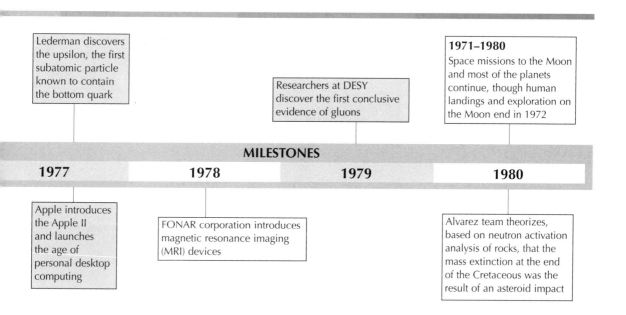

Lederman discovers the upsilon, the first subatomic particle known to contain the bottom quark

Researchers at DESY discover the first conclusive evidence of gluons

1971–1980
Space missions to the Moon and most of the planets continue, though human landings and exploration on the Moon end in 1972

MILESTONES

1977 **1978** **1979** **1980**

Apple introduces the Apple II and launches the age of personal desktop computing

FONAR corporation introduces magnetic resonance imaging (MRI) devices

Alvarez team theorizes, based on neutron activation analysis of rocks, that the mass extinction at the end of the Cretaceous was the result of an asteroid impact

Burton Richter (right), codiscoverer of the charm quark, views a subatomic particle event display with Martin Perl (center) and Gerson Goldhaber. (Courtesy Interactions.org, Copyright SLAC)

Particle physicists started congratulating themselves for completing matter's family tree. Up and down quarks combined with the familiar leptons—electrons and electron-neutrinos—to make up normal matter. Strangeness and charm made up a more massive quark duo and had lepton counterparts known as the muon and the muon-neutrinos. That scheme seemed to include all known subatomic particles. But at the same time that Richter, Ting, and others were discovering the J/psi and deducing that it was charmed, a team of SLAC researchers led by Martin Perl (1927–) was detecting the first of a series of puzzling events. They finally realized that they had discovered a new lepton about 17 times as heavy as a muon and about 3,500 times as heavy as an electron. They named it for the Greek let-ter tau. Its discovery led to Perl's sharing the Nobel Prize in physics in 1995 "for pioneering contributions to lepton physics" with Frederick Reines, who with Clyde Cowan first detected the electron-neutrino (see chapter 6).

The new lepton did not have any known matching quarks or a cor-responding neutrino, but the patterns of particle physics suggested that there ought to be both. The neutrino would be hard to find but easy to name (tau-neutrino). The quarks soon had symbols t and b, corresponding to one of two sets of names: top and bottom, or truth and beauty. No mat-ter what they were called, it would take higher energies to bring them into existence. (Eventually, physicists settled on top and bottom.) In 1977, a team led by Leon Lederman (1922–   ) at the Fermi National Accelerator Laboratory (Fermilab) in Batavia, Illinois, near Chicago detected a particle they called upsilon and soon established that it was the beautiful counterpart of the charming J/psi. It is a meson composed of a bottom quark and its corresponding antiquark. Fermilab teams also eventually found the top quark in 1995 and the tau-neutrino in 2000. Lederman shared the Nobel Prize in physics in 1988, not for the discovery of the bottom quark, but for his earlier prediction of the existence of the muon-neutrino. His corecipients were Melvin Schwartz (1932–2006) and Jack Steinberger (1921–   ), both of Columbia University in New York City, who detected muon-neutrinos in an experiment at Brookhaven in 1962.

One other notable discovery in particle physics came in 1979 at the Deutsches Elektronen Synchrotron laboratory (DESY) in Hamburg, Germany. Researchers there observed the first conclusive evidence for gluons, the gauge bosons presumed to be exchanged by quarks as the carriers of the strong force.

Grand Unified Theories

The discovery of charm was the experimental evidence that theorists, like Sheldon Glashow and his colleagues (see preceding chapter), needed to support their unification of the electromagnetic and weak forces. The details of their electroweak theory are too advanced for this book but can be described in general terms. Like Gell-Mann's theory of the strong force, the theory that unified electromagnetism and the weak nuclear force was based on mathematical symmetry. For mathematical physicists, that success led them to seek an even deeper symmetry that encompassed the strong nuclear force as well. They referred to that goal as the *Grand Unification Theory*, or *GUT*.

Glashow and many others proposed a number of different approaches to achieving a GUT, but none proved successful. Some formulations seemed unnecessarily complex and made predictions that were not possible to test experimentally. One very intriguing—and testable—attempt at a GUT led physicists to a series of experiments in which they used neutrino detectors to search for proton decays. Before that theory was developed, physicists viewed protons as stable forever, but now some wondered if protons would decay on extremely rare occasions—so rare that perhaps one proton in the body of a human being would decay during that person's lifetime. Large neutrino detectors would have revealed such rare events, but after a number of major experiments, not a single proton decay was confirmed.

The GUT efforts were not abandoned entirely. In fact one approach has led to several decades of theoretical research and is thus worthy of mention here and in later chapters. Led by John H. Schwarz (1941–   ),

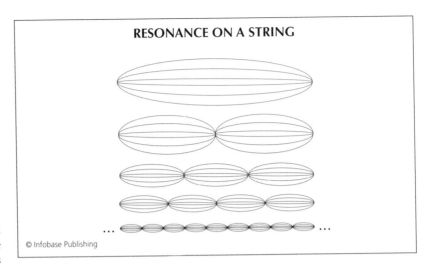

RESONANCE ON A STRING

© Infobase Publishing

String theory describes subatomic particles as resonances on a many-dimensional string, just as a musical string can vibrate in many modes to produce different notes. The modes of the one-dimensional string shown here all have nodes (fixed points) at the end of the string, but the wavelengths of the vibration can vary. The fundamental note at the top resonates with one up-and-down segment in the string. The first overtone, immediately below it with two segments, has a wavelength half as long as the fundamental. Other overtones have two, three, four, . . . , nine, and more segments. A similar mathematical approach with many dimensions yields the properties of subatomic particles, such as protons and neutrons, and their resonances, such as the delta particles discussed in chapter 7.

who joined the physics faculty at Caltech after completing his doctorate at the University of California, Berkeley, the approach is called *string theory*. That theory describes elementary particles by a mathematical analogy to a string, which is a one-dimensional object that can vibrate in three-dimensional space. The early versions of string theory had 10 dimensions (a nine-dimensional space plus time), and it predicts subatomic particles as a set of allowed vibrations of that string.

Specifically, the string can vibrate in many modes and produce different tones—the fundamental note plus a series of overtones. (See drawing above.) By analogy, each of the nine dimensions of string theory corresponds to a property of matter, and the allowed modes of vibration correspond to different subatomic particles. A major reason for the high level of interest in string theory is that it encompasses not only the electroweak and strong interactions but also gravity.

Schwarz published his first paper on string theory in 1971, but it has yet to achieve the broad acceptance of quantum mechanics or relativity. String theory was then and is still in the intermediate stage between proposal and experimental confirmation. It is like Planck's quantum before Einstein's work on the photoelectric effect or Dirac's prediction of antimatter before the discovery of the positron. Its mathematical results seem to apply to physics, but there are no experimental phenomena that can be tied to it directly.

Quantum Entanglement

In 1969, John F. Clauser (1942–   ) of Columbia University, along with colleagues from Boston University and Harvard, suggested a way to use polarized light to test one of the most unusual and contentious predictions of quantum mechanics, the phenomenon of *entanglement*. Albert Einstein had another name for it, "spooky action at a distance." It was, in fact, his major criticism of quantum theory, even going beyond his famous "God does not play dice." (See chapter 5.) Entanglement is best understood by looking at a particular example. This is not the experiment that Clauser proposed, because to explain that would require a section to explain polarized light and the spin of photons. This example describes the entanglement of spin-½ particles, such as protons, neutrons, or electrons. Suppose two particles, which pass the same point while moving in opposite directions, interact so that their spins align in opposite directions, one pointing east and the other west. Some time later, they each pass a detector that measures spin along the north-south direction.

According to quantum mechanics, the single-particle wave function for each particle is an equal mix of spin-north and spin-south states. Each detector is thus equally likely to register a northward-pointing spin as a southward-pointing spin. The spin of the particle along the north-south direction is not determined until the measurement takes place. Since the two particles are now separated in space but have their spins measured at the same time, there is no way for one north-south spin detector to influence the other. Thus using single-particle wave functions, the analysis produces equal likelihood for the two spin measurements to be in the same direction (both north or both south) as to be in opposite directions (one north, one south).

But when the analysis is done using a two-particle wave function, the result is that the spins remain opposite. Before the particles enter their respective detectors, neither one has a particular north-south preference. But the detection of one spin as northward-pointing forces the other to point southward. The particles, though separated, have their spins permanently entangled. To Einstein, that action was "spooky" because there is no time to communicate a message from one particle across the distance to its partner, yet the partner responds instantaneously to the other's measurement. In 1974, Clauser and his team built the apparatus that he and his Harvard and Boston colleagues had suggested in 1969. They expected to rule out quantum entanglement, because it seemed to violate the relativistic rules of cause and effect, but they instead discovered that it was a real phenomenon.

To the present day, some scientists argue that the experiment was flawed, but as each criticism is addressed, the phenomenon of quantum entanglement survives. That discovery has opened up a number of important technological possibilities, especially in the area known today as quantum computing.

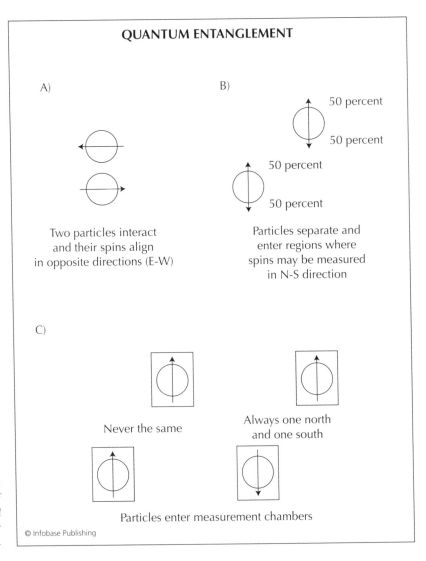

QUANTUM ENTANGLEMENT

A)

Two particles interact
and their spins align
in opposite directions (E-W)

B)

50 percent

50 percent

50 percent

50 percent

Particles separate and
enter regions where
spins may be measured
in N-S direction

C)

Never the same

Always one north
and one south

Particles enter measurement chambers

© Infobase Publishing

Quantum entanglement, which Einstein called "spooky action at a distance," has been confirmed in experiments like this one. If a property of two particles can be set into a particular relationship when the particles interact, such as the aligning of the direction of their spins oppositely in the east-west direction, quantum entanglement states that relationship continues even when the particles are separated. For example, if the spin of either particle is later measured along the north-south direction, quantum mechanics predicts that it will be equally as likely to point north as south. If the particles' quantum wave functions were independent, their north-south spins would thus be equally likely to be the same as opposite. But it turns out that the particles' spins are entangled through a two-particle quantum wave function. Thus measuring one as north forces the other to be south, even if there is not enough time to send a message from one to the other at the speed of light.

Applications of Physics and Connections to Other Sciences in the 1970s

Physics made news in the 1970s not only for continued discoveries in the subatomic realm but also for many applications of physics in other sciences, engineering, and technology. In electronics, new micro-fabrication techniques, many of which relied on development of new materials and improved devices such as lasers, led to integrated circuits of increasing complexity. Entire central processing units of computers could be laid out on silicon chips. Calculating power that once required huge air-conditioned rooms with their own electrical service could now be placed in devices small enough to carry. In 1971, Texas Instruments began selling the first pocket electronic calculators. Engineers, who once could be identified by the precision slide rules that hung on their belts, now had handheld electronic gadgets that could calculate faster and to greater precision. By mid-decade, the age of personal computing had begun, with the 1977 Apple II leading the way.

The availability of additional computing power also led to a new medical application of a technique that physicists and chemists had been using to investigate the internal structure of solids, nuclear magnetic resonance, or NMR. The technique relies on the fact that protons and neutrons, like electrons, have spin. The familiar magnetic properties of some substances, such as iron, result from the spin of electrons. In the quantum scheme of things, spin-up electrons tend to form pairs with spin-down electrons, but especially if there is an odd number of electrons, not all of an atom's electrons have partners. When the crystal structure is right, the unpaired electron spins tend to align, producing strong magnetism. Meanwhile, in the nucleus, protons and neutrons with opposite spins also pair off. Again, especially when there is an odd number of protons or neutrons, the nucleus is left with one or more unpaired spins and thus can act as a tiny magnet.

The nuclear magnets align with the material's internal magnetic fields, and they also respond to applied magnetic fields from the outside. If those applied fields rotate, a nucleus can behave like a tilted spinning top. Its magnetic axis will trace out a circular path at a particular natural frequency. When the frequency of the rotating field matches the natural frequency, the nucleus absorbs energy. That is a resonance phenomenon—in this case, nuclear magnetic resonance—like those discussed earlier in the book. The natural frequencies and directions of NMR

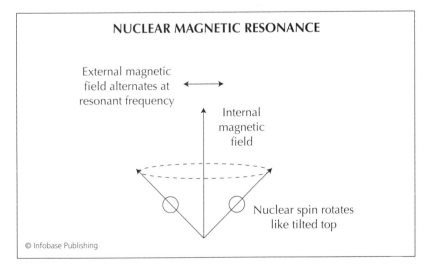

NUCLEAR MAGNETIC RESONANCE

External magnetic field alternates at resonant frequency

Internal magnetic field

Nuclear spin rotates like tilted top

© Infobase Publishing

The phenomenon of nuclear magnetic resonance (NMR), illustrated here, is the key to the valuable medical technique of magnetic resonance imaging (MRI).

enable scientists to determine the internal magnetic fields of the material and thus understand more about its crystal structure. The discovery of NMR and its usefulness for understanding the properties of solids led to the Nobel Prize in physics in 1952, awarded to Felix Bloch (1905–83) and Edward Purcell (1912–97).

But outside of the scientific research community, NMR was not of great interest in the 1970s until Paul Lauterbur (1929–2007) of the State University of New York at Stony Brook suggested a technique that used NMR measurements to create images of a slice of material. Peter Mansfield (1933–) of the University of Nottingham, England, extended Lauterbur's techniques to the resonances of hydrogen nuclei in living matter and developed techniques for rapid imaging. Raymond Damadian (1936–) founded the FONAR Corporation in 1978 to manufacture the first NMR scanners. Because of the public's tendency to connect the word *nuclear* with heath risks and weapons, the medical devices were quickly designated magnetic resonance imaging (MRI) devices. Lauterbur and Mansfield were awarded the 2003 Nobel Prize in physiology or medicine. Damadian, believing that his technological contributions to MRI deserved the same recognition as Lauterbur's and Mansfield's scientific ones, ran a full-page ad in the *New York Times* claiming that the awards committee had treated him unfairly by leaving him out.

Another major scientific development with a strong connection to physics was the announcement by Nobel Prize–winning physicist Luis Alvarez of the University of California, Berkeley, that he; his son, Berkley geologist Walter Alvarez (1940–); and Berkeley chemists Frank Asaro (1927–) and Helen Michel (1933?–) had uncovered the cause of the mass extinction at the end of the Cretaceous period, 65 million years ago. Their conclusion was that an asteroid as large as Mount Everest had slammed into Earth and set off a series of global calamities that wiped out many species, including the dinosaurs.

The research began when Walter Alvarez returned from Italy with a piece of rock that contained a thin layer of sediment separating distinctly different fossils of the Cretaceous and Tertiary periods of Earth's history, the so-called K-T boundary. He asked his father if there was a way to measure how long it took for that layer to be deposited. Luis Alvarez was an expert in cosmic rays, and he realized he could make use of the steady rain of particles from space to answer his son's question. In particular, the rare element iridium, a member of the platinum family, could be detected using a technique called neutron activation analysis (see chapter 4). When a high-energy neutron strikes an iridium nucleus, the iridium produces a distinctive gamma ray. Measuring the amount of iridium in the layer, he concluded, would enable them to compute how long the layer took to build up.

From other geological evidence, Walter Alvarez knew that the layer took at most a few thousand years to accumulate. Using Luis Alvarez's

Luis Alvarez (right), with his team of son Walter Alvarez, Frank Asaro, and Helen Michel (right to left), used neutron activation analysis to discover the so-called iridium anomaly that led to the widely accepted theory that an asteroid impact caused the mass extinction that ended the Cretaceous period and the era of the dinosaurs. (Ernest Orlando Lawrence Berkeley National Laboratory, courtesy AIP Emilio Segrè Visual Archives)

estimate of how much iridium that would represent, neutron activation experts Asaro and Michel were not sure there would be enough to measure. Still, they had just gotten an improved neutron-activation system in their laboratory and were eager to try it out. Their measurement was astounding. There was as much iridium in that thin layer as would normally accumulate in about a half-million years. They checked and confirmed their measurements. Then they started tossing out hypotheses for what could cause that "iridium anomaly." The only idea that held up to scrutiny was the asteroid hypothesis. It seemed outrageous, yet it could be tested by measuring other K-T boundary rocks from other locations. So in 1980, they published their results and waited for other measurements to support or challenge their hypothesis.

Other K-T layers from around the world showed similar results. Ultimately, scientists not only accepted the Berkeley group's conclusions but also found what they believe to be the asteroid's impact crater, eroded but still discernable by subtle magnetic and gravitational deviations, at Chicxulub on the coast of Mexico's Yucatán Peninsula.

One other area where physics played a prominent role in the 1970s was the exploration of space, especially the solar system. Apollo Moon missions continued until 1972, several spacecraft explored Venus and Mars, and two *Voyager* missions explored the giant outer planets Jupiter, Saturn, Uranus, and Neptune and their moons. For more information on these missions, readers should consult the Further Reading section below.

Scientist of the Decade: Luis Alvarez (1911–1988)

In a word, Luis Walter Alvarez was inventive. Whether he was involved in the quest for subatomic particles, the defense of his country, the investigation into the murder of President John F. Kennedy, the search for hidden chambers in an Egyptian pyramid, or the discovery and interpretation of clues about the extinction of the dinosaurs in a thin layer of sediment, "Luie" (as he was known to almost everyone in the scientific community) had a unique way of viewing problems, which led to uniquely creative solutions.

Born in San Francisco on June 13, 1911, Luis traced his ancestry to Spain, where his paternal grandfather was born before coming to Los Angeles by way of Cuba, and Ireland, where his mother's missionary family had roots. His father, Walter Clement Alvarez, was a successful physician and medical researcher who allowed young Luie to discover the tools and equipment in his laboratory. By age 10, the boy knew how to use all the lab's small tools and could wire together electrical circuits.

In 1925, the Alvarez family moved to Rochester, Minnesota, where Dr. Alvarez took a position at the famous Mayo Clinic. During high school, Luis worked at the clinic as a summer apprentice in the instrument shop, and after graduation, he enrolled at the University of Chicago, where he discovered physics. There he had the rare opportunity to use the equipment and work with the technicians of legendary physicist Albert A. Michelson (1852–1931), whose precise measurements of the speed of light first cast doubt on the existence of the luminiferous ether (see Introduction and chapter 1). Blessed with an outstanding memory and a passion for his subject, he read and digested every article Michelson had written.

While still a college student in 1934, Luis took flying lessons and was able to begin soloing after only three hours of instruction. His experience in the cockpit came in handy during World War II (see below), and he remained an active pilot until he was 73 years old.

After his 1936 graduation from Chicago, Luis Alvarez accepted an invitation from Ernest Orlando Lawrence (see chapter 4) to continue his studies at Berkeley, where he eventually became a faculty member. Family connections helped, since Luis's father had helped raise money for one of Lawrence's cyclotrons, and his sister worked for Lawrence as a part-time secretary. But his talents quickly justified the offer. He devoured every journal article ever written about nuclear physics. Years later, he would astonish other scientists by reproducing a graph or recalling an obscure fact, then citing the original reference by authors, journal, and year of publication. Sometimes he could tell them precisely where the journal was located in the library and whether they would find the item on a left- or right-hand page.

But more than memory was at work with Luis Alvarez. For his research, he decided to make a measurement that Hans Bethe (see chapter 4) said could not be done, and he proved Bethe wrong. In four years, he made several other major discoveries, including the radioactivity of the hydrogen isotope tritium (atomic mass 3: one proton plus two neutrons) and a form of radioactive change called electron capture, in which a proton unites with one of an atom's inner electrons to form a neutron. In 1940, World War II interrupted his work on nuclear physics. He went to the Massachusetts Institute of Technology (MIT) Radiation Laboratories, where he worked on radar systems until 1943. He developed two important inventions, one for a radar bombing system and another that fooled the crews of surfacing enemy submarines into thinking that an attacking airplane was going away. He then went to Chicago and then Los Alamos to apply his inventive mind to the problem of how to detonate atomic bombs (see chapter 5). In 1946, the British honored Alvarez with the prestigious Collier Air Trophy for his work at MIT.

When the war ended, Alvarez returned to Berkeley, where he invented or developed several techniques to accelerate subatomic particles and

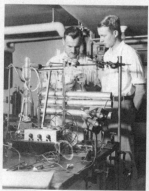  

The varied career of Luis Alvarez. Left to right: As a graduate student studying cosmic rays in 1933 with his adviser, Arthur Compton at the University of Chicago (Brookhaven National Laboratory) *With bubble chamber display at Berkeley* (Brookhaven National Laboratory) *Receiving National Medal of Science from president Lyndon B. Johnson* (Ernest Orlando Lawrence Berkeley National Laboratory, courtesy AIP Emilio Segrè Visual Archives)

detect the products of the resulting high-energy interactions. Most notable was an improvement to bubble chamber technology, which led to the discovery of many subatomic particles and resonances. Without those discoveries, which led to his 1968 Nobel Prize in physics, Murray Gell-Mann would never have been able to devise his eightfold way.

Alvarez had broad interests and knowledge, which led him to several fascinating projects later in his career. In 1964, the Warren Commission, which was investigating the 1963 assassination of President John F. Kennedy, brought him in to analyze a famous amateur motion picture of the shooting. At about the same time, bemoaning his need for bifocal glasses, he invented the variable focus lens, which led to a successful optical instrument company. A few years later, he devised a way to use cosmic-ray muons to probe the interior of the Pyramid of Chefren for secret passages. His results showed there were no hidden chambers, but the project still captured the imagination of all who heard about it.

In 1977, as he was entering retirement, Luis Alvarez began what was to prove his most memorable and exciting work. It started with a rock presented to him as a gift from his son Walter, a geology professor at Berkeley. The rock contained a layer of clay or sediment that marked the boundary between two geologic periods, the Cretaceous and the Tertiary. The Cretaceous period apparently ended abruptly with the extinction of many species, including the dinosaurs. But how abruptly, Walter wondered. Was there anything in that layer that might provide a hint? As related in the main body of this chapter, Luis's knowledge of cosmic rays led them to a surprising theory and a new understanding of the history of life on Earth and the role that cosmic impacts might play in it.

Near the end of a memorial appreciation, Richard A. Muller, a Berkeley colleague and one of Alvarez's most successful students wrote this:

> I shall always remember Luis Alvarez as a man who loved thinking above all else. . . . Only one out of ten ideas, he said, was worth pursuing. Only one out of ten of these would last a month. Only one out of ten of those would lead to a discovery. If these figures are true, then Luis must have had tens of thousands of ideas.

The many ideas of Luis Alvarez—Nobel laureate, recipient of the National Medal of Science, and a man enshrined in the National Inventor's Hall of Fame—changed physics and changed the world.

Further Reading

Books

Alvarez, Luis W. *Alvarez, Adventures of a Physicist*. New York: Basic Books, 1987. Luis Alvarez's adventurous life in his own words.

Alvarez, Walter. *T-Rex and the Crater of Doom*. Princeton, N.J.: Princeton University Press, 1997. A lively account of the scientific investigation that led to a radical new understanding of the mass extinction that killed the dinosaurs.

Bortz, Fred. *Collision Course! Cosmic Impacts and Life on Earth*. Brookfield, Conn.: Millbrook Press, 2001. For younger readers, this book discusses several planetary impacts of comets and asteroids, including the one that killed the dionosaurs.

———. "What Killed the Dinosaurs?" Chap. 2, *To the Young Scientist: Reflections on Doing and Living Science*. Danbury, Conn.: Franklin Watts, 1997. This chapter is based on an interview with Frank Asaro and Helen Michel, who did the neutron activation analysis that led to Luis Alvarez's theory that the dinosaurs' extinction was due to the impact of an asteroid.

Burrows, William E. *The Infinite Journey: Eyewitness Accounts of NASA and the Age of Space*. New York: Discovery Books, 2000. A vivid pictorial account of NASA's exploration of the Moon and the Planets.

———. *This New Ocean: The Story of the First Space Age*. New York: Random House, 1998. A detailed history of space exploration.

Cernan, Eugene, with Don Davis. *The Last Man on the Moon*. New York: St. Martin's, 1999. A description of *Apollo 17*, the last manned mission to the Moon, written by the astronaut who was the last to board the lunar module for its return trip.

Cole, K. C. *The Hole in the Universe: How Scientists Peered over the Edge of Emptiness and Found Everything*. New York: Harcourt, 2001. A description of modern theories of subatomic particles and cosmology.

Cropper, William H. *Great Physicists: The Life and Times of Leading Physicists from Galileo to Hawking*. New York: Oxford University Press, 2001. The life and times of many great physicists, including Gell-Mann.

Dauber, Philip M., and Richard A. Muller. *The Three Big Bangs: Comet Crashes, Exploding Stars, and the Creation of the Universe*. New York: Perseus Books, 1997. A clear and interesting look at the origin and history of life on Earth by one of Luis Alvarez's best-known students.

Gell-Mann, Murray. *The Quark and the Jaguar: Adventures in the Simple and the Complex*. New York: W. H. Freeman, 1994. The story of the eight-fold way and quarks in Murray Gell-Mann's own words.

Hawking, Stephen. *The Universe in a Nutshell*. New York: Bantam, 2001. Insight into cosmology and string theory by own of the world's greatest theoretical physicists.

Heppenheimer, T. A. *Countdown: A History of Space Flight.* New York: John Wiley, 1997. A detailed history of manned spaceflight.

Johnson, George. *Strange Beauty: Murray Gell-Mann and the Revolution in Twentieth-Century Physics.* New York: Random House, 1999. A definitive and readable biography of Murray Gell-Mann and an explanation of his major scientific ideas.

Kragh, Helge. *Quantum Generations: A History of Physics in the Twentieth Century.* Princeton, N.J.: Princeton University Press, 1999. An in-depth history of 20th-century physics and physicists.

Launius, Roger D., and Howard McCurdy. *Imagining Space: Achievements * Predictions * Possibilities, 1950–2050.* San Francisco, Calif.: Chronicle, 2001. An illustrated history of and future of spaceflight.

McCurdy, Howard E. *Space and the American Imagination.* Washington, D.C.: Smithsonian, 1997. A history of the United States space program.

Morton, Oliver. *Mapping Mars: Science, Imagination, and the Birth of a World.* New York: Picador, 2002. A detailed history of the discoveries from various Mars missions.

Schumm, Bruce A. *Deep Down Things: The Breathtaking Beauty of Particle Physics.* Baltimore: Johns Hopkins University Press, 2005. A look at the mathematical ideas that underlie particle physics and string theory.

Seife, Charles. *Alpha & Omega: The Search for the Beginning and the End of the Universe.* New York: Viking, 2003. A look at the connections between particle physics and the cosmology of the big bang.

Siegfried, Tom. *Strange Matters: Undiscovered Ideas at the Frontiers of Space and Time.* Washington, D.C.: Joseph Henry Press, 2002. A book discussing ideas, such as string theory, which the author refers to as "prediscoveries" because they are likely to produce insights into particle physics and cosmology.

Suplee, Curt. *Physics in the 20th Century.* New York: Harry N. Abrams, 1999. A pictorial history of 20th-century physics.

Web Sites

American Institute of Physics, Center for History of Physics. Available online. URL: http://www.aip.org/history. Accessed March 27, 2006. Follow pull-down menu for special online exhibits or browse for a variety of written resources and images.

Feynman Online. Available online. URL: http://www.feynman.com. Accessed April 3, 2006. A tribute to Richard Feynman with many useful links to all aspects of his life and science, including streaming video of four lectures on QED in New Zealand in 1979.

Garwin, Richard L. "Memorial Tribute for Luis W. Alvarez." In *Memorial Tributes*, National Academy of Engineering, vol. 5. Washington D.C.: National Academy Press, 1992. Also available online. URL: http://www.fas.org/rlg/alvarez.htm. Accessed April 20, 2006. A detailed obituary and memorial tribute for Luis Alvarez.

National Inventors Hall of Fame. Available online. URL: http://www.
invent.org. Accessed April 18, 2006. Search Web site by name of inventor or invention.

Nobelprize.org. Available online. URL: http://nobelprize.org. Accessed
March 27, 2006. The official Web site of the Nobel Foundation contains
brief biographies of Nobel Prize winners, summaries of their prize-winning work, and their acceptance speeches.

Schwarz, Patricia. The Official String Theory Web Site. Available online.
URL: http://www.superstringtheory.com. Accessed April 21, 2006. A
comprehensive Web site about string theory, the physicists who have
worked on it, and its history.

The Science Museum. Available online. URL: http://www.sciencemu-
seum.org.uk. Accessed March 27, 2006. A British online science
education resource that includes useful exhibits on Atomic Firsts;
Life, the Universe, and the Electron; Marie Curie and the History of
Radioactivity; and many other topics discussed in this book.

The Science Shelf, Books for the World Year of Physics 2005. Available
online. URL: http://www.scienceshelf.com/WorldYearofPhysics.htm.
Accessed April 26, 2006. This page on the book review site of Fred
Bortz has brief comments about a number of books published in recognition of the World Year of Physics, plus links to reviews of a number of
other physics books for nonspecialist readers.

Watt, Robert D., W. Peter Trower, M. Lynn Stevenson, Richard A. Muller,
and Walter Alvarez. "Luis W. Alvarez, Physics: Berkeley." In *University
of California: In Memoriam, 1988*, edited by David Krogh. Also available
online. URL: http://ark.cdlib.org/ark:/13030/hb967nb5k3. Follow link
to "View Options: Standard" and choose "Luis W. Alvarez." Accessed
April 20, 2006. A memorial essay about Luis Alvarez by many individuals
who knew him best.

World Year of Physics 2005. Available online. URL: http://www.phys-
ics2005.org. Accessed March 27, 2006. An online resource developed in
honor of the centennial of Albert Einstein's "Miracle Year."

9

1981–1990:
Broadening Public Discourse

As noted in the previous chapter, the last 20 years of the 20th century appear to be marked more by applications of physics rather than by mind-boggling new theories or breakthrough experiments. The word *appear* in the preceding sentence is important. It is legitimate to ask if that is really a historical trend or if it merely reflects a lack of historical perspective. Twenty years may simply not be enough time to recognize the revolutionary nature of a new theory or discovery. However, a look back on the 1980s from early in the 21st century does reveal increased public interest in physics and the role of physicists in society. In part, that can be attributed to the nature of the discoveries, such as the Alvarez team's hypothesis of an asteroid impact. It can also be related to changing politics, which led to government funding for applications of science rather than for new research. But perhaps the most important factor in the public's perception resulted from a change within the physics community itself. Many physicists realized that public support for their science would benefit if they made more direct connections with the many nonscientists who were intensely curious about the century's great new ideas and discoveries in physics and astronomy.

In particular, two very different physicists with very different approaches and interests capitalized on that curiosity in notable ways. Largely through his *Cosmos* television series but also through his books, Cornell University astronomy professor Carl Sagan (1934–96) promoted a sense of wonder about the universe. Across the Atlantic at Cambridge University in England, Stephen Hawking (1942–   ), holding the title of Lucasian Professor of Mathematics that had once been Isaac Newton's, capitalized on the public's interest in relativity and quantum mechanics by writing a book that became a surprise best seller, *A Brief History of Time.*

Television viewers loved Sagan's genuine enthusiasm about the cosmos, and he became a celebrity; but his fame also brought criticism. His detractors saw his broadcast work as self-promotion, designed as much to inspire awe in Carl Sagan's genius as in the wonders of the universe. But they were in the minority. Regardless of his motives, Sagan made the most of his public acclaim to encourage interest in science. He also used it to promote a political agenda, as described below. Hawking's celebrity developed in part because he dared to try to explain the challenging concepts of quantum mechanics and relativity to general readers without recourse to complicated mathematics and in part because he had a compelling life story. For that reason, and because Sagan's work was primarily astronomy rather than physics, Hawking is this chapter's scientist of the decade.

Particle Physics and Quantum Effects

Progress in particle physics continued in the 1980s with the building or improvement of particle accelerators that produced more energetic collisions or had better particle detection techniques. The new particles discovered in the 1980s were not unexpected. Rather, their detection confirmed previous predictions. For example, in 1983, research teams at CERN detected the W and Z particles, the gauge bosons that are exchanged in the weak interaction. Even though these had been anticipated, their detection was exciting. As noted in chapter 7, the theory of the weak interaction required positive and negative Ws. The work by Sheldon Glashow's team that combined the weak interaction with electromagnetism also led to predictions of a new quark flavor (charm) and the neutral Z particle. The discovery of the J/psi in 1974 had confirmed the existence of charm, so the detection of the Z was eagerly awaited as the final piece of supporting evidence for the electroweak unification.

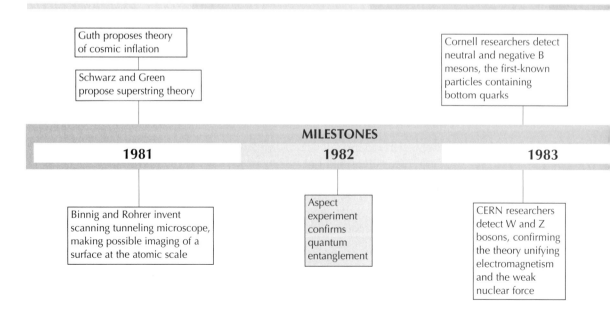

Guth proposes theory of cosmic inflation

Schwarz and Green propose superstring theory

Cornell researchers detect neutral and negative B mesons, the first-known particles containing bottom quarks

MILESTONES

1981	1982	1983

Binnig and Rohrer invent scanning tunneling microscope, making possible imaging of a surface at the atomic scale

Aspect experiment confirms quantum entanglement

CERN researchers detect W and Z bosons, confirming the theory unifying electromagnetism and the weak nuclear force

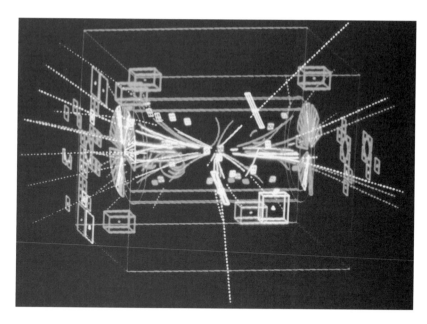

Decay of a Z into an electron and position, the first Z event recorded by the UA1 detectors at CERN on April 30, 1983 (CERN)

Another discovery came from Cornell University, where researchers had built a device called the Cornell Electron Storage Ring (CESR) in the late 1970s. In 1979, CESR produced its first electron-positron collisions. The high energy produced when an electron and positron annihilate each other made it possible to create and detect particles

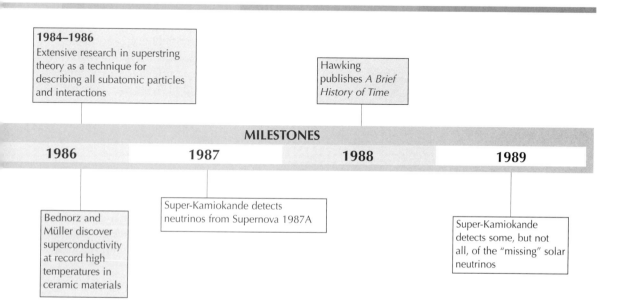

1984–1986
Extensive research in superstring theory as a technique for describing all subatomic particles and interactions

Hawking publishes *A Brief History of Time*

MILESTONES

1986	1987	1988	1989

Bednorz and Müller discover superconductivity at record high temperatures in ceramic materials

Super-Kamiokande detects neutrinos from Supernova 1987A

Super-Kamiokande detects some, but not all, of the "missing" solar neutrinos

containing the bottom quark, in particular the two types of B meson detected in 1983: the electrically neutral B-zero (a bottom plus an anti-down) and the negatively charged B-minus (a bottom plus an anti-up). Physicists were especially interested in a particular property known as CP symmetry violation, which was expected in and was indeed exhibited by the B-zero. (CP stands for "charge parity," referring to a combination of electric charge reversal and mirror imaging.) That property was first observed in K-zero mesons (down plus anti-strange) and was essential for developing an understanding of the distinction between matter and antimatter.

Also in the 1980s, the slow accumulation of data in the large, underground neutrino detectors continued to support Raymond Davis's early results (see chapter 6). With improvements in equipment, the number of solar neutrino detections had reached 2,000, and the rate was still about a third of what was expected. In 1987, light reached Earth from a supernova event in the neighboring Large Magellanic Cloud (170,000 light-years away). According to astrophysical theories of supernovas, a blast of neutrinos was also expected. Physicists led by Masatoshi Koshiba at Japan's new Super-Kamiokande detected 12 neutrinos from the distant exploding star, confirming astrophysicists' understanding of the supernova process and giving credibility to their giant detector's data. In 1989, Koshiba reported that his group was detecting solar neutrinos at a rate greater than Davis had, but still far less than expected. The detection of neutrinos from Supernova 1987A demonstrated that the detector could not be blamed for the missing solar neutrinos, and the theory of nuclear processes in stars seemed sound. Thus physicists realized their understanding of neutrino behavior was incomplete. Something was happening to the neutrinos between the Sun and the detector, but what?

Evidence supporting another puzzling phenomenon, quantum entanglement, also grew in the 1980s. In 1982, at the Institut d'Optique in Orsay, France, Alain Aspect (1947–   ) devised an experiment to test entanglement in a different way than the Clauser group had done (see preceding chapter). Both the Aspect and Clauser experiments are examples of tests of Bell inequalities, devised in 1964 by Belfast-born CERN physicist John Bell (1928–90) to determine whether quantum entanglement actually occurred. The Aspect experiment addressed certain doubts about the validity of Clauser's experiment and its interpretation. To explain those concerns here would require a philosophical and mathematical discussion that is beyond the scope of this book. The important point, however, is that the Aspect group's results supported Clauser's original conclusion. The experiment persuaded most doubters that nature is indeed governed by quantum mechanical principles that lead to entanglement, no matter how "spooky" that may seem to some people.

GUTs, Superstrings, and Cosmic Inflation

Quantum entanglement was not the only discovery of the 1970s and 1980s that many physicists considered puzzling, odd, or spooky. Detailed measurements of the cosmic microwave background (see chapter 7) in different directions were remarkably consistent with each other. Why is that puzzling? Consider an earthbound observer looking in opposite directions in the sky and measuring the temperature of the cosmic background. At the most extreme, the two locations are separated by twice the distance that light would have traveled since the big bang. That same situation would have always been true for those regions at all times in the past as the universe expanded, unless that expansion was faster than light. Since the theory of relativity prohibits particles from moving faster than light, those regions never should have been able to exchange energy or influence one another. Statistical mechanical analysis of the big bang predicts a certain amount of random variation in temperature between different regions of space. For regions that are close enough to communicate or exchange energy with one another, their temperature differences will diminish; that is, they will approach thermal equilibrium with one another. For those widely separated regions, however, the variation that existed at the big bang should still be apparent. Yet it is not. The measured variation in temperature of the cosmic background indicates that even the most widely separated regions have reached thermal equilibrium. They may not be able to communicate with one another now, but they must have exchanged energy sometime in the past.

How could that be? In 1981, Alan Guth (1947–   ), a physics professor at the Massachusetts Institute of Technology, proposed an explanation for that odd result. His idea, which he called *inflation*, blended a grand unified theory (GUT) with the physics of phase transitions, such as freezing or melting. As he explained it, during an unimaginably short time after the big bang, the entire universe underwent a phase change during which space itself expanded at a rate much greater than the speed of light. Before that phase transition, all matter/energy was unified. That led to thermal equilibrium between all regions of the universe, including those regions that were too far apart to communicate after that transition. At about the same time as Guth proposed cosmic inflation, John Schwarz and Michael Green (1946–   ) modified string theory by adding another dimension and calling it superstring theory. As the decade proceeded, other physicists added even more dimensions—the precise number depending on the particular version of superstring theory that the physicists preferred. The number of physicists involved in string theory research increased rapidly in the 1984–86 period, as they realized the mathematics could describe all the subatomic particles and their interactions.

GUTs, superstrings, and cosmic inflation provide useful mathematical descriptions that tie together cosmology—the study of the behavior of the universe as an entity—and the physics of subatomic particles. Those approaches were developed to provide a foundation for a wide variety of observed physical phenomena, but none of them has yet led to a prediction of a testable but unobserved phenomenon. Until that happens, some physicists are reluctant to consider any of those approaches as a full-blown "theory," since scientists usually reserve that term for ideas that are not only supported by a large body of evidence but have also demonstrated their predictive power. This book follows the common terminology, using "string theory" and "grand unified theory" for example, even though calling them theories probably overstates the case.

A Brief History of Physics Books and Scientific Celebrity in the 1980s

By the late 1980s, physics had reached a point in its history that resembled the late 19th century. Quantum mechanics, relativity, and the theories of the nuclear interactions had replaced Newtonian mechanics, Maxwell's equations, and atomic theory as the fundamental foundation of physics, but superstrings and cosmic inflation suggested that other fundamental ideas were yet to be discovered. Would new theories complete the tapestry of physics, or would they cause it to unravel, just as radioactivity and Planck's quantum had done in the early decades of the 20th century? Questions like that drove Stephen Hawking's research at Cambridge. Hawking also sensed a deep fascination in those questions among educated non-physicists, and he set about to respond to that interest. The result was a 1988 book entitled *A Brief History of Time: From the Big Bang to Black Holes.*

As readers worked through its pages, they encountered many ideas that challenged their intuitive view of space, time, and matter. For many, the book provided a fascinating intellectual ride, but in the end, they had a difficult time explaining what, if anything, they had learned. Still, Hawking's engaging writing style led people to recommend it to their friends. The book became a best seller, though most people who bought it never read most of its pages or fully grasped its key points. To them, it was enough to share Hawking's enthusiasm for his questions and speculations about space, time, matter, and energy. Readers also found the book remarkable because of the effort that went into producing it. Hawking is a quadriplegic who communicates with the help of a computer and voice synthesizer, which he controls with the help of a device that responds to slight movements of his hand. For a profoundly disabled person to fulfill the obligations of his professorship and to write such a book for the general public was remarkable indeed.

Even though *A Brief History of Time* captured the public's interest, Hawking was not the best-known celebrity-scientist of the 1980s. That

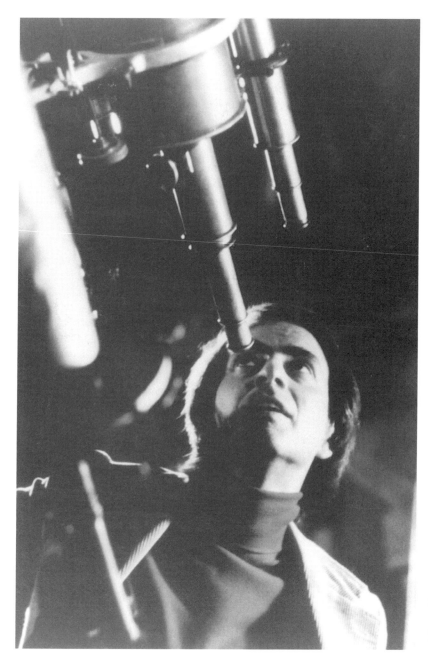

Carl Sagan, known for his popular books and the TV series Cosmos *(Cornell University, courtesy AIP Emilio Segrè Visual Archives)*

distinction belonged to Carl Sagan, who was a prolific author of popular books and magazine articles about science, including his 1979 book, *Broca's Brain*, with speculations about alien life and artificial intelligence, which won a Pulitzer Prize, one of the highest honors in the world of art and literature. Sagan had also become a television personality for his frequent guest appearances on NBC's *Tonight Show with Johnny Carson* and as the host of his own public television series *Cosmos*, which led to a best-selling book by the same name.

Sagan's greatest scientific interest was the quest for life on other worlds, which he frequently connected to environmental concerns on Earth. His doctoral thesis in the late 1950s included an analysis of the atmosphere of Venus, which he argued was so rich in carbon dioxide that it caused a runaway *greenhouse effect*, a phenomenon in which a planet's atmosphere acts like a glass greenhouse. The atmosphere is transparent to solar energy in the form of visible light, which passes through and heats the planet's surface, but it traps the infrared radiation emitted by the hot surface. On Venus, Sagan concluded, that phenomenon led to surface temperatures hot enough to melt aluminum. Could a similar fate befall Earth? Long before global warming became a major political topic around the world, Sagan was among the first scientists to raise the alarm about the increased rate of burning fossil fuel. That burning had already produced a measurable increase in atmospheric carbon dioxide on Earth. Future increases posed a risk of serious global warming and a disruption of Earth's climate. In the late 1980s, some scientists saw worrisome signs that the changes had already begun, although the observations could also be interpreted as normal variation. Even if a trend had begun, it was too soon to make the case that human activities, such as burning of petroleum and coil, were responsible for the changes.

Meanwhile, Sagan and his colleagues saw an even greater threat to life on Earth, a phenomenon called nuclear winter that they speculated would result from a nuclear war in which the major powers detonated their full arsenals of thermonuclear weapons. In a scientific paper that became known as TTAPS after the initials of its five authors (the *S* stood for Sagan), the researchers drew on the analysis by Alvarez's team and others about the global climate changes that followed the Cretaceous-ending asteroid impact. That event created a global cloud of dust and a storm of glowing rock that had been blasted into space and fell back to Earth as meteors, setting off forest fires around the globe. For years, a pall of dust and smoke blocked most sunlight and created wintry conditions everywhere on the planet. TTAPS argued that a nuclear war could raise a similar dust cloud with an equally catastrophic outcome.

As is usually the case with such dramatic claims, the TTAPS paper had many critics who disagreed about the extent of climate disruption a nuclear war would cause. Still, the TTAPS predictions added a new dimension to international discussions about nuclear arms. It is generally considered an important factor in moving the major nations toward nuclear arms reduction treaties in the 1980s. Sagan may have been the fifth of five authors of the study, but he was clearly its major public advocate. Ironically, his arguments in favor of the study's conclusions broke a rule for which he is widely known: "Extraordinary claims require extraordinary evidence." The evidence favoring nuclear winter was not extraordinary, and Sagan knew it. But in his view, the consequences were dire—far worse than the unimaginable devastation that the bombs themselves would cause. The world could not afford to take the chance that the extraordinary TTAPS result would be right.

Breakthroughs in Condensed Matter Physics

By the early 1980s, most physicists had begun calling solid-state physics by a new name, condensed matter physics, following the lead of 1977 Nobel laureate Philip W. Anderson (1923–   ), who changed the name of his research group in 1967, and the American Physical Society, which renamed the former Division of Solid State Physics in 1978. No matter what the field was called, it was responsible for two of the most significant breakthroughs in physics in the 1980s, both of which were promptly recognized with Nobel Prizes.

The first came in 1981, when two researchers at IBM Zurich Research Laboratory in Switzerland, Gerd Binnig (1947–   ) and Heinrich Rohrer (1933–   ) invented a device that enabled scientists to create images of individual atoms on the surface of a material, the scanning tunneling microscope (STM). The STM takes advantage of the quantum mechanical phenomenon known as tunneling, which results from the wave nature of objects that are usually considered particles. For example, most electrons at the surface of a solid are usually viewed as belonging to particular atoms, but in fact, their wave function extends beyond the atom. When

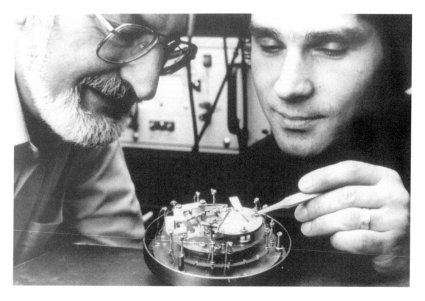

Gerd Binnig (right) and Heinrich Rohrer, with the apparatus that led to the development of the scanning tunneling microscope (AIP Emilio Segrè Visual Archives)

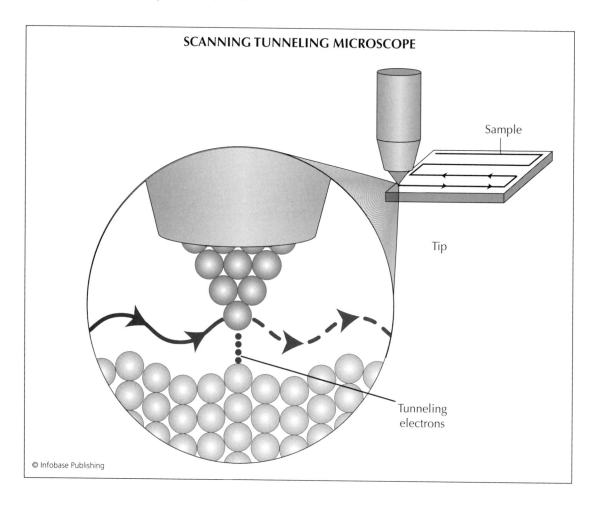

SCANNING TUNNELING MICROSCOPE

Sample

Tip

Tunneling
electrons

© Infobase Publishing

The scanning tunneling microscope takes advantage of the quantum phenomenon known as tunneling to create an image of the atoms on the surface of a sample.

the point of a very sharp metal needle is placed very close to the surface, the wave functions of the electrons at the needle's tip and of electrons on the material's surface overlap. Quantum mechanical calculations yield this result: At any time, there is a chance of finding an electron from the needle in the material or vice versa. The closer the needle is to the surface, the greater the chance for that to occur. Normally, a certain ionizing voltage would be necessary to draw an electron out of the needle tip or the surface and across the gap between them, but the quantum mechanical phenomenon permits that transfer to happen even if there is a much smaller voltage. It is as if electrons tunnel through a barrier that they do not have enough energy to surmount and emerge on the other side. The smaller the gap, the larger the tunneling current becomes. Thus if a needle scans back and forth across a surface, the size of the tunneling

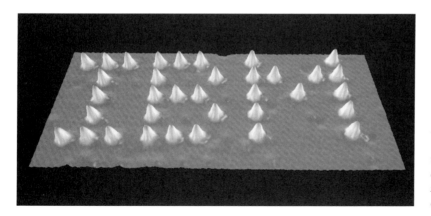

Using the same principles that led to the development of the scanning tunneling microscope (STM), it is possible to manipulate individual atoms, as shown in this STM image of xenon atoms spelling out IBM on a crystal of nickel. (IBM)

current reflects how close the needle is to an individual atom. Binnig and Rohrer perfected a technique that detected that tunneling current and displayed it like a television picture.

By the time the pair was awarded the Nobel Prize in physics in 1986, a number of variations of the STM technique were yielding valuable results. Atomic force microscopes were measuring and displaying the variation of the electric force between the needle and the surface, and other devices were even moving individual atoms to form artificial arrangements. (To demonstrate that capability, IBM wrote its corporate name with xenon atoms on nickel in dot-matrix letters a few atoms high.)

Winning a Nobel Prize within five years of a discovery is remarkable, and Binnig and Rohrer's scientific colleagues at IBM Zurich celebrated the news. Little did they suspect that they would be having a similar party the next year for J. Georg Bednorz (1950–) and K. Alexander Müller (1927–), who had just cooked up a recipe for another Nobel Prize–winning discovery. Their work in 1986 led to a worldwide flurry of research into new superconducting materials and a Nobel Prize in 1987. Unlike most researchers in superconductivity who were studying metal alloys, Bednorz and Müller were researching the phenomenon in ceramic materials, which are hard but brittle compounds of metals and nonmetals, including oxides.

To most scientists interested in superconductivity, that seemed to be an odd choice, because both theory and experiments indicated that the temperature at which ceramics became superconducting was even colder than that needed for metals. As noted in chapter 2, Heike Kamerlingh Onnes had discovered the phenomenon in 1911 in a thin wire of frozen mercury at a temperature so low—barely more than 4°C (39°F) above absolute zero—that all gases, even helium, turn to liquid. When discussing superconductivity, physicists and other scientists describe temperatures in kelvins, or degrees Celsius above absolute zero, and this book

J. Georg Bednorz (left) and K. Alexander Müller, whose work on superconductivity in ceramic materials earned them a Nobel Prize in 1987, a year after their IBM colleagues Binnig and Rohrer (IBM Corporate Archives)

will follow that choice. For example, the superconducting transition temperature of mercury is 4.3K. The Bardeen, Cooper, and Schrieffer (BCS) theory of 1957 (see chapter 6) revealed that the quantum mechanical mechanism underlying superconductivity was the exchange of phonons (quanta of vibrational or sound energy) between Cooper pairs of electrons. BCS theory led materials scientists and engineers (researchers who specialized in the fabrication and study of new materials) to alloys that became superconducting at steadily higher temperatures. By the

1970s, they had developed alloys with transition temperatures as high as 23K. At that still frigid temperature, progress stalled. The hoped-for goal of producing superconductivity at a temperature that could be achieved with liquid nitrogen (77K or higher) seemed to be out of reach.

The reason for that goal is simple. Liquid helium is much more expensive to make than liquid nitrogen. To slow the evaporation of the precious helium, all practical liquid helium systems are surrounded by liquid nitrogen. That limited the technological applications of super-conductivity to those few that benefited from a very high magnetic field produced by electromagnets made from coils of superconducting wire. In particular, superconducting alloys were economically practical in mag-netic resonance imaging (see chapter 8) and in powerful magnets needed to control the beams in particle accelerators. Eliminating the need for liquid helium would make those magnets much less complex and less costly to build and operate.

So why did Bednorz and Müller look at ceramics rather than alloys? Part of it was simple curiosity, wondering whether the BCS theory applied to other materials as well as alloys. They soon found that it did not. One of the ceramics they were looking at had a superconduct-ing transition temperature significantly higher than that predicted by BCS theory. Since the transition temperature was still very low, the difference measured in kelvins was tiny; but it was significant on a percentage basis. They saw that result as a hint of a different route to superconductivity beyond Cooper pairs and phonons, and they began looking for other ceramics with significantly higher transition points. In early 1986, they discovered superconductivity in a class of ceramics called perovskites. One in particular, lanthium-barium-copper oxide, was superconducting up to 35K, a 50 percent increase above any previ-ously discovered superconductor. That set off a race to find ceramics that were superconducting at above the temperature of liquid nitrogen. Within months, materials scientists succeeded. Suddenly, the new goal was room temperature (roughly 300K), but progress stalled again at about 130K, not far above the maximum transition temperature that had been achieved when Bednorz and Müller accepted the 1987 Nobel Prize in physics.

Because ceramics are brittle, they are hard to form into wires, which has limited their practical applications to date. Room temperature super-conductivity still seems to be an unreachable goal for two reasons. First, physicists have yet to develop a new theory or a refinement of the BCS theory to explain what is happening in these ceramics. Second, there has been no progress toward superconductivity at higher temperatures since the late 1980s. Based on the history of superconductivity, the field may well yield more Nobel Prizes if someone makes a breakthrough in either of those two areas.

Scientist of the Decade: Stephen Hawking (1942–)

On January 8, 1942, Stephen Hawking was born in a hospital in Oxford, England. His parents, Frank and Isobel Hawking chose to have their child delivered in Oxford rather than staying closer to their home in Highgate, a northern suburb of London, to escape the risk from German bombing. Despite the ongoing World War II, the German and British air forces had agreed not to bomb each other's great university centers of Oxford and Cambridge, Heidelberg and Göttingen. Both those places and the date of Hawking's birth were significant. He would attend college at Oxford and earn his doctorate at Cambridge, where he would later occupy a faculty position once held by Sir Isaac Newton, whose 300th birthday year had just begun.

Perhaps an even more remarkable coincidence is that January 8 was the 300th anniversary of the death of the great Galileo Galilei. By turning his telescope to the skies, Galileo had transformed humanity's view of other planets and of Earth's place in the cosmos. In his career, Hawking would become one of the 20th-century physicists who transformed the scientific understanding of the cosmos itself. To his colleagues, Hawking's insights and scientific publications are his most important contributions, but to the broader society, he is known and appreciated for his popular books and for his unquenchable optimism in the face of profound disability.

Stephen came by his great intelligence and free spirit naturally. Both of his parents had graduated from Oxford but discovered each other at the medical institute where Frank was studying tropical medicine and Isobel was working as a secretary. They were viewed as somewhat eccentric in St. Albans, 20 miles farther north of London, where they moved when Stephen was eight. Isobel was an intellectual with a strong social conscience and an attraction to left-wing political causes, while Frank was frugal to a fault. He spent little on his personal appearance or on the family car, which was a former London taxi that he bought for £50.

During Stephen's secondary education (equivalent to junior high school in the United States) at the prestigious St. Albans school, he was a satisfactory but not outstanding student. He did better on exams than his coursework, since he preferred

Stephen Hawking, the celebrated physicist, whose book A Brief History of Time: From the Big Bang to Black Holes *won him popular acclaim* (AIP Emilio Segrè Visual Archives, Physics Today Collection)

building models and inventing complex games to homework. Looking ahead, he aimed to be a research scientist like his father. Stephen preferred mathematics and physics, but Frank persuaded him to substitute chemistry, which he saw as more practical, for math. When Stephen began to study general relativity, the lack of formal mathematics courses caused him some difficulty, but it allowed him to think more pictorially rather than in equations. That proved to be a great advantage for him when disease struck and writing mathematical expressions became increasingly difficult.

Hawking entered Oxford in 1959 at age 17 at a time when a student's brilliance was valued above hard work. The only required examinations were the finals, and like many of his classmates, he coasted through his courses. After three years, he was ready to graduate. Oxford offered four levels of degrees, and he was on the borderline between first- and second-class degrees. He told a panel of examiners that he intended to do research at Cambridge if he earned a first-class degree, and the examiners agreed to give it to him.

As Hawking began to settle into his research at Cambridge, tragedy struck in the form of a medical diagnosis. He learned he had amyotrophic lateral sclerosis (ALS), a disease that attacks the muscles, eventually leading to paralysis and death. It is the same disease that killed the famous baseball star Lou Gehrig and has come to be named for Gehrig in the United States. The physician's prognosis was that he had about two years to live. At first Hawking saw no reason to continue his Ph.D. project, since he would not have time to finish it. However, his inherent optimism eventually took hold. He realized that as long as he was alive and had an active mind, he had something to live for. He knew he would need help, but he was determined to make the most of whatever time he had left. No one helped him more than Jane Wilde, whom he had met at a party in 1963 soon after his ALS symptoms had started. Not even his dire prognosis could stand in the way of love, and he and Jane soon became engaged. His ALS symptoms progressed but at a much slower pace than expected, and he completed his Ph.D. in the summer of 1965. The couple married in July of that year.

Hawking was offered a research fellowship in theoretical physics at Cambridge, which he accepted. Despite his increasing disability, he and Jane managed a remarkably normal life, which included children. At work, it did not take him long to capture the attention of fellow physicists. He elected to study black holes, which had been predicted in the 1930s (see chapter 4) but had never been observed. He wanted to reconcile the mathematical description of a black hole, which predicted a "singularity" of infinite density at its center, with a physical world in which infinities are not possible. In collaboration with Roger Penrose (1931–) of Oxford University, whose mathematical skills complemented his physical insights, Hawking developed a theory that described the physics of black holes yet avoided the singularity.

In the early 1970s, astronomers discovered an X-ray emitting object in the constellation Cygnus, which they named Cygnus X-1. By 1974, Hawking and most astrophysicists expressed 80 percent confidence that the object was a black hole with a star in orbit around it. The X-rays were the result of emissions from the star's gases as they were drawn into the black hole and heated to exceedingly high temperatures. Impishly, Hawking decided to provide himself some "insurance" if he were wrong. He made a bet with his good friend Kip Thorne (1940–), an astrophysicist at Caltech, promising Thorne a one-year subscription to *Penthouse* magazine if Cygnus X-1 turned out to contain a black hole. If not, he would have the consolation of a four-year subscription to the British magazine *Private Eye.* In 1990, the confidence level that Cygnus X-1 was a black hole had risen to 95 percent, and Hawking paid off the bet.

In 1982, faced with large expenses for his medical care and for his children's school tuition, Hawking was looking for additional income. He had always enjoyed sharing his research with a wider audience than just his academic colleagues and students, and he was confident he could write a short book for general audiences about his unique perspectives on the universe. The book, *A Brief History of Time: From the Big Bang to Black Holes,* did not come as easily as he thought—it was not published until 1988, but its success exceeded even his own most optimistic expectations.

Despite his medical condition, Hawking has always considered his life "normal," even after an emergency tracheotomy cost him the remaining use of his voice in 1985. Normal people sometimes divorce, as Jane and Stephen Hawking did in 1990. He and one of his nurses, Elaine Mason, left their spouses to live together and eventually marry. Elaine's husband, David, had designed the computer hardware for Hawking's wheelchair.

Today Stephen Hawking continues his research and writing. In 2002, Cambridge University celebrated his 60th birthday with a symposium entitled *The Future of Theoretical Physics and Cosmology,* published the lectures as a book, and broadcast them on BBC television. Hawking offered no bets as to how many more birthdays he would celebrate, but he clearly intends to outlive any predictions anyone cares to make.

Further Reading

Books

Alvarez, Luis W. *Alvarez, Adventures of a Physicist*. New York: Basic Books, 1987. Luis Alvarez's adventurous life in his own words.

Alvarez, Walter. *T-Rex and the Crater of Doom*. Princeton, N.J.: Princeton University Press, 1997. A lively account of the scientific investigation that led to a radical new understanding of the mass extinction that killed the dinosaurs.

Bortz, Fred. *Collision Course! Cosmic Impacts and Life on Earth*. Brookfield, Conn.: Millbrook Press, 2001. For younger readers, this book discusses several planetary impacts of comets and asteroids, including the one that killed the dionosaurs.

———. "What Killed the Dinosaurs?" Chap. 2, *To the Young Scientist: Reflections on Doing and Living Science*. Danbury, Conn.: Franklin Watts, 1997. This chapter is based on an interview with Frank Asaro and Helen Michel, who did the neutron activation analysis that led to Luis Alvarez's theory that the dinosaurs' extinction was due to the impact of an asteroid.

Burrows, William E. *The Infinite Journey: Eyewitness Accounts of NASA and the Age of Space*. New York: Discovery Books, 2000. A vivid pictorial account of NASA's exploration of the Moon and the Planets.

———. *This New Ocean: The Story of the First Space Age*. New York: Random House, 1998. A detailed history of space exploration.

Cernan, Eugene, with Don Davis. *The Last Man on the Moon*. New York: St. Martin's, 1999. A description of *Apollo 17*, the last manned mission to the Moon, written by the astronaut who was the last to board the lunar module for its return trip.

Close, Frank, Michael Marten, and Christine Sutton. *The Particle Odyssey: A Journey to the Heart of Matter*. New York: Oxford University Press, 2002. A detailed and colorfully illustrated overview of the discovery of subatomic particles.

Cole, K. C. *The Hole in the Universe: How Scientists Peered over the Edge of Emptiness and Found Everything*. New York: Harcourt, 2001. A description of modern theories of subatomic particles and cosmology.

Cropper, William H. *Great Physicists: The Life and Times of Leading Physicists from Galileo to Hawking*. New York: Oxford University Press, 2001. The life and times of many great physicists, including Hawking.

Dauber, Philip M., and Richard A. Muller. *The Three Big Bangs: Comet Crashes, Exploding Stars, and the Creation of the Universe*. New York: Perseus Books, 1997. A clear and interesting look at the origin and history of life on Earth by one of Luis Alvarez's best-known students.

Gell-Mann, Murray. *The Quark and the Jaguar: Adventures in the Simple and the Complex*. New York: W. H. Freeman, 1994. The story of the eightfold way and quarks in Murray Gell-Mann's own words.

Hawking, Stephen. *A Brief History of Time.* New York: Bantam, 1988. Hawking's most famous book about the nature of matter, energy, space-time, and cosmology for nonscientists.

———. *The Universe in a Nutshell.* New York: Bantam, 2001. Insight into cosmology and string theory by one of the world's greatest theoretical physicists.

Heppenheimer, T. A. *Countdown: A History of Space Flight.* New York: John Wiley, 1997. A detailed history of the manned spaceflight.

Johnson, George. *Strange Beauty: Murray Gell-Mann and the Revolution in Twentieth-Century Physics.* New York: Random House, 1999. A definitive and readable biography of Murray Gell-Mann and an explanation of his major scientific ideas.

Kragh, Helge. *Quantum Generations: A History of Physics in the Twentieth Century.* Princeton, N.J.: Princeton University Press, 1999. An in-depth history of 20th-century physics and physicists.

Launius, Roger D., and Howard McCurdy. *Imagining Space: Achievements * Predictions * Possibilities, 1950–2050.* San Francisco, Calif.: Chronicle, 2001. An illustrated history of and future of spaceflight.

McCurdy, Howard E. *Space and the American Imagination.* Washington, D.C.: Smithsonian, 1997. A history of the United States space program.

Morton, Oliver. *Mapping Mars: Science, Imagination, and the Birth of a World.* New York: Picador, 2002. A detailed history of the discoveries from various Mars missions.

Schumm, Bruce A. *Deep Down Things: The Breathtaking Beauty of Particle Physics.* Baltimore: Johns Hopkins University Press, 2005. A look at the mathematical ideas that underlie particle physics and string theory.

Seife, Charles. *Alpha & Omega: The Search for the Beginning and the End of the Universe.* New York: Viking, 2003. A look at the connections between particle physics and the cosmology of the big bang.

Siegfried, Tom. *Strange Matters: Undiscovered Ideas at the Frontiers of Space and Time.* Washington, D.C.: Joseph Henry Press, 2002. A book discussing ideas, such as string theory, which the author refers to as "prediscoveries" because they are likely to produce insights into particle physics and cosmology.

Suplee, Curt. *Physics in the 20th Century.* New York: Harry N. Abrams, 1999. A pictorial history of 20th-century physics.

White, Michael, and John Gribbin. *Stephen Hawking: A Life in Science.* New York: Dutton, 1992. A definitive and readable biography of Hawking's first 50 years.

Web Sites

American Institute of Physics, Center for History of Physics. Available online. URL: http://www.aip.org/history. Accessed March 27, 2006. Follow pull-down menu for special online exhibits or browse for a variety of written resources and images.

National Inventors Hall of Fame. Available online. URL: http://www.invent.org. Accessed April 18, 2006. Search Web site by name of inventor or invention.

Nobelprize.org. Available online. URL: http://nobelprize.org. Accessed March 27, 2006. The official Web site of the Nobel Foundation contains brief biographies of Nobel Prize winners, summaries of their prize-winning work, and their acceptance speeches.

Schwarz, Patricia. The Official String Theory Web Site. Available online. URL: http://www.superstringtheory.com. Accessed April 21, 2006. A comprehensive Web site about string theory, the physicists who have worked on it, and its history.

The Science Museum. Available online. URL: http://www.sciencemuseum.org.uk. Accessed March 27, 2006. A British online science education resource that includes useful exhibits on Atomic Firsts; Life, the Universe, and the Electron; Marie Curie and the History of Radioactivity; and many other topics discussed in this book.

The Science Shelf, Books for the World Year of Physics 2005. Available online. URL: http://www.scienceshelf.com/WorldYearofPhysics.htm. Accessed April 26, 2006. This page on the book review site of Fred Bortz has brief comments about a number of books published in recognition of the World Year of Physics, plus links to reviews of a number of other physics books for nonspecialist readers.

World Year of Physics 2005. Available online. URL: http://www.physics2005.org. Accessed March 27, 2006. An online resource developed in honor of the centennial of Albert Einstein's "Miracle Year."

10

1991–2000:
Cosmic Connections

The decade of the 1990s did little to resolve the dangling questions of string theory and other attempts at unifying the fundamental physical forces. There was some progress but no surprises in particle physics. The detection of the top quark and the tau-neutrino at the Fermi National Accelerator Lab (Fermilab) in Batavia, Illinois, completed the standard model of particle physics, culminating work begun by Gell-Mann more than 30 years earlier. It was also a time of important discoveries in other sciences made possible by continued technological progress. People who read Hawking's popular books had new cosmological questions to savor, raised by an orbiting observatory called the *Cosmic Background Explorer* (*COBE*) and early results from the ambitious Sloan Digital Sky Survey (SDSS) project. Those who shared Sagan's enthusiasm for extraterrestrial life bubbled over with interest in a Martian rock, while those who shared his environmental concerns (often the same people) were troubled by increasing evidence of global warming caused by human activity. An understanding of physics became increasingly important in the global politics of energy and environmental policy.

In the United States especially, science education became a hot political issue. This chapter's featured scientist, former Fermilab director Leon Lederman, had always valued learning. In retirement, he redirected his energy and seized upon opportunities to make a difference in the way young people learned science. He used the prestige of his Nobel Prize and his leadership in the physics community to great advantage in his new work that led to both a model science education program in the Chicago public schools and a national educational resource about subatomic physics at Fermilab and online.

Subatomic Physics: Completing the Standard Model

After the discovery of the J/psi meson and the charm quark in 1974, physicists had a short-lived sense that they had completed the subatomic picture (see chapter 8). At that point, they knew of two "generations" of fundamental particles. The first generation was composed of the particles of ordinary matter: up and down quarks that combined to produce protons, neutrons, and the pions of Yukawa's theory of the strong force; plus two leptons, the electron and its neutrino. The second generation of two more quarks (strange and charm) and two more leptons (the muon and its neutrino) accounted for the property Gell-Mann called strangeness and the property of charm that was necessary to unify the electroweak force. The sense of completeness was shattered in 1975 with the discovery of a new lepton, the tau particle. That suggested that a third generation of fundamental particles existed, including another pair of quarks (top/truth and bottom/beauty) and a tau-neutrino. Would that generation complete what was coming to be known as the standard model of subatomic particles? Accelerators were achieving higher and higher energies, so this question naturally arose: Would there be a fourth generation of fundamental particles, then a fifth, and so on?

As the 1990s began, the top quark and the tau-neutrino still had not been detected, and it had been 15 years since Lederman and his team had spotted evidence of the bottom quark in the form of the upsilon (see chapter 7). Physicists began to suspect that the third generation might be the last, but they were mindful of an important adage in science: "The absence of evidence is not evidence of absence." By the end of the decade

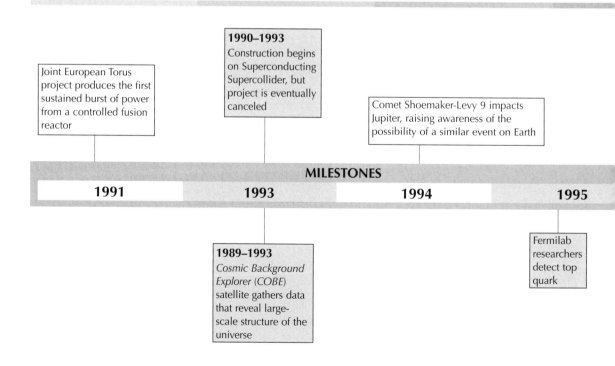

1990–1993
Construction begins on Superconducting Supercollider, but project is eventually canceled

Joint European Torus project produces the first sustained burst of power from a controlled fusion reactor

Comet Shoemaker-Levy 9 impacts Jupiter, raising awareness of the possibility of a similar event on Earth

MILESTONES

| 1991 | 1993 | 1994 | 1995 |

1989–1993
Cosmic Background Explorer (COBE) satellite gathers data that reveal large-scale structure of the universe

Fermilab researchers detect top quark

and the century, they still lacked evidence that three generations were enough, but they had ideas of where to look: deep underground in the large neutrino detectors (see chapter 11).

The various major accelerator laboratories around the world continued to develop new detection techniques and devices and to examine increasingly more energetic collisions. As more energy was available, it opened the possibility of producing more massive particles. The top quark was expected to be about 40 times as massive as the bottom, but by 1995, the technology to detect it was available. That year, two teams at Fermilab teams found conclusive evidence of top quarks in their high-energy collision experiments. To complete the third generation of fundamental subatomic particles, only the elusive tau-neutrino remained to be found. Again, it was Fermilab researchers who made the critical discovery in 2000, the last year of the 20th century.

No signs of another generation of fundamental subatomic particles were on the horizon, but there was still international interest in building particle accelerators with the power needed in the search for the Higgs boson (see chapter 7). In the United States, the Superconducting Supercollider (SSC) project began to take shape in the 1980s and won government approval in 1987. It required huge superconducting magnets that would enable beams of particles to travel through a circular tunnel 54 miles (87 km) in circumference. By mid-1990, a full engineering

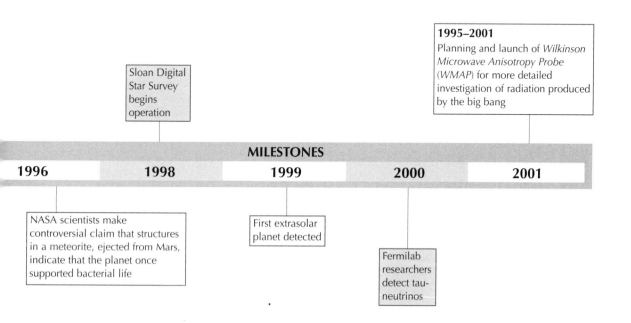

1995–2001
Planning and launch of *Wilkinson Microwave Anisotropy Probe* (*WMAP*) for more detailed investigation of radiation produced by the big bang

Sloan Digital Star Survey begins operation

MILESTONES

| 1996 | 1998 | 1999 | 2000 | 2001 |

NASA scientists make controversial claim that structures in a meteorite, ejected from Mars, indicate that the planet once supported bacterial life

First extrasolar planet detected

Fermilab researchers detect tau-neutrinos

THE STANDARD MODEL

Three generations of matter

	First generation	Second generation	Third generation	Force carriers
Quarks	Up	Charm	Top	Photon (Electro-magnetic force)
	Down	Strange	Bottom	Gloun (Strong nuclear force)
Leptons	Electron-neutrino	Muon-neutrino	Tau-neutrino	Z Boson (Electro-weak force)
	Electron	Muon	Tau	W Boson (Weak nuclear force)

© Infobase Publishing

The detection of the tau neutrino in 2000 completed the third generation of the standard model of subatomic particles, with no other quarks, leptons, or force carriers looming on the horizon.

design was in place, and construction began soon afterward. In 1993, after spending $2 billion on the project and with 14 miles (22.5 km) of tunneling completed, the U.S. Congress canceled the project. Scientists turned to CERN for the next advance in energy, where the Large Hadron Collider is expected to be operational in 2007.

Meanwhile, theorists were puzzling over the missing neutrino problem and the question of whether the neutrino has mass. Neutrino mass can go a long way to explaining the problem of missing solar neutrinos. In the last years of the 1990s, a number of physicists had begun viewing the electron-neutrino, muon-neutrino, and the tau-neutrino not as three different particles but as three modes of the same particle. For that hypothesis to fit with physical theory, the neutrino (or neutrinos) must have mass and that mass must change as the neutrino changes its mode. If the neutrinos are indeed just modes rather than separate particles, they would oscillate between modes as they travel through space. Such oscillation would mean that solar neutrinos, emitted as electron-neutrinos, would arrive at Earth as an equal mix of all three modes. If the neutrino detectors respond only to electron-neutrinos, two-thirds of those solar neutrinos would escape detection. That indeed proved to be the case, but the definitive result did not come until the new century (see chapter 11). That result also rules out a fourth generation of subatomic particles, which would require a fourth neutrino mode, contradicting the now strong evidence for three modes. The standard model of subatomic particles appears to be complete with three generations of four particles: a lepton and its corresponding neutrino mode plus a pair of quarks.

Surprises in Cosmology

The discoveries in particle physics during the 1990s were predictable, but the most closely related field, cosmology, turned out to be full of surprises. How can the physics of the universe as a whole be considered a close relative of subatomic physics? The answer lies in trying to understand the big bang itself. During the first instants of time as science knows it, all the matter in the universe was concentrated into a very small volume. The period of cosmic inflation ended when the universe was about a hundredth of a millionth of a millionth of a millionth of a millionth of a millionth of a second old. Then, for the rest of the first few microseconds (millionths of a second), its matter was so hot and compressed that even mesons and baryons could not stay together. Instead, all the matter in the universe was in a form known as "quark-gluon plasma." By the mid-1990s, the world's most powerful particle accelerators were capable of producing a similar state of matter. Physicists do not all agree that actual quark-gluon plasmas have been produced in those accelerators, but they certainly expect the Large Hadron Collider to create one. When that happens, they hope to be able to design experiments to study the conditions that existed before mesons and baryons—the fundamental particles of matter as we know it—came into being.

In other words, the goal is to test theories of the entire cosmos in the laboratories of one small planet. Interest in that work grew substantially in the 1990s as astronomers developed tools to refine their picture of the big bang by studying the very earliest light and the first stars. How long ago did that first light leave its sources? To answer that requires a deeper discussion of the events that followed the period of the cosmic quark-gluon plasma, when quarks in the cooling universe formed pairs (mesons) and triplets (baryons). As that matter became cooler and more spread out, electromagnetism and gravity began to play a more important role. After about 380,000 years (about 1/36,000 of the 13.7-billion-year age of the universe), cosmic matter had cooled to the point that atoms could form. At that point, the universe became transparent, so that is the age of the oldest glow in the cosmic background. Gravity then drew atoms together to form gas clouds and stars. That took about 200 million years—less than 2 percent of the age of the universe.

The cosmic background radiation contains information about those early events, so they can be studied directly. For the period before that, from the time the universe was a quark-gluon plasma until the time it became transparent, 1990s physicists were developing theories to describe its evolution. Particle physicists hoped to study the quark-gluon plasma in their accelerators, and astronomers were hoping to detect the earliest light and first stars with their latest technological advances. A theory that successfully explains both sets of observations could unify all the fundamental forces, all matter and energy, and cover the history of the entire universe from the fundamental to the cosmic. That would be quite an accomplishment, a theory of everything, indeed!

A theory is no stronger than the data on which it is based. Cosmologists realized that they needed a much more detailed picture of the distant universe, including the cosmic background. On November 18, 1989, NASA launched the *Cosmic Background Explorer* (*COBE*) satellite into a nearly polar orbit of Earth that permitted its three major instruments to survey the entire sky over the course of a year. It continued in operation through the end of 1993. It not only produced clear evidence supporting the big bang theory, but it also revealed that the universe had a structure that resembled joined soap bubbles. Astronomers were already aware that galaxies formed clusters, but *COBE* revealed signs of superclusters—clusters of clusters—that stretched like great thin sheets of matter surrounding vast empty voids. The most likely explanation for that structure is that it resulted from irregularities in the distribution of the earliest matter formed in the big bang, exaggerated by gravitational attraction. These discoveries resulted in the award of the Nobel Prize in physics in 2006 to *COBE* team leaders John C. Mather (1946–) and George F. Smoot (1945–).

COBE's results were tantalizing, and cosmologists wanted more. In 1995, they began planning an ambitious project, the *Wilkinson Microwave Anisotropy Probe* (*WMAP*), to map the cosmic background in sharper detail. NASA approved the mission for development in 1997, and it was launched on June 30, 2001. The remarkable early results of this ongoing project, which include reconsidering the need for Einstein's cosmological constant (see chapters 2–3), are described in chapter 11.

Neither *COBE* nor *WMAP* was intended to detect or measure individual galaxies. In effect, they are studies of a giant network of forests, but unless someone examines the individual trees, the conclusions remain in doubt. That was the impetus for the Sloan Digital Sky Survey (SDSS) that began in 1998 as a five-year project to take a galactic census over one-quarter of the sky. It included a large number of the world's greatest land-based observatories and the *Hubble Space Telescope*, all probing to the limits of observation. Like *WMAP*, the SDSS has produced significant results (see chapter 11), and both are continuing to illuminate cosmological study.

Other Physics-Related Developments in the 1990s

Research and progress continued in a number of physics-related technologies in the 1990s, but none had significant breakthroughs. The growth in electronics continued its remarkable trajectory, but the advancements were largely in techniques in processing of materials that led to increasing miniaturization and speed, not in new physics. Those advances fueled spectacular increases in the use and number of cellular telephones and the rise of the Internet and the World Wide Web. People who had never heard of e-mail and "surfing the 'net" in 1991 were regular users only a few years later. Likewise, research continued in superconductivity, but no one made breakthroughs either in finding new classes of superconducting materials or in developing a BCS-like theory that applied to the new high-temperature superconductors of the 1980s.

The decade began with hope for nuclear fusion as an eventual source of electric power. In 1991, the Joint European Torus (JET) project produced the first sustained burst of power from a controlled fusion reactor. The project continues, but its future commercial feasibility remains dubious at best. That is unfortunate, because by the late 1990s, a number of major scientific organizations had declared that burning of fossil fuels was a serious global problem. Many scientists warned that increasing temperatures, especially in the Arctic, were signs of major problems to come for political stability and economic development in the 21st-century world. It was important to find sources of energy that did not produce carbon dioxide.

Elsewhere in the physical sciences, several major events in planetary astronomy captured the public's attention. In 1994, the odd "string-of-pearls" comet Shoemaker-Levy 9, which had been discovered the previous year, plunged into the cloud tops of Jupiter, providing a dramatic reminder that space rocks regularly collide with planets. By then, the Alvarez team's interpretation of the iridium anomaly as the result of a 65-million-year-old asteroid impact was widely accepted. Most scientists regarded the Chicxulub crater as the "smoking gun." The combination of the two spectacular events raised public awareness of the very real but remote danger of cosmic impacts. Fiction writers produced books and movie scripts (including *Deep Impact* and *Armageddon*) based on impacts from space, but more important, a number of governments increased funding for projects that identified so-called near-earth objects that could eventually collide with the planet.

Another headline-grabbing planetary discovery came in 1996, when a group of NASA scientists made a dramatic announcement about a meteorite they had been studying. Called Meteorite ALH84001, the rock had previously been identified as a piece of Mars that had been launched into space by a meteoric impact and eventually reached Earth. It was an ancient and complex rock with an interesting geological history, including small sedimentary globules deposited by flowing water in early Martian history. Electron micrographs and micro-chemical analysis revealed minerals and structures that would be interpreted as signs of bacterial life in an Earth rock. Could life have originated on Mars around the same time as it did on Earth? The evidence was tantalizing but not conclusive. Critics suggested alternative explanations, and arguments about the original conclusions have continued ever since. Though neither side is willing to concede the argument, both agree that more evidence is needed to draw firm conclusions. Such evidence will probably come within a few decades as a result of robot (and possibly human) missions to Mars.

Scientist of the Decade: Leon Lederman (1922–)

To Leon Lederman, success begins with a sense of humor. As he told an interviewer for the Academy of Achievement in 1992, humor is "a shock effect that's bizarre, a twist to a story that you tell, and that's the way it is in research." As most of the profiles in this book illustrate, successful scientists usually do not solve difficult problems with superior skills alone. Many bright people have those skills yet fail to find a solution. It is that unusual twist of mind, the ability to see a problem from a different angle that, more often than not, opens a door that no one ever noticed before. In a life that has been successful on many levels—scientifically, administratively, and in public service—Lederman has always had the knack of getting to the heart of a problem and persuading others that they can solve it too.

Leon Lederman was born in New York City on July 15, 1922, the second son of Russian-Jewish immigrants. Though neither of his parents went to college, they valued education and encouraged Leon to go to the City College of New York, where he majored in chemistry and graduated in 1943. After that, he served three years in the U.S. Army,

Leon Lederman on the morning of the 1988 Nobel Prize ceremony, where he was honored with the award for physics. (Interactions.org and Fermilab Visual Media Services)

where he worked on radars. When he got out of the military, he went to Columbia University and studied physics. Adjusting to graduate school was difficult after wartime military service, and his first-year grades were poor. He soon found his footing, earned his master's degree in 1948, and continued on for his doctorate in 1951.

He had a number of job offers, including one to stay on at Columbia, where they were just beginning to develop a program in particle physics. He had started some projects in that area and decided to stay there for a few years to keep his momentum going. Those few years turned into most of a career. Thanks in large part to Lederman's work, Columbia became one of the world's leading high-energy physics research centers. During the late 1950s and early 1960s, he was part of the team that discovered CP symmetry violation in the decay of the kaon (described briefly in the previous chapter with regard to the B meson). In 1962, Lederman and his colleagues at Columbia developed an approach to creating and detecting muon-neutrinos, for which they won the Nobel Prize in physics 26 years later.

Lederman was one of the leaders of the effort to establish Fermilab, and he began working there while still head of Columbia's famed Nevis Laboratories for high-energy physics. In 1977, he led the team that found the upsilon particle, demonstrating the existence of the bottom quark. He left Columbia in 1979 to become director of Fermilab, a position he held for 10 years. As director, Lederman was a natural leader. He used his trademark humor to declare that he did not take himself too seriously, but the projects were important business and demanded everyone's best and most creative work.

Lederman approached research as a scientist's most important educational experience, an education that never ended as long as the researcher remained active. As a professor, he taught and learned from more than 50 graduate students. At Columbia, if he took a semester off from the classroom to tend to his experimental work, he would make up for it with an increased teaching load when he got back. He believed that every young person deserved an education and began to notice that many elementary and high schools were not fulfilling that obligation when it came to science. He wanted to do something about it, and winning the 1988 Nobel Prize made that possible.

"I didn't expect the awe with which people treat this thing," he told the interviewer from the Academy of Achievement. "It really has an aura about it. First of all, you become an expert on everything. You get interviewed. 'What do you think about the Brazilian debt, or Social Security, or women's dresses?'" He realized that he now had an opportunity. "If you ever want to do anything in the way of education, or science policy, or . . . change laws or move people to be active, then boy, having a Nobel Prize helps a lot! You get into places that normally would be very difficult to get into."

It was not the Nobel Prize alone that opened those doors for Leon Lederman. Soon after he left Columbia to run Fermilab, he began to miss teaching, and he quickly found a way to get involved in education again. He started a program for gifted high school students called Saturday Morning Physics. As usual, Lederman not only taught, but he learned. He discovered that many teachers were not prepared to handle such talented young people. He began to look into the educational system whenever his job permitted him the time. In 1988, he moved to Chicago, where the public school system had 400,000 students, and decided to try to make a difference.

Lederman's talent for seeing things differently led him to this question: With so many students in the school system, why are so few of them going into science? Most youngsters enter school full of questions, and questions are the essence of science. What happens to them along the way? Lederman realized that all too often, it was not what happened but rather what did not happen. Too few teachers were prepared in math and science, and so they did not know how to encourage the students. Often they found the questions intimidating, and they actively discouraged the students' curiosity. They were not bad teachers, just unprepared. Lederman led an effort to show teachers the joy of science through a model program called The Teachers Academy. If it worked in Chicago, it could work in other cities as well.

Leon Lederman shows his playful side while posing with a Fermilab exhibit of a cryostat, a device necessary to maintain very low temperatures necessary for the superconducting electromagnets used to create the fields that control paths of subatomic particles in accelerators. (Fermilab Visual Media Services)

If Lederman's leadership works as well with The Teachers Academy as it did at Fermilab, his impact will continue long after he is no longer personally involved. In 1995, six years after he retired as lab director, Fermilab scientists detected the long-sought top quark, and in 2000, other Fermilab researchers completed the standard model of particle physics with their detection of the tau-neutrino. Such strong research is only one element of the influence and legacy of Leon Lederman. In Fermilab's Lederman Science Center and its Teacher Resource Center, volunteers and professional staff are carrying out his educational vision; and in the public schools of many American cities, teachers and students are seeing science in new ways. His parents, who taught him about the value of education, would be proud.

Public attention went to planets far beyond Mars and Jupiter in the mid-1990s. Several teams of astronomers developed techniques to identify extrasolar planets, that is, planetary companions of stars other than the Sun. By the end of the 20th century, tens of stars were known to have planets, and it was clear that planetary systems were common. Telescope technology had not yet reached the point of being able to detect planetary systems that might include Earthlike bodies, but a number of new Earth-based and space-based planet-finding instruments were under development as the new century and millennium began in 2001.

Further Reading

Books

Bortz, Fred. *Martian Fossils on Earth? The Story of Meteorite ALH84001.* Brookfield, Conn.: Millbrook Press, 2001. For younger readers, this book discusses the claims and controversies about evidence for ancient Martian bacterial life.

Close, Frank, Michael Marten, and Christine Sutton. *The Particle Odyssey: A Journey to the Heart of Matter.* New York: Oxford University Press, 2002. A detailed and colorfully illustrated overview of the discovery of subatomic particles.

Kragh, Helge. *Quantum Generations: A History of Physics in the Twentieth Century.* Princeton, N.J.: Princeton University Press, 1999. An in-depth history of 20th-century physics and physicists.

Schumm, Bruce A. *Deep Down Things: The Breathtaking Beauty of Particle Physics.* Baltimore: Johns Hopkins University Press, 2005. A look at the mathematical ideas that underlie particle physics and string theory.

Seife, Charles. *Alpha & Omega: The Search for the Beginning and the End of the Universe.* New York: Viking, 2003. A look at the connections between particle physics and the cosmology of the big bang.

Siegfried, Tom. *Strange Matters: Undiscovered Ideas at the Frontiers of Space and Time.* Washington, D.C.: Joseph Henry Press, 2002. A book discussing ideas, such as string theory, which the author refers to as "prediscoveries" because they are likely to produce insights into particle physics and cosmology.

Suplee, Curt. *Physics in the 20th Century.* New York: Harry N. Abrams, 1999. A pictorial history of 20th-century physics.

Web Sites

Academy of Achievement. Available online. URL http://www.achievement.org. Accessed April 21, 2006. Find Leon Lederman's story by following link from pull-down menu of achievers.

American Institute of Physics, Center for History of Physics. Available online. URL: http://www.aip.org/history. Accessed March 27, 2006.

Follow pull-down menu for special online exhibits or browse for a variety of written resources and images.

Fermilab Education Office. Available online. URL: http://www-ed.fnal.gov/ed_home.html. Accessed April 21, 2006. Official Web site of the educational outreach organization founded by Leon Lederman at Fermilab.

Nobelprize.org. Available online. URL: http://nobelprize.org. Accessed March 27, 2006. The official Web site of the Nobel Foundation contains brief biographies of Nobel Prize winners, summaries of their prize-winning work, and their acceptance speeches.

Robbins, Stuart. *Journey through the Galaxy*. Available online. URL: http://home.cwru.edu/~sjr16. Click "History" for "A Brief History of the Universe," or go to http://home.cwru.edu/~sjr16/advanced/cosmos_history.html. Accessed April 21, 2006. A Web site with a number of useful pages on cosmology.

Schwarz, Patricia. The Official String Theory Web Site. Available online. URL: http://www.superstringtheory.com. Accessed April 21, 2006. A comprehensive Web site about string theory, the physicists who have worked on it, and its history.

The Science Museum. Available online. URL: http://www.sciencemuseum.org.uk. Accessed March 27, 2006. A British online science education resource that includes useful exhibits on Atomic Firsts; Life, The Universe, and the Electron; Marie Curie and the History of Radioactivity; and many other topics discussed in this book.

The Science Shelf, Books for the World Year of Physics 2005. Available online. URL: http://www.scienceshelf.com/WorldYearofPhysics.htm. Accessed April 26, 2006. This page on the book review site of Fred Bortz has brief comments about a number of books published in recognition of the World Year of Physics, plus links to reviews of a number of other physics books for nonspecialist readers.

Sloan Digital Sky Survey. SDSS Sky Survey/SkyServer. Available online. URL: http://cas.sdss.org/dr4/en. Accessed April 21, 2006. The official Web site of the SDSS program.

Wilkinson Microwave Anisotropy Probe (WMAP). Available online. URL: http://wmap.gsfc.nasa.gov. Accessed April 21, 2006. Official WMAP Web site.

World Year of Physics 2005. Available online. URL: http://www.physics2005.org. Accessed March 27, 2006. An online resource developed in honor of the centennial of Albert Einstein's "Miracle Year."

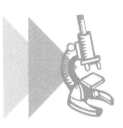

Conclusion:
Cosmic and Terrestrial Challenges
for the Twenty-first Century

Though the number 100 has no particular significance in nature, 10-fingered humans treat new centuries and centennials as auspicious events, as times to consider both history and the future. That is always a good thing, because understanding the past provides valuable insights for the future. New centuries and centennial observances often lead to books like this one and the others in the Twentieth Century Science reference set. The year 2005 was of particular note for physicists. Major scientific societies declared 2005 as the "World Year of Physics" in recognition that 100 years earlier an obscure patent clerk named Albert Einstein published three major papers that shook the foundations of physics. Their understanding of space, time, matter, and energy changed fundamentally and led to a revolution in science and technology that continues today.

Sudbury neutrino detector confirms neutrino oscillation, thereby establishing that there are no further generations of subatomic particles beyond the three sets of leptons, baryons, and gauge bosons of the standard model

MILESTONES

2002

2005

Physicists celebrate "World Year of Physics" in the centennial of Einstein's "miracle year"

At the beginning of the 20th century, physical theory based on Newton's laws of motion and gravitation, Maxwell's equations of electromagnetism, and the atomic nature of matter seemed to provide a nearly complete understanding of nature. Those theories explained almost everything, except for a few new phenomena like X-rays, radioactivity, Planck's mathematical device called the quantum, the subatomic "corpuscles" that made up cathode rays, and experiments that failed to detect the luminiferous ether. Still, no one expected any of those to require fundamental changes in physics itself. Most physicists felt that they and their science had a firm theoretical foundation and were closing in on theories for everything.

Today the new foundations of physics are relativity, quantum theory, and the standard model of subatomic particles. These have been remarkably successful in describing and predicting most natural phenomena, even as measurements and instruments become capable of producing previously unimagined detail. Now many physicists think that a single "theory of everything" may be within their reach. That theory would combine the grainy quantum world with the smooth spacetime of relativity, and it would unite the subatomic universe with the cosmos by joining all three fundamental forces—gravity, the electroweak interaction (electromagnetism plus the weak nuclear force), and the strong nuclear force—into one. Yet there is a great difference between today's physicists who are seeking a theory of everything and their counterparts in the early 20th century who thought physics had already achieved theories for everything. That difference is the history recounted in this book. Looking back on the astonishing developments in 20th-century physics, few physicists would be surprised if another reformulation of the foundations of their science lies ahead in the 21st. The early years of this new century have already demonstrated how much physicists have learned about the universe and how much they still do not understand.

The Nature of Matter Revisited

In the years since 2000, many of the most significant new results in physics have come from astronomical observations. New orbiting telescopes have enabled astronomers to view the universe in regions of the electronic spectrum that were previously inaccessible due to absorption in the atmosphere. Even in spectral regions where astronomy has been traditionally done, astronomers now are gathering a wealth of new data and images from larger land-based telescopes, with capabilities enhanced by modern high-speed communication and innovative observational techniques. Projects such as the *Wilkinson Microwave Anisotropy Probe* (*WMAP*) and the Sloan Digital Sky Survey (SDSS), described in the previous chapter, have led physicists to new questions about the nature of matter. In contrast, neutrino astronomy solidified their confidence that the third generation of quarks and leptons had completed the standard model of particle physics.

As noted in the last chapter, theoretical physicists had begun to regard electron-, muon-, and tau-neutrinos not as distinct particles but as different modes of the same particle. According to their theories, the neutrinos emitted by the Sun would start out as electron-neutrinos but would oscillate among modes on their way to Earth. By the time they reached the neutrino detector in the Homestake gold mine, only one-third of them would be electron-neutrinos, with the remainder being muon-neutrinos and tau-neutrinos in equal numbers. That detector was only sensitive to electron-neutrinos and thus would be expected to record only a third as many neutrinos as it would without mode oscillation. That result was confirmed more strongly as physicists refined the theory of solar fusion reactions. Meanwhile, the Super Kamiokande neutrino detector in Japan was somewhat sensitive to muon-neutrinos. That accounted for its larger number of detections. Physicists needed more data to confirm neutrino oscillation and that came in 2001 from the Sudbury Neutrino Observatory in Canada, where scientists had designed and built a neutrino detector that was sensitive to all three neutrino modes. The standard model was indeed complete with three generations of quarks and leptons.

The standard model seems complete, but is it possible that there are entire undiscovered classes of matter in the universe, each with its own set of fundamental particles? As far-fetched as that question seems, many physicists are treating it seriously. Their reasons come both from theory and observation. The theory is string theory. Because it envisions extra dimensions, it also allows for additional symmetries, which leads to theoretical possibilities called mirror matter and super matter. The observations come largely from *WMAP* and SDSS and what they say about the amount of mass in the universe, but the earliest discussions date back to a landmark paper by astronomers Vera Rubin (1928–   ) and William K. Ford in 1970. Observing the rotation rate of a nearby galaxy, they were able to estimate the gravitational attraction needed to hold onto its outer stars. From that acceleration, they were able to determine the galaxy's mass. Then, by taking a census of the stars in that galaxy, they were able to estimate how much of that mass was luminous. To their surprise, the mass of the stars was only a little more than 10 percent of the total. Nearly 90 percent was dark matter of unknown composition. As the decades have passed since the Rubin/Ford result, dark matter seems to be part of every galaxy for which rotation can be measured.

Though it is reasonable to assume that much of that dark matter is made up of fundamental particles of the standard model, no one has yet found a way to test that assumption. It could be something more exotic. That possibility seems even more credible in light of recent conclusions from *WMAP* and SDSS data. As soon as scientists realized that the universe is expanding, they began to wonder about its ultimate fate. As the galaxies spread apart, their mutual gravitational attraction should slow down the recession rate. There were three possible scenarios that depended on the total mass of the universe. The scenarios can be understood by comparing them to the possible fate of a projectile launched upward from the surface of the Earth. If the projectile is traveling at less than escape velocity (about 25,000 [40,000 km] miles per hour when launched from the surface), it will eventually stop its outward motion and fall back to the ground. If it is traveling faster than escape velocity, it will slow down toward a certain minimum velocity but continue to move away forever. If it is traveling exactly at escape velocity, it does not fall back but its recession rate slows toward zero. Escape velocity depends on Earth's mass and size. If the planet were the same size but heavier, the projectile would need to be launched at a higher speed to escape.

The Sudbury Neutrino Observatory, which confirmed the phenomenon of neutrino mode oscillation in 2001. For scale, notice the people on the catwalk. (Ernest Orlando Lawrence Berkeley National Laboratory)

The same is true of the universe. Is its mass large enough to reverse the expansion that began with the big bang and lead to a big crunch (a "closed" universe)? Is the mass so small that the expansion will continue without limit (an open universe)? Or is its mass just right, a so-called Goldilocks or flat universe, so that it will reach a near steady state? When the 20th century ended, the best measurements suggested that the universe was improbably close to flat, and *WMAP* data seemed to confirm that conclusion. Could there be an unknown physical law that led inevitably to a flat universe rather than an open or closed one?

However, some SDSS measurements of distant supernovas suggest a dramatically different conclusion. Instead of slowing down, the expansion rate of the universe seems to be speeding up! If that is so, something besides gravity is acting. Perhaps there is another form of unknown, unseen matter that produces a repulsion or anti-gravitational effect, which scientists are calling dark energy. Perhaps the strange expansion is simply due to the cosmological constant of Einstein's general relativity theory. He called that constant his greatest blunder once the expansion of the universe was discovered, but perhaps the blunder was actually being too quick to dismiss adding the constant to his equations. Perhaps there are unknown physical effects that are leading to a misinterpretation of the data. The theory clearly has some loose ends. What will people discover as they tug on those strands with new mathematical approaches and new measurements? Clearly history does not stop at the end of a century!

What Is "Everything"?

Those puzzling results also influence progress toward a "theory of everything." As string theory has evolved, it has come to describe a multiplicity of possible universes, each of which has a different set of fundamental constants (like Planck's constant, the constant relating masses to the gravitational force between them, the speed of light, the basic unit of electric charge, and the masses of the fundamental particles). Is the known universe the only one in existence, or is the spacetime in which humans live merely a four-dimensional slice of a much larger realm? If this is the only universe, why does it have the particular constants that it does?

Some physicists view the many possibilities embodied in string theory as encouraging. Others consider it as dubious precisely because it can be adjusted to fit any observations and has not yet led to testable predictions. Perhaps the loose ends in string theory are related to the recent peculiar discoveries in cosmology. What does that mean for the future of string theory and, indeed, all of physics? The only reasonable conclusion is that the future of the science is as unpredictable now as it was 100 years ago.

David Gross (1941–   ) of the Kavli Institute for Theoretical Physics at the University of California, Santa Barbara, would agree. Gross shared the 2004 Nobel Prize in physics for the development of quantum chromodynamics (the strong-force version of quantum electrodynamics) during the 1970s and has been a strong proponent of string theory. His work made him a natural selection to give the closing address at the 23rd Solvay Conference in Physics, held in Brussels, Belgium, in December 2005, a prestigious event with a history going back to the 1911, the year that Rutherford announced his discovery of the atomic nucleus. "Many of us believed that string theory was a very dramatic break with our previous notions of quantum theory. But now we learn that string theory, well, is not that much of a break."

He compared the present state of the theory with the puzzling discoveries of radioactivity, which was discovered by Becquerel in 1896, described in detail by Rutherford and Soddy in the first decade of the 20th century, but was not explained until quantum mechanics was well developed. Physicists "were missing something absolutely fundamental" at the time of the first Solvay Conference, he noted. "We are missing perhaps something as profound as they were back then."

Some might view Gross's words about the future of physics as discouraging, but they should not be interpreted that way. The missing theoretical ingredient is a challenge, not a failure. Physicists are, as always, engaging in difficult quests. New Einsteins, Rutherfords, Paulis, Meitners, Feynmans, Bardeens, Gell-Manns, Alvarezes, Hawkings, and Ledermans are already at work, looking for new ways to view old problems. Will 21st-century physics yield the Higgs particle, a theory of high-temperature superconductivity, or a theory of everything? Will physics-based technologies lead to fusion power, quantum computers, and remarkable materials?

The answer to many of those questions is almost certain to be yes.

Further Reading

Books

Close, Frank, Michael Marten, and Christine Sutton. *The Particle Odyssey: A Journey to the Heart of Matter.* New York: Oxford University Press, 2002. A detailed and colorfully illustrated overview of the discovery of subatomic particles.

Schumm, Bruce A. *Deep Down Things: The Breathtaking Beauty of Particle Physics.* Baltimore: Johns Hopkins University Press, 2005. A look at the mathematical ideas that underlie particle physics and string theory.

Seife, Charles. *Alpha & Omega: The Search for the Beginning and the End of the Universe.* New York: Viking, 2003. A look at the connections between particle physics and the cosmology of the big bang.

Siegfried, Tom. *Strange Matters: Undiscovered Ideas at the Frontiers of Space and Time.* Washington, D.C.: Joseph Henry Press, 2002. A book discussing ideas, such as string theory, which the author refers to as "prediscoveries" because they are likely to produce insights into particle physics and cosmology.

Smolin, Lee. *The Trouble with Physics: The Rise of String Theory, the Fall of a Science, and What Comes Next.* New York: Houghton Mifflin, 2006. A noted string theorist concludes that string theory is deeply flawed and must be abandoned to clear the way for the development of new approaches to "the theory of everything."

Woit, Peter. *Not Even Wrong: The Failure of String Theory and the Search for Unity in Physical Law.* New York: Basic Books, 2006. String theory is increasingly coming under attack as a nontheory for its failure to make testable predictions. This author makes his point by using a disdainful phrase from Wolfgang Pauli (see chapter 3) as the book's title.

Web Sites

American Institute of Physics, Center for History of Physics. Available online. URL: http://www.aip.org/history. Accessed March 27, 2006. Follow pull-down menu for special online exhibits or browse for a variety of written resources and images.

Nobelprize.org. Available online. URL: http://nobelprize.org. Accessed March 27, 2006. The official Web site of the Nobel Foundation contains brief biographies of Nobel Prize winners, summaries of their prize-winning work, and their acceptance speeches.

Robbins, Stuart. *Journey through the Galaxy.* Available online. URL: http://home.cwru.edu/~sjr16. Click "History" for "A Brief History of the Universe," or go to http://home.cwru.edu/~sjr16/advanced/cosmos_history.html.

Accessed April 21, 2006. A Web site with a number of useful pages on cosmology.

Schwarz, Patricia. *The Official String Theory Web Site.* Available online. URL: http://www.superstringtheory.com. Accessed April 21, 2006. A comprehensive Web site about string theory, the physicists who have worked on it, and its history.

The Science Museum. Available online. URL: http://www.sciencemuseum.org.uk. Accessed March 27, 2006. A British online science education resource that includes useful exhibits on Atomic Firsts; Life, the Universe, and the Electron; Marie Curie and the History of Radioactivity; and many other topics discussed in this book.

The Science Shelf, Books for the World Year of Physics 2005. Available online. URL: http://www.scienceshelf.com/WorldYearofPhysics.htm. Accessed April 26, 2006. This page on the book review site of Fred Bortz has brief comments about a number of books published in recognition of the World Year of Physics, plus links to reviews of a number of other physics books for nonspecialist readers.

Sloan Digital Sky Survey. *SDSS Sky Survey/SkyServer.* Available online. URL: http://cas.sdss.org/dr4/en. Accessed April 21, 2006. The official Web site of the SDSS program.

Wilkinson Microwave Anisotropy Probe (WMAP). Available online. URL: http://wmap.gsfc.nasa.gov. Accessed April 21, 2006. Official WMAP Web site.

World Year of Physics 2005. Available online. URL: http://www.physics2005.org. Accessed March 27, 2006. An online resource developed in honor of the centennial of Albert Einstein's "Miracle Year."

The Periodic Table of the Elements

In 1869, Dmitry Mendeleyev devised a rows-and-columns of the chemical elements that grouped them according to their properties. He called it the periodic table of the elements. Beginning at the upper left with the lightest atom, hydrogen, he placed chemical symbols down the first column of a grid in the order of increasing atomic mass. Then he moved rightward from one column to the next, placing atoms with similar chemical and physical properties next to each other in rows.

The modern periodic table, which appears on the following pages, reverses the roles of rows and columns but otherwise follows Mendeleyev's approach. The arrangement has now served scientists for nearly a century and a half, providing spaces to add new elements as they have been discovered or synthesized.

The periodic table was a great achievement, but important questions remained. What distinguishes atoms of one element from those of another, and how do those differences result in the regularity of the periodic table? The answers came from breakthroughs in physics in the last years of the 19th and first quarter of the 20th century—specifically, the discoveries of the electron and the atomic nucleus and the development of quantum mechanics.

The final pieces of the puzzle were Wolfgang Pauli's 1924 proposal of electron spin and his exclusion principle of 1925. Together these provide the basis for the periodic behavior of the elements.

PERIODIC TABLE OF THE ELEMENTS

1 IA																	18 VIIIA
1 H 1.00794	2 IIA											13 IIIA	14 IVA	15 VA	16 VIA	17 VIIA	2 He 4.0026
3 Li 6.941	4 Be 9.0122											5 B 10.81	6 C 12.011	7 N 14.0067	8 O 15.9994	9 F 18.9984	10 Ne 20.1798
11 Na 22.9898	12 Mg 24.3051	3 IIIB	4 IVB	5 VB	6 VIB	7 VIIB	8 VIIIB	9 VIIIB	10 VIIIB	11 IB	12 IIB	13 Al 26.9815	14 Si 28.0855	15 P 30.9738	16 S 32.067	17 Cl 35.4528	18 Ar 39.948
19 K 39.0938	20 Ca 40.078	21 Sc 44.9559	22 Ti 47.867	23 V 50.9415	24 Cr 51.9962	25 Mn 54.938	26 Fe 55.845	27 Co 58.9332	28 Ni 58.6934	29 Cu 63.546	30 Zn 65.409	31 Ga 69.723	32 Ge 72.61	33 As 74.9216	34 Se 78.96	35 Br 79.904	36 Kr 83.798
37 Rb 85.4678	38 Sr 87.62	39 Y 88.906	40 Zr 91.224	41 Nb 92.9064	42 Mo 95.94	43 Tc (98)	44 Ru 101.07	45 Rh 102.9055	46 Pd 106.42	47 Ag 107.8682	48 Cd 112.412	49 In 114.818	50 Sn 118.711	51 Sb 121.760	52 Te 127.60	53 I 126.9045	54 Xe 131.29
55 Cs 132.9054	56 Ba 137.328	57- 70 ☆	72 Hf 178.49	73 Ta 180.948	74 W 183.84	75 Re 186.207	76 Os 190.23	77 Ir 192.217	78 Pt 195.08	79 Au 196.9655	80 Hg 200.59	81 Tl 204.3833	82 Pb 207.2	83 Bi 208.9804	84 Po (209)	85 At (210)	86 Rn (222)
87 Fr (223)	88 Ra (226)	89- 102 ★	104 Rf (261)	105 Db (262)	106 Sg (266)	107 Bh (262)	108 Hs (263)	109 Mt (268)	110 Ds (271)	111 Rg (272)	112 Uub (277)	113 Uut (284)	114 Uuq (285)	115 Uup (288)	116 Uuh (292)		118 Uuo (294)

Atomic number — Symbol — Atomic weight

3 **Li** 6.941

☆ Lanthanoids	57 La 138.9055	58 Ce 140.115	59 Pr 140.908	60 Nd 144.24	61 Pm (145)	62 Sm 150.36	63 Eu 151.966	64 Gd 157.25	65 Tb 158.9253	66 Dy 162.500	67 Ho 164.9303	68 Er 167.26	69 Tm 168.9342	70 Yb 173.04
★ Actinoids	89 Ac (227)	90 Th 232.0381	91 Pa 231.036	92 U 238.0289	93 Np (237)	94 Pu (244)	95 Am 243	96 Cm (247)	97 Bk (247)	98 Cf (251)	99 Es (252)	100 Fm (257)	101 Md (258)	102 No (259)

Numbers in parentheses are atomic mass numbers of most stable isotopes

Periodic table of elements

THE CHEMICAL ELEMENTS

(g) none (c) metallics

element	symbol	a.n.	element	symbol	a.n.	element	symbol	a.n.
aluminum	Al	13	lead	Pb	82	scandium	Sc	21
bohrium	Bh	107	lutetium	Lu	71	seaborgium	Sg	106
cadmium	Cd	48	manganese	Mn	25	silver	Ag***	47
chromium	Cr	24	meitnerium	Mt	109	tantalum	Ta	73
cobalt	Co	27	mercury	Hg	80	technetium	Tc	43
copper	Cu***	29	molybdenum	Mo	42	thallium	Tl	81
darmstaduim	Ds	110	nickel	Ni	28	titanium	Ti	22
dubnium	Db	105	niobium	Nb	41	tin	Sn	50
gallium	Ga	31	osmium	Os****	76	tungsten	W	74
gold	Au***	79	palladium	Pd****	46	ununbium	Uub	112
hafnium	Hf	72	platinum	Pt****	78	ununtrium	Uut	113
hassium	Hs	108	rhenium	Re	75	ununquadium	Uuq	114
indium	In	49	rhodium	Rh****	45	vanadium	V	23
iridium	Ir****	77	roentgenium	Rg	111	yttrium	Y	39
iron	Fe	26	ruthenium	Ru****	44	zinc	Zn	30
lawrencium	Lr	103	rutherfordium	Rf	104	zirconium	Zr	40

(g) actinoid (c) metallics

element	symbol	a.n.
actinium	Ac	89
americium	Am	95
berkelium	Bk	97
californium	Cf	98
curium	Cm	96
einsteinium	Es	99
fermium	Fm	100
mendelevium	Md	101
neptunium	Np	93
nobelium	No	102
plutonium	Pu	94
protactinium	Pa	91
thorium	Th	90
uranium	U	92

(g) halogens (c) nonmetallics

element	symbol	a.n.	element	symbol	a.n.
astatine	At*	85	fluorine	F	9
bromine	Br	35	iodine	I	53
chlorine	Cl	17			

(g) pnictogen (c) metallics

element	symbol	a.n.	element	symbol	a.n.
arsenic	As*	33	nitrogen	N**	7
antimony	Sb*	51	phosophorus	P**	15
bismuth	Bi	83	ununpentium	Uup	115

a.n. = atomic number
(g) = group
(c) = classification

* = semimetallics (c)
** = nonmetallics (c)
*** = coinage metal (g)
**** = precious metal (g)

(g) alkali metal (c) metallics

element	symbol	a.n.	element	symbol	a.n.
cesium	Cs	55	potassium	K	19
francium	Fr	87	rubidium	Rb	37
lithium	Li	3	sodium	Na	11

(g) alkaline earth metal (c) metallics

element	symbol	a.n.	element	symbol	a.n.
barium	Ba	56	magnesium	Mg	12
beryllium	Be	4	radium	Ra	88
calcium	Ca	20	strontium	Sr	38

(g) chalcogen (c) nonmetallics

element	symbol	a.n.	element	symbol	a.n.
oxygen	O	8	sulfur	S	16
polonium	Po	84	tellurium	Te	52
selenium	Se	34	ununhexium	Uuh	116

(g) lanthanoid (c) metallics

element	symbol	a.n.
cerium	Ce	58
dysprosium	Dy	66
erbium	Er	68
europium	Eu	63
gadolinium	Gd	64
holmium	Ho	67
lanthanum	La	57
neodymium	Nd	60
praseodymium	Pr	59
promethium	Pm	61
samarium	Sm	62
terbium	Tb	65
thulium	Tm	69
ytterbium	Yb	70

(g) none (c) semimetallics

element	symbol	a.n.
boron	B	5
germanium	Ge	32
silicon	Si	14

(g) noble (c) nonmetallics gases

element	symbol	a.n.
argon	Ar	18
helium	He	2
krypton	Kr	36
neon	Ne	10
radon	Rn	86
xenon	Xe	54
unococtium	Uuo	118

(g) none (c) nonmetallics

element	symbol	a.n.
carbon	C	6
hydrogen	H	1

© Infobase Publishing

The chemical elements

Nobel Prize Winners

Physics does not stand alone as a science. It has strong connections to chemistry through atomic theory, to biology through important measurement techniques such as spectroscopy and crystallography, to astronomy through cosmology and nuclear fusion, and to other physical sciences such as geology and meteorology. Likewise, significant technological or engineering accomplishments have their roots in physics. Thus the Nobel Prize in physics has often been awarded to scientists who work primarily in other fields, and some great physicists have won Nobel Prizes in other sciences as well as the prestigious Nobel Peace Prize.

The following list of Nobel Prize winners in physics between 1901 and 2000 provides a useful catalog of many of the greatest 20th-century physicists and their accomplishments. Many of the great scientific accomplishments of the later years of the century have yet to earn Nobel Prizes and may never earn such recognition. Others, such as Raymond Davis's work in neutrino astronomy, have earned Nobel Prizes since 2000.

The Nobel Foundation Web site (http://nobelprize.org) provides full information including biographies and Nobel Prize lectures for all laureates. The brief descriptions of the specific awards are quoted from pages on this site. The nationalities listed are the laureates' citizenship at the time of the award.

1901

Wilhelm Conrad Röntgen (1845–1923), Germany

"In recognition of the extraordinary services he has rendered by the discovery of the remarkable rays subsequently named after him"

1902

Hendrik Antoon Lorentz (1853–1928), the Netherlands, and Pieter Zeeman (1865–1943), the Netherlands

"In recognition of the extraordinary service they rendered by their researches into the influence of magnetism upon radiation phenomena"

1903

Antoine-Henri Becquerel (1852–1908), France

"In recognition of the extraordinary services he has rendered by his discovery of spontaneous radioactivity"

and Pierre Curie (1859–1906), France, and Marie Curie, née Sklodowska (1867–1934), France

"In recognition of the extraordinary services they have rendered by their joint researches on the radiation phenomena discovered by Professor Henri Becquerel"

1904

Lord Rayleigh (John William Strutt, 1842–1919), United Kingdom

"For his investigations of the densities of the most important gases and for his discovery of argon in connection with these studies"

1905

Philipp Eduard Anton von Lenard (1862–1947), Germany

"For his work on cathode rays"

1906

Joseph John Thomson (1856–1940), United Kingdom

"In recognition of the great merits of his theoretical and experimental investigations on the conduction of electricity by gases"

1907

Albert Abraham Michelson (1852–1931), United States

"For his optical precision instruments and the spectroscopic and metrological investigations carried out with their aid"

1908

Gabriel Lippmann (1845–1921), France

"For his method of reproducing colours photographically based on the phenomenon of interference"

1909

Guglielmo Marconi (1874–1937), Italy, and Karl Ferdinand Braun (1850–1918), Germany

"In recognition of their contributions to the development of wireless telegraphy"

1910

Johannes Diderik van der Waals (1837–1923), the Netherlands

"For his work on the equation of state for gases and liquids"

1911

Wilhelm Wien (1864–1928), Germany

"For his discoveries regarding the laws governing the radiation of heat"

1912

Nils Gustaf Dalén (1869–1937), Sweden

"For his invention of automatic regulators for use in conjunction with gas accumulators for illuminating lighthouses and buoys"

1913

Heike Kamerlingh Onnes (1853–1926), the Netherlands

"For his investigations on the properties of matter at low temperatures which led, inter alia, *to the production of liquid helium"*

1914

Max von Laue (1879–1960), Germany

"For his discovery of the diffraction of X-rays by crystals"

1915

Sir William Henry Bragg (1862–1942), United Kingdom, and William Lawrence Bragg (1890–1971), United Kingdom

"For their services in the analysis of crystal structure by means of X-rays"

1916

No prize awarded

1917

Charles Glover Barkla (1877–1944), United Kingdom

"For his discovery of the characteristic Röntgen radiation of the elements"

1918

Max Karl Ernst Ludwig Planck (1858–1947), Germany

"In recognition of the services he rendered to the advancement of Physics by his discovery of energy quanta"

1919

Johannes Stark (1874–1957), Germany

"For his discovery of the Doppler effect in canal rays and the splitting of spectral lines in electric fields"

1920

Charles-Édouard Guillaume (1861–1938), Switzerland

"In recognition of the service he has rendered to precision measurements in Physics by his discovery of anomalies in nickel steel alloys"

1921

Albert Einstein (1879–1955), Germany and Switzerland

"For his services to Theoretical Physics, and especially for his discovery of the law of the photoelectric effect"

1922

Niels Henrik David Bohr (1885–1962), Denmark

"For his services in the investigation of the structure of atoms and of the radiation emanating from them"

1923

Robert Andrews Millikan (1868–1953), United States

"For his work on the elementary charge of electricity and on the photo-electric effect"

1924

Karl Manne Georg Siegbahn (1886–1978), Sweden

"For his discoveries and research in the field of X-ray spectroscopy"

1925

James Franck (1882–1964), Germany, and Gustav Ludwig Hertz (1887–1975), Germany

"For their discovery of the laws governing the impact of an electron upon an atom"

1926

Jean-Baptiste Perrin (1870–1942), France

"For his work on the discontinuous structure of matter, and especially for his discovery of sedimentation equilibrium"

1927

Arthur Holly Compton (1892–1962), United States

"For his discovery of the effect named after him"

and Charles Thomson Rees Wilson (1869–1959), United Kingdom

"For his method of making the paths of electrically charged particles visible by condensation of vapour"

1928

Owen Willans Richardson (1879–1959), United Kingdom

"For his work on the thermionic phenomenon and especially for the discovery of the law named after him"

1929

Prince Louis-Victor-Pierre-Raymond de Broglie (1892–1987), France

"For his discovery of the wave nature of electrons"

1930

Sir Chandrasekhara Venkata Raman (1888–1970), India

"For his work on the scattering of light and for the discovery of the effect named after him"

1931

No prize awarded

1932

Werner Karl Heisenberg (1901–76), Germany

> *"For the creation of quantum mechanics, the application of which has,* inter alia, *led to the discovery of the allotropic forms of hydrogen"*

1933

Erwin Schrödinger (1887–1961), Austria, and Paul Adrien Maurice Dirac (1902–84), United Kingdom

> *"For the discovery of new productive forms of atomic theory"*

1934

No prize awarded

1935

James Chadwick (1891–1974), United Kingdom

> *"For the discovery of the neutron"*

1936

Victor Franz Hess (1883–1964), Austria

> *"For his discovery of cosmic radiation"*

and Carl David Anderson (1905–91), United States

> *"For his discovery of the positron"*

1937

Clinton Joseph Davisson (1881–1958), United States, and George Paget Thomson (1891–1975), United Kingdom

> *"For their experimental discovery of the diffraction of electrons by crystals"*

1938

Enrico Fermi (1901–54), Italy

> *"For his demonstrations of the existence of new radioactive elements produced by neutron irradiation, and for his related discovery of nuclear reactions brought about by slow neutrons"*

1939

Ernest Orlando Lawrence (1901–58), United States

"For the invention and development of the cyclotron and for results obtained with it, especially with regard to artificial radioactive elements"

1940–42

No prizes awarded

1943

Otto Stern (1888–1969), United States

"For his contribution to the development of the molecular ray method and his discovery of the magnetic moment of the proton"

1944

Isidor Isaac Rabi (1898–1988), United States

"For his resonance method for recording the magnetic properties of atomic nuclei"

1945

Wolfgang Pauli (1900–58), Austria

"For the discovery of the Exclusion Principle, also called the Pauli Principle"

1946

Percy Williams Bridgman (1882–1961), United States

"For the invention of an apparatus to produce extremely high pressures, and for the discoveries he made therewith in the field of high pressure physics"

1947

Sir Edward Victor Appleton (1892–1965), United Kingdom

"For his investigations of the physics of the upper atmosphere especially for the discovery of the so-called Appleton layer"

1948

Patrick Maynard Stuart Blackett (1897–1974), United Kingdom

"For his development of the Wilson cloud chamber method, and his discoveries therewith in the fields of nuclear physics and cosmic radiation"

1949

Hideki Yukawa (1907–81), Japan

"For his prediction of the existence of mesons on the basis of theoretical work on nuclear forces"

1950

Cecil Frank Powell (1903–69), United Kingdom

"For his development of the photographic method of studying nuclear processes and his discoveries regarding mesons made with this method"

1951

Sir John Douglas Cockcroft (1897–1967), United Kingdom, and Ernest Thomas Sinton Walton (1903–95), Ireland

"For their pioneer work on the transmutation of atomic nuclei by artificially accelerated atomic particles"

1952

Felix Bloch (1905–83), United States, and Edward Mills Purcell (1912–97), United States

"For their development of new methods for nuclear magnetic precision measurements and discoveries in connection therewith"

1953

Frits (Frederik) Zernike (1888–1966), the Netherlands

"For his demonstration of the phase contrast method, especially for his invention of the phase contrast microscope"

1954

Max Born (1882–1970), United Kingdom

"For his fundamental research in quantum mechanics, especially for his statistical interpretation of the wavefunction" and

Walther Bothe (1891–1957), Federal Republic of Germany

"For the coincidence method and his discoveries made therewith"

1955

Willis Eugene Lamb (1913–   ), United States

"For his discoveries concerning the fine structure of the hydrogen spectrum" and

Polykarp Kusch (1911–93), United States

"For his precision determination of the magnetic moment of the electron"

1956

William Bradford Shockley (1910–89), United States, John Bardeen (1908–91), United States, and Walter Houser Brattain (1902–87), United States

"For their researches on semiconductors and their discovery of the transistor effect"

1957

Chen Ning Yang (1922–), China, and Tsung-Dao Lee (1926–), China

"For their penetrating investigation of the so-called parity laws which has led to important discoveries regarding the elementary particles"

1958

Pavel Alekseyevich Cherenkov (1904–90), USSR, Ilya Mikhailovich Frank (1908–90), USSR, and Igor Yevgenyevich Tamm (1895–71), USSR

"For the discovery and the interpretation of the Cherenkov effect"

1959

Emilio Gino Segrè (1905–89), United States, and Owen Chamberlain (1920–2006), United States

"For their discovery of the antiproton"

1960

Donald Arthur Glaser (1926–), United States

"For the invention of the bubble chamber"

1961

Robert Hofstadter (1915–90), United States

"For his pioneering studies of electron scattering in atomic nuclei and for his thereby achieved discoveries concerning the structure of the nucleons" and

Rudolf Ludwig Mössbauer (1929–), Federal Republic of Germany

"For his researches concerning the resonance absorption of gamma radiation and his discovery in this connection of the effect which bears his name"

1962

Lev Davidovich Landau (1908–68), USSR

"For his pioneering theories for condensed matter, especially liquid helium"

1963

Eugene Paul Wigner (1902–95), United States

"For his contributions to the theory of the atomic nucleus and the elementary particles, particularly through the discovery and application of fundamental symmetry principles" and

Maria Goeppert-Mayer (1906–72), United States, and J. Hans D. Jensen (1907–73), Federal Republic of Germany

"For their discoveries concerning nuclear shell structure"

1964

Charles Hard Townes (1915–   ), United States, Nicolay Gennadiyevich Basov (1922–2001), USSR, and Aleksandr Mikhailovich Prokhorov (1916–2002), USSR

"For fundamental work in the field of quantum electronics, which has led to the construction of oscillators and amplifiers based on the maser-laser principle"

1965

Sin-Itiro Tomonaga (1906–79), Japan, Julian Schwinger (1918–94), United States, and Richard P. Feynman (1918–88), United States

"For their fundamental work in quantum electrodynamics, with deep-ploughing consequences for the physics of elementary particles"

1966

Alfred Kastler (1902–84), France

"For the discovery and development of optical methods for studying Hertzian resonances in atoms"

1967

Hans Albrecht Bethe (1906–2005), United States

"For his contributions to the theory of nuclear reactions, especially his discoveries concerning the energy production in stars"

1968

Luis Walter Alvarez (1911–88), United States

"For his decisive contributions to elementary particle physics, in particular the discovery of a large number of resonance states, made possible through his development of the technique of using hydrogen bubble chamber and data analysis"

1969

Murray Gell-Mann (1929–   ), United States

"For his contributions and discoveries concerning the classification of elementary particles and their interactions"

1970

Hannes Olof Gösta Alfvén (1908–95), Sweden

"For fundamental work and discoveries in magneto-hydrodynamics with fruitful applications in different parts of plasma physics"

and Louis-Eugène-Félix Néel (1904–2000), France

"For fundamental work and discoveries concerning antiferromagnetism and ferrimagnetism which have led to important applications in solid state physics"

1971

Dennis Gabor (1900–79), United Kingdom

"For his invention and development of the holographic method"

1972

John Bardeen (1908–91), United States, Leon Neil Cooper (1930–   ), United States, and John Robert Schrieffer (1931–   ), United States

"For their jointly developed theory of superconductivity, usually called the BCS-theory"

1973

Leo Esaki (1925–   ), Japan, and Ivar Giaever (1929–   ), United States

"For their experimental discoveries regarding tunneling phenomena in semiconductors and superconductors, respectively," and

Brian David Josephson (1940–   ), United Kingdom

"For his theoretical predictions of the properties of a supercurrent through a tunnel barrier, in particular those phenomena which are generally known as the Josephson effects"

1974

Sir Martin Ryle (1918–84), United Kingdom, and Antony Hewish (1924–), United Kingdom

"For their pioneering research in radio astrophysics: Ryle for his observations and inventions, in particular of the aperture synthesis technique, and Hewish for his decisive role in the discovery of pulsars"

1975

Aage Niels Bohr (1922–), Denmark, Ben Roy Mottelson (1926–), Denmark, and Leo James Rainwater (1917–86), United States

"For the discovery of the connection between collective motion and particle motion in atomic nuclei and the development of the theory of the structure of the atomic nucleus based on this connection"

1976

Burton Richter (1931–), United States, and Samuel Chao Chung Ting (1936–), United States

"For their pioneering work in the discovery of a heavy elementary particle of a new kind"

1977

Philip Warren Anderson (1923–), United States, Sir Nevill Francis Mott (1905–96), United Kingdom, and John Hasbrouck van Vleck (1899–1980), United States

"For their fundamental theoretical investigations of the electronic structure of magnetic and disordered systems"

1978

Pyotr Leonidovich Kapitsa (1894–1984), USSR

"For his basic inventions and discoveries in the area of low-temperature physics" and

Arno Allan Penzias (1933–), United States and Robert Woodrow Wilson (1936–), United States

"For their discovery of cosmic microwave background radiation"

1979

Sheldon Lee Glashow (1932–), United States, Abdus Salam (1926–96), Pakistan, and Steven Weinberg (1933–), United States

"For their contributions to the theory of the unified weak and electromag-netic interaction between elementary particles, including, inter alia, *the prediction of the weak neutral current"*

1980

James Watson Cronin (1931–), United States, and Val Logsdon Fitch (1923–), United States

"For the discovery of violations of fundamental symmetry principles in the decay of neutral K-mesons"

1981

Nicolaas Bloembergen (1920–), United States, and Arthur Leonard Schawlow (1921–99), United States

"For their contribution to the development of laser spectroscopy" and

Kai M. Siegbahn (1918–), Sweden

"For his contribution to the development of high-resolution electron spectroscopy"

1982

Kenneth G. Wilson (1936–), United States

"For his theory for critical phenomena in connection with phase transitions"

1983

Subramanyan Chandrasekhar (1910–95), United States

"For his theoretical studies of the physical processes of importance to the structure and evolution of the stars"

and William Alfred Fowler (1911–95), United States

"For his theoretical and experimental studies of the nuclear reactions of importance in the formation of the chemical elements in the universe"

1984

Carlo Rubbia (1934–), Italy, and Simon van der Meer (1925–), the Netherlands

"For their decisive contributions to the large project, which led to the discov-ery of the field particles W and Z, communicators of weak interaction"

1985

Klaus von Klitzing (1943–), Federal Republic of Germany

"For the discovery of the quantized Hall effect"

1986

Ernst Ruska (1906–88), Federal Republic of Germany

"For his fundamental work in electron optics, and for the design of the first electron microscope" and

Gerd Binnig (1947–   ), Federal Republic of Germany, and Heinrich Rohrer (1933–   ), Switzerland

"For their design of the scanning tunneling microscope"

1987

J. Georg Bednorz (1950–   ), Federal Republic of Germany, and K. Alexander Müller (1927–   ), Switzerland

"For their important break-through in the discovery of superconductivity in ceramic materials"

1988

Leon M. Lederman (1922–   ), United States, Melvin Schwartz (1932–2006), United States, and Jack Steinberger (1931–   ), Switzerland

"For the neutrino beam method and the demonstration of the doublet structure of the leptons through the discovery of the muon neutrino"

1989

Norman F. Ramsey (1915–   ), United States

"For the invention of the separated oscillatory fields method and its use in the hydrogen maser and other atomic clocks" and

Hans G. Dehmelt (1932–   ), United States, and Wolfgang Pauli (1913–93), Federal Republic of Germany

"For the development of the ion trap technique"

1990

Jerome I. Friedman (1930–   ), United States, Henry W. Kendall (1926–99), United States, and Richard E. Taylor (1929–   ), Canada

"For their pioneering investigations concerning deep inelastic scattering of electrons on protons and bound neutrons, which have been of essential importance for the development of the quark model in particle physics"

1991

Pierre-Gilles de Gennes (1932–   ), France

"For discovering that methods developed for studying order phenomena in simple systems can be generalized to more complex forms of matter, in particular to liquid crystals and polymers"

1992

Georges Charpak (1924–   ), France

"For his invention and development of particle detectors, in particular the multiwire proportional chamber"

1993

Russell A. Hulse (1950–   ), United States, and Joseph H. Taylor, Jr. (1941–   ), United States

"For the discovery of a new type of pulsar, a discovery that has opened up new possibilities for the study of gravitation"

1994

Bertram N. Brockhouse (1918–2003), Canada, and Clifford G. Shull (1915–2001), United States

"For pioneering contributions to the development of neutron scattering techniques for studies of condensed matter," Brockhouse *"for the development of neutron spectroscopy,"* and Shull *"for the development of the neutron diffraction technique"*

1995

Martin L. Perl (1927–   ), United States, and Frederick Reines (1918–98), United States

"For pioneering experimental contributions to lepton physics," Perl *"for the discovery of the tau lepton"* and Reines *"for the detection of the neutrino"*

1996

David M. Lee (1931–   ), United States, Douglas D. Osheroff (1945–   ), United States, and Robert C. Richardson (1937–   ), United States

"For their discovery of superfluidity in helium-3"

1997

Steven Chu (1948–   ), United States, Claude Cohen-Tannoudji (1933–   ), France, and William D. Phillips (1948–   ), United States

"For development of methods to cool and trap atoms with laser light"

1998

Robert B. Laughlin (1950–), United States, Horst L. Störmer (1949–), Federal Republic of Germany, and Daniel C. Tsui (1939–), United States

"For their discovery of a new form of quantum fluid with fractionally charged excitations"

1999

Gerardus 't Hooft (1946–), the Netherlands, and Martinus J. G. Veltman (1931–), the Netherlands

"For elucidating the quantum structure of electroweak interactions in physics"

2000

Zhores I. Alferov (1930–), Russia, Herbert Kroemer, (1928–), Federal Republic of Germany, and Jack S. Kilby (1923–2005), United States

"For basic work on information and communication technology," Alferov and Kroemer *"for developing semiconductor heterostructures used in high-speed- and opto-electronics,"* and Kilby *"for his part in the invention of the integrated circuit"*

Glossary

absolute frame of reference   see FRAME OF REFERENCE

alpha decay   see ALPHA RAYS

alpha rays (or **alpha particles**)   the least penetrating form of radioactivity. Alpha particles are helium nuclei, and the process that produces them is often called alpha decay

amorphous   a kind of solid in which the atoms lack the orderly arrangement of a crystal

annihilation   an event in which two particles interact and destroy each other, such as the combination of an electron and a hole in a semiconductor or the combination of a particle and its antiparticle

antimatter   a type of matter with identical properties to its normal matter counterpart except for carrying an opposite electric charge and parity.

atom   the smallest particle of a substance that can be identified as a chemical element

atomic mass   a number that specifies the mass of a nucleus, equal to the total number of protons and neutrons it contains

atomic number   a number that specifies an element's position in the periodic table, equal to the number of protons in the element's nucleus

baryon   a subatomic particle at least as heavy as a proton that is composed of three quarks and responds to the strong nuclear force

beta decay   see BETA RAYS

beta rays (or **beta particles**)   a form of radioactivity that is more penetrating than alpha rays but less penetrating than gamma rays. Beta particles are electrons, and the process that produces them in nuclei is often called beta decay

blackbody radiation   the electromagnetic energy emitted by an object as a consequence of its temperature

black hole   a collapsed star so dense that nothing can escape from it, including light

boson (gauge boson)   generally, a subatomic particle with integral spin; particularly, a gauge boson which is exchanged to create a fundamental force, such as photons for the electromagnetic force, gluons for the strong nuclear force, and W and Z particles for the weak force

Brownian motion   a phenomenon in which small particles, such as grains of dust or pollen, move in irregular paths when suspended in a gas or liquid

cathode ray   a stream of negative electricity emitted from a hot electrode in a vacuum tube, discovered in 1897 to be composed of electrons

chain reaction   a sequence of nuclear fissions in which neutrons emitted in one fission event cause one or more additional nuclei to split, resulting in a rapid and intense release of energy

cloud chamber   a device in which condensation of a vapor reveals a trail of ions such as those produced along the path of a charged subatomic particles; cloud chambers were used in early studies of cosmic rays and subatomic particles

color   the property of a quark that interacts with the strong nuclear force, equivalent to positive or negative charge for the electromagnetic force

compound   a chemical substance made up of a particular combination of elements

condensed matter physics   a subfield of physics, a generalization of solid-state physics to include all substances whose properties depend on the mutual interaction of large assemblies of atoms, including liquids, crystalline solids, and amorphous solids

conduction band   a set of closely spaced electron energy levels in a solid in which the electrons belong to no particular atoms and thus move freely through the material

continuous spectrum   see SPECTRUM

cosmic rays   energetic particles that come to Earth from distant parts of the universe or result from interaction of such particles with the upper reaches of Earth's atmosphere

cosmological constant   a quantity that arose in Einstein's mathematical description of general relativity; its value and algebraic sign determined whether and how fast the universe was expanding or contracting

cosmology   the scientific study of the universe as an entity

covalent bond   a type of chemical bond in which the participating atoms share electrons

crystal   a solid substance that is characterized by a regularly repeating, three-dimensional arrangement of its atoms

cyclotron   a device that accelerates subatomic particles to very high energies as they follow a spiraling path in a very large magnetic field

diode   an electronic device that permits an electric current to pass through in only one direction

eightfold way   a term borrowed from Buddhism to describe the mathematical symmetry underlying the various bosons

electrical resistance   a property of matter that impedes the flow of electricity through it

electromagnetism   a basic force of nature that includes both electricity and magnetism and is the basis for electromagnetic waves, including light

electron   a small negatively charged subatomic particle discovered in cathode rays in 1897 and later found to determine an atom's chemical and electrical behavior and to be useful as the basis for electronic technology

element   a chemical substance made up of only one kind of atom

entanglement   see QUANTUM ENTANGLEMENT

ferromagnetism   a property of certain types of matter, such as iron, that enables it to develop and maintain a permanent magnetic field

fission   a radioactive process in which a nucleus splits into two smaller nuclei and several neutrons

flavor   a term used to distinguish the different types of quarks; a quark's flavor can be up, down, strange, charm, top, or bottom

frame of reference   a point of origin and set of directions in space (such as north-south, east-west, up-down) against which the relative position and motion of an object can be specified. The luminiferous ether was presumed to be an absolute, unmoving frame of reference until Einstein's special theory of relativity demonstrated that no such frame exists

gamma rays (or **gamma radiation**)   the most penetrating form of radioactivity. Gamma rays are high-energy photons

gluon   the gauge boson exchanged between quarks thereby acting as the carrier of the strong nuclear force

grand unification theory (GUT)   a goal of theoretical physicists who are seeking a theory to unify all the fundamental forces

gravity   a basic force of nature that creates an attraction between any two bodies that have mass

greenhouse effect   a phenomenon in which the atmosphere of a planet permits solar energy to enter but blocks outgoing infrared radiation, leading to a considerably higher planetary temperature than would occur if the planet had no atmosphere

hole   a region in a semiconductor in which an electron is missing and behaves as if it is a mobile, positive charge

inflation   a theory that explains the unexpected uniformity of the cosmic background radiation by a very brief period just after the big bang when the cosmos and spacetime itself expanded at a rate much faster than the speed of light

interference   a phenomenon that occurs when waves overlap; for two light waves of the same wavelength, this results in a series of bright and dark bands

ionic bond a type of chemical bond in which the participating atoms exchange electrons, thereby becoming oppositely charged ions held together by electrical attraction

ionization the creation of electrically charged atoms called **ions**

isospin a quantum mechanical property of baryons that has the same kind of reflection symmetry as a rotation or magnetization: for example, a proton has isospin +½, while a neutron has isospin -½

isotope one of several nuclei with the same atomic number but different atomic masses

kaon (K meson) a type of meson discovered in 1947 and later found to contain a "strange" quark

Lamb shift a slight splitting in the spectrum of hydrogen, first observed by Willis Lamb and critical to understanding quantum electrodynamics

lepton a light subatomic particle that does not respond to the strong nuclear force; leptons include electrons, muons, taus, and their neutrinos and antiparticles

line spectrum see SPECTRUM

luminiferous ether a hypothetical substance once presumed to permeate all space as the carrier of electromagnetic waves

many-body problem analysis of a physical model that involves the interaction of more than two bodies, such as they behavior of electrons in solids

Maxwell's equations a set of four formulas that describes the interrelationships between electricity and magnetism and predicts the existence of electromagnetic waves that travel at the speed of light

meson a middle-weight subatomic particle that consists of a quark and an antiquark; the first usage of the term referred to pions

mesotron a name originally used for the muon, the first particle discovered with mass in the intermediate range between the electron's and the proton's

molecule a particular combination of atoms making up the smallest particle of a substance that can be identified as a particular compound

muon a subatomic particle that is the second-generation equivalent of the electron in the standard model

neutron a subatomic particle with slightly more mass than a proton but without electric charge; nuclei are made up of protons and neutrons bound together by the strong nuclear force

neutron activation analysis a technique used to determine the chemical and isotopic composition of a material by bombarding it with neutrons and measuring the resulting radioactivity

neutron star a super-dense star in which all its matter has been compressed into neutrons (see PULSAR)

***n*-type semiconductor** a semiconductor with an excess of electrons over holes

nucleon   a proton or neutron; the atomic mass of a nucleus is the total number of nucleons it contains

nucleus (plural: **nuclei**)   the tiny, positively charged central part of an atom that contains most of its mass

parity   an inherent left- or right-handedness of a subatomic particle that is only observable in processes, such as beta decay, that involve the weak nuclear force

periodic table of the elements   an arrangement of the chemical elements in rows and columns that reveals similarities in their physical and chemical properties

perturbation   a minor change in physical circumstances that often results in a minor correction to a well-known theory, often the first step in a many-body analysis

phonon   a quantum or packet of vibrational energy

photoelectric effect   a phenomenon in which shining a light can cause electrons to be emitted from a metal surface

photon   a quantum or packet of light energy

pion   a meson that is exchanged between nucleons, creating the strong nuclear force

Planck's constant   a fundamental ratio in nature that relates the energy of a quantum to the frequency of its corresponding electromagnetic wave

positron   the antimatter counterpart of an electron

proton   a subatomic particle having one unit of positive electric charge and one unit of atomic mass; the nucleus of normal hydrogen is a single proton

p **-type semiconductor**   a semiconductor with an excess of holes over electrons

pulsar   a type of star that produces light that pulsates at very regular intervals, now known to be a rapidly rotating neutron star

quark   a type of subatomic particle that is considered the fundamental building block of baryons and mesons, that is, particles that interact via the strong nuclear force

quantum (plural: **quanta**)   a packet of energy devised by Planck to explain the shape of blackbody radiation; later generalized to be a packet of any physical entity, such as electric charge or a particle's angular momentum, that varied in steps rather than continuously

quantum chromodynamics (QCD)   a theory that describes the strong nuclear force as a result of quarks exchanging a type of bosons called gluons

quantum electrodynamics (QED)   a subfield of physics that restructures Maxwell's theory so that it is consistent with the quantum nature of matter and energy

quantum entanglement   a phenomenon in which determination of the quantum state of one particle immediately affects the quantum state of another particle some distance away because a relationship between those states had been established previously; Einstein referred to the phenomenon, when first predicted, as "spooky action at a distance"

quantum mechanics   a subfield of physics based on the quantum description of matter and energy as having a dual wave-particle nature

quantum number   a value that describes a physical property that can take on integer multiples of a fundamental value, such as Planck's constant (or half-integer values, in the case of spin)

radioactivity   a subatomic process in which a nucleus emits energetic particles or gamma rays

relative frame of reference   see FRAME OF REFERENCE

renormalization   a mathematical technique applied to quantum electrodynamics that enables the equation to handle infinities that were problems in previous approaches

resonance   a phenomenon with a natural frequency that occurs in response to stimulation, such as the vibration of a string or the air column of a musical instrument

scattering   a phenomenon in which a stream of particles or energy is diverted by interaction with a target. The resulting pattern reveals details of the target, as the scattering of alpha particles revealed the nuclear structure of atoms

semiconductor (adj.: **semiconducting**) a material with electrical properties between that of an insulator and a conductor; the electrical conductivity of a semiconductor can be controlled by making small changes to its composition

shell   a set of energy levels corresponding to particular quantum numbers. The chemical properties of elements and certain physical properties of nuclei show periodic behavior because of the way electrons, protons, and neutrons fill shells

solid-state physics   a subfield of physics dealing with the properties of solid matter: later included in the broader category of condensed matter physics

spacetime   a four-dimensional combination of space and time that resulted from Einstein's theory of relativity

spectral line splitting   a phenomenon in which a single spectral line splits into several with the application of an external influence such as an electric or magnetic field

spectroscope   an optical device that splits light (or another electromagnetic wave) into its component wavelengths and measures their intensities

spectrum   the various colors contained in light, or more generally the various wavelength in any energy-carrying waves, often displayed as a continuous graph of intensity v. wavelength or as a series of lines specifying intensity at specific wavelengths

spin   a fundamental property of subatomic particles, represented by a quantum number designated s, that corresponds to their inherent magnetism

standard model of particle physics   a description of the fundamental particles that make up all matter as we know it as three generations of leptons and quarks plus gauge bosons as carriers of the fundamental subatomic forces

standing wave   an unmoving pattern of oscillation that results from steady interference of two other waves or as a resonance phenomenon

statistical mechanics   a mathematical approach to physics that connects microscopic properties such as the motion of individual atoms or molecules in a gas to macroscopic (overall) properties such as temperature and pressure

strangeness   a quantum mechanical property that was found to be conserved during transformations of subatomic particles under the influence of the strong nuclear force; later recognized as the total number of strange quarks

string theory   a mathematical approach devised to unify the fundamental forces and explain fundamental particles as allowed vibrations on a 10-dimensional string

strong nuclear force   a fundamental force of nature that acts between quarks and is responsible for binding protons and neutrons together in nuclei

superconductivity   a quantum mechanical property of certain substances that causes them to lose all resistance to electric current below a certain critical temperature

superfluidity   a quantum mechanical property observed in liquid helium in which it loses all viscosity, or resistance to flowing, below a certain critical temperature

superstring theory   an improvement on string theory that adds an 11th dimension

transistor   an electronic device made of semiconducting material that can function as an amplifier or a controllable switch

transmutation   the transformation of one nucleus into another by a radioactive emission

transuranic elements   chemical elements with atomic numbers greater than uranium's 92

uncertainty principle   a consequence of the quantum nature of matter and energy discovered by Werner Heisenberg, stating the existence of natural limits on the precision of measurement of the paired quantities energy and time or position and momentum

valence   a property of an atom expressed as a positive or negative number that describes the way that atom accepts or contributes electrons in a chemical reaction

valence band   a set of closely spaced electron energy levels in a solid in which the electrons are shared among a few atoms and thus are involved in chemical bonding within the material

wave function   a mathematical representation used in the Schrödinger equation that describes the position of an object by a wavelike variation in space rather than as a fixed point

weak nuclear force   a fundamental force of nature that acts within the nucleus and governs the process of beta decay

X-ray diffraction   a phenomenon in which the interaction of X-rays with a solid produce a pattern that reveals information about the solid's crystal structure

Further Resources

Books

Adams, Steve. *Frontiers: Twentieth-Century Physics.* New York: Taylor and Francis, 2000. A survey of 20th-century physics written for high school students.

Alvarez, Luis W. *Alvarez, Adventures of a Physicist.* New York: Basic Books, 1987. Luis Alvarez's adventurous life in his own words.

Alvarez, Walter. *T-Rex and the Crater of Doom.* Princeton, N.J.: Princeton University Press, 1997. A lively account of the scientific investigation that led to a radical new understanding of the mass extinction that killed the dinosaurs.

Bodanis, David, with a new foreword by Simon Singh. *E=mc^2: The Biography of the World's Most Famous Equation.* 2001. Reprint, New York: Walker, 2005. A term-by-term discussion of the elements of Einstein's best-known formula.

Bortz, Fred. *Collision Course! Cosmic Impacts and Life on Earth.* Brookfield, Conn.: Millbrook Press, 2001. For younger readers, this book discusses several planetary impacts of comets and asteroids, including the one that killed the dinosaurs.

————. *The Electron.* New York: Rosen Publishing, 2004. An easy-to-read history of the electron and its applications.

————. *Martian Fossils on Earth? The Story of Meteorite ALH84001.* Brookfield, Conn.: Millbrook Press, 2001. For younger readers, this book discusses the claims and controversies about evidence for ancient Martian bacterial life.

————. *The Neutrino.* New York: Rosen Publishing, 2004. An easy-to-read history of the neutrino and its significance.

————. *The Neutron.* New York: Rosen Publishing, 2004. An easy-to-read history of the neutron and its applications.

————. *The Photon.* New York: Rosen Publishing, 2004. An easy-to-read history of the photon and its applications.

————. *The Proton.* New York: Rosen Publishing, 2004. An easy-to-read history of the proton and its applications.

————. "What Killed the Dinosaurs?" Chap. 2, *To the Young Scientist: Reflections on Doing and Living Science.* Danbury, Conn.: Franklin Watts, 1997. This chapter is based on an interview with Frank Asaro and Helen Michel, who did the neutron activation analysis that led to Luis Alvarez's theory that the dinosaurs' extinction was due to the impact of an asteroid.

Breithaupt, Jim. *Teach Yourself Physics.* Chicago: NTC/Contemporary Publishing, 2002. A compact introduction to the key concepts, major discoveries, and current challenges in physics.

Bromley, D. Allan. *A Century of Physics.* New York: Springer, 2002. A tour from the last century of physics growth, impact, and directions. Numerous photos and illustrations.

Burrows, William E. *The Infinite Journey: Eyewitness Accounts of NASA and the Age of Space.* New York: Discovery Books, 2000. A vivid pictorial account of NASA's exploration of the Moon and the planets.

————. *This New Ocean: The Story of the First Space Age.* New York: Random House, 1998. A detailed history of space exploration.

Calaprice, Alice. *The Einstein Almanac.* Baltimore: Johns Hopkins University Press, 2005. An overview of Einstein's life and work in concise snippets.

Calaprice, Alice, ed. with a foreword by Freeman Dyson. *The New Quotable Einstein.* Princeton, N.J.: Princeton University Press, 2005. Einstein's human side as shown in his often witty and warm letters to colleagues, friends, family, and lovers.

Calder, Nigel. *Einstein's Universe: The Layperson's Guide.* New York: Penguin, 2005. A reissue of a 1979 guide to relativity, with a new author's note and afterword.

Cassidy, David. *Uncertainty: The Life and Science of Werner Heisenberg.* New York: W. H. Freeman, 1991. An interesting personal history of Heisenberg's life and science, with the theme of uncertainty in both.

Cathcart, Brian. *The Fly in the Cathedral: How a Group of Cambridge Scientists Won the International Race to Split the Atom.* New York: Farrar, Straus and Giroux, 2004. A fascinating story of Cockroft and Walton's achievement, with insights into Rutherford's leadership and Chadwick's discovery of the neutron.

Cernan, Eugene, with Don Davis. *The Last Man on the Moon.* New York: St. Martin's, 1999. A description of *Apollo 17,* the last manned mission to the Moon, written by the astronaut who was the last to board the lunar module for its return trip.

Chapple, Michael. *Schaum's A to Z Physics.* New York: McGraw-Hill, 2003. Defines 650 key concepts with diagrams and graphs, intended for high school students and college freshman.

Charap, John M. *Explaining the Universe: The New Age of Physics.* Princeton, N.J.: Princeton University Press, 2002. A description of the field of physics at the beginning of the 21st century.

Chown, Marcus. *The Magic Furnace: The Search for the Origin of Atoms.* New York: Oxford University Press, 2001. A readable history of the quest to understand the composition of the universe.

Close, Frank, Michael Marten, and Christine Sutton. *The Particle Odyssey: A Journey to the Heart of Matter.* New York: Oxford University Press, 2002. A detailed and colorfully illustrated overview of the discovery of subatomic particles.

Cole, K. C. *The Hole in the Universe: How Scientists Peered over the Edge of Emptiness and Found Everything.* New York: Harcourt, 2001. A description of modern theories of subatomic particles and cosmology.

Cornwell, John. *Hitler's Scientists: Science, War, and the Devil's Pact.* New York: Viking, 2003. Provides insight into the political forces that shaped research in physics and the lives of physicists in the 1930s and 1940s.

Cropper, William H. *Great Physicists: The Life and Times of Leading Physicists from Galileo to Hawking.* New York: Oxford University Press, 2001. The life and times of many great physicists.

Dauber, Philip M., and Richard A. Muller. *The Three Big Bangs: Comet Crashes, Exploding Stars, and the Creation of the Universe.* New York: Perseus Books, 1997. A clear and interesting look at the origin and history of life on Earth by one of Luis Alvarez's best-known students.

Dennis, Johnnie T. *The Complete Idiot's Guide to Physics.* Indianapolis, Ind.: Alpha Books, 2003. A friendly review of high school–level classical physics.

The Diagram Group. *The Facts On File Physics Handbook.* New York: Facts On File, 2000. Convenient resource containing a glossary of terms; short biographical profiles of celebrated physicists; a chronology of events and discoveries; and useful charts, tables, and diagrams.

Dyson, Marianne. *Space and Astronomy: Decade by Decade.* New York: Facts On File, 2007. A fine overview of the notable personnel and events in the field of space and astronomy in the 20th century.

Einstein, Albert, with a new introduction by Brian Green. *The Meaning of Relativity.* 5th ed. 1954. Reprint, Princeton, N.J.: Princeton University Press, 2005. A readable presentation of Einstein's most famous theory in his own words.

Falk, Dan. *Universe on a T-Shirt: The Quest for the Theory of Everything.* New York: Arcade Publishing, 2002. A story outlining developments in the search for the theory that will unify all four natural forces.

Fleisher, Paul. *Relativity and Quantum Mechanics: Principles of Modern Physics.* Minneapolis, Minn.: Lerner Publications, 2002. An introduction to the concepts of relativity and quantum mechanics written for middle school students.

Fermi, Laura. *Atoms in the Family: My Life with Enrico Fermi.* Chicago: University of Chicago Press, 1954. A memoir by Fermi's wife, providing insights into the life of a fascinating man and scientist.

Feynman, Michelle. *Perfectly Reasonable Deviations from the Beaten Path: The Letters of Richard P. Feynman.* New York: Basic Books, 2005. A collection of Feynman's correspondence, selected and edited by his daughter.

Feynman, Richard. *The Feynman Lectures on Physics.* 3 vols. Reprint, Boston: Addison-Wesley Longman, 1970. A classic set of lectures that captures Feynman's unique approach and teaching style.

———. *QED: The Strange Theory of Light and Matter.* Princeton, N.J.: Princeton University Press, 1986. Based on a series of lectures at UCLA in which Feynman explained quantum electrodynamics to a broad audience.

——— (as told to Ralph Leighton). *Surely You're Joking, Mr. Feynman: Adventures of a Curious Character.* New York: W. W. Norton, 1985. The first of two popular memoirs.

——— (———). *What Do You Care What Other People Think? Further Adventures of a Curious Character.* New York: W. W. Norton, 1988. Feynman's second memoir published just months before his death.

Frisch, Otto. *What Little I Remember.* Cambridge: Cambridge University Press, 1979. A very readable autobiography of Lisa Meitner's nephew and a great physicist in his own right.

Gell-Mann, Murray. *The Quark and the Jaguar: Adventures in the Simple and the Complex.* New York: W. H. Freeman, 1994. The story of the eightfold way and quarks in Murray Gell-Mann's own words.

Gleick, James. *Genius: The Life and Science of Richard Feynman.* New York: Pantheon, 1992. One of two definitive Feynman biographies.

Gribbin, John with Mary Gribbin. *Stardust: Supernovae and Life; The Cosmic Connection.* New Haven, Conn.: Yale University Press, 2001. Covers similar material as Marcus Chown's *The Magic Furnace* (above), with a greater emphasis on science and a lesser emphasis on history.

Griffith, W. Thomas. *The Physics of Everyday Phenomena.* 4th ed. Boston: WCB/McGraw Hill, 2004. A conceptual text for nonscience college students.

Gundersen, P. Erik. *The Handy Physics Answer Book.* Detroit: Visible Ink Press, 1999. Answers numerous questions about physics using a conceptual approach.

Hahn, Otto. *Otto Hahn: My Life, The Autobiography of a Scientist,* translated by Ernst Kaiser and Eithne Wilkins. New York: Herder and Herder, 1970.

Hawking, Stephen. *A Brief History of Time.* New York: Bantam, 1988. Hawking's most famous book about the nature of matter, energy, space-time, and cosmology for nonscientists.

———. *The Universe in a Nutshell.* New York: Bantam, 2001. Insight into cosmology and string theory by own of the world's greatest theoretical physicists.

Heppenheimer, T. A. *Countdown: A History of Space Flight.* New York: John Wiley, 1997. A detailed history of the manned spaceflight.

Hoddeson, Lillian, Ernest Braun, Jürgen Teichmann, and Spencer Weart. *Out of the Crystal Maze: Chapters from the History of Solid-State Physics.* New York: Oxford University Press, 1992. A comprehensive history of condensed matter physics written for professional physicists and historians of physics.

Hoddeson, Lillian and Vicki Daitsch. *True Genius: the Life and Science of John Bardeen.* Washington, D.C.: Joseph Henry Press, 2002. The definitive biography of John Bardeen, including considerable detail about his scientific work.

Holton, Gerald James, and Stephen G. Brush. *Physics, the Human Adventure: From Copernicus to Einstein and Beyond.* New Brunswick, N.J.: Rutgers University Press, 2001. Comprehensive introduction intended for non-science college students. Difficult reading but covers a lot of material.

James, Ioan. *Remarkable Physicists: From Galileo to Yukawa.* New York: Cambridge University Press, 2004. Contains brief biographies of 50 physicists spanning a period of 250 years, focusing on the lives rather than the science.

Johnson, George. *Strange Beauty: Murray Gell-Mann and the Revolution in Twentieth-Century Physics.* New York: Random House, 1999. A definitive and readable biography of Murray Gell-Mann and an explanation of his major scientific ideas.

Kragh, Helge. *Quantum Generations: A History of Physics in the Twentieth Century.* Princeton, N.J.: Princeton University Press, 1999. An in-depth history of 20th-century physics and physicists.

Launius, Roger D., and Howard McCurdy. *Imagining Space: Achievements * Predictions * Possibilities, 1950–2050.* San Francisco, Calif.: Chronicle, 2001. An illustrated history of and future of spaceflight.

Leighton, Ralph, ed. *Classic Feynman: All the Adventures of a Curious Character,* by Richard Feynman. New York: W. W. Norton, 2005. A compilation of Feynman's two memoirs in chronological order, with a foreword by Freeman Dyson.

Leiter, Darryl J. *A to Z of Physicists.* New York: Facts On File, 2003. Profiles more than 150 physicists, discussing their research and contributions. Includes bibliography, cross-references, and chronology.

Lightman, Alan. *The Discoveries: Great Breakthroughs in 20th Century Science, Including the Original Papers.* New York: Pantheon, 2005. Includes many papers discussed in this book plus commentaries on their significance.

McCurdy, Howard E. *Space and the American Imagination.* Washington, D.C.: Smithsonian, 1997. A history of the United States space program.

McGrath, Kimberley A., ed. *World of Physics.* Farmington Hills, Mich.: Thomson Gale, 2001. Contains 1,000 entries on concepts, theories, discoveries, pioneers, and issues related to physics.

Mehra, Jagdish. *The Beat of a Different Drum: The Life and Science of Richard Feynman.* Oxford: Oxford University Press, 1994. One of two definitive Feynman biographies.

Moore, Walter. *Schrödinger: Life and Thought.* Cambridge: Cambridge University Press, 1989. A biography that captures the human and scientific complexities of the man who captured the wave-particle duality of matter and energy in a famous equation.

Morton, Oliver. *Mapping Mars: Science, Imagination, and the Birth of a World.* New York: Picador, 2002. A detailed history of the discoveries from various Mars missions.

Rhodes, Richard. *The Making of the Atomic Bomb.* New York: Simon & Schuster, 1986. A history of the Manhattan Project.

Rigden, John S. *Einstein 1905: The Standard of Greatness.* Cambridge, Mass.: Harvard University Press, 2005. Accessible discussion of Einstein's three 1905 masterworks.

Rosen, Joe. *Encyclopedia of Physics.* New York: Facts On File, 2004. Comprehensive one-volume overview containing more than 600 entries and 11 prose essays on different current topics.

Schumm, Bruce A. *Deep Down Things: The Breathtaking Beauty of Particle Physics.* Baltimore: Johns Hopkins University Press, 2005. A look at the mathematical ideas that underlie particle physics and string theory.

Seife, Charles. *Alpha & Omega: The Search for the Beginning and the End of the Universe.* New York: Viking, 2003. A look at the connections between particle physics and the cosmology of the big bang.

Siegfried, Tom. *Strange Matters: Undiscovered Ideas at the Frontiers of Space and Time.* Washington, D.C.: Joseph Henry Press, 2002. A book discussing ideas, such as string theory, which the author refers to as "prediscoveries" because they are likely to produce insights into particle physics and cosmology.

Sime, Ruth Lewin. *Lise Meitner: A Life in Physics.* Berkeley: University of California Press, 1996. A thorough treatment of the scientist.

Smolin, Lee. *The Trouble with Physics: The Rise of String Theory, the Fall of a Science, and What Comes Next.* New York: Houghton Mifflin, 2006. A noted string theorist concludes that string theory is deeply flawed and must be abandoned to clear the way for the development of new approaches to "the theory of everything."

Suplee, Curt. *Physics in the 20th Century.* New York: Harry N. Abrams, 1999. A pictorial history of 20th-century physics.

Trefil, James. *From Atoms to Quarks: An Introduction to the Strange World of Particle Physics.* Rev. ed. New York: Anchor Books, 1994. A primer on this complex subject written for general readers.

White, Michael, and John Gribbin. *Stephen Hawking: A Life in Science.* New York: Dutton, 1992. A definitive and readable biography of Hawking's first 50 years.

Woit, Peter. *Not Even Wrong: The Failure of String Theory and the Search for Unity in Physical Law.* New York: Basic Books, 2006. String theory is increasingly coming under attack as a nontheory for its failure to make testable predictions. This author makes his point by using a disdainful phrase from Wolfgang Pauli (see chapter 3) as the book's title.

Web Sites

Academy of Achievement. Available online. URL http://www.achievement. org. Accessed April 21, 2006. Find Leon Lederman's story by following link from pull-down menu of achievers.

American Institute of Physics, Center for History of Physics. Available online. URL: http://www.aip.org/history. Accessed March 27, 2006. Follow pull-down menu for special online exhibits on Albert Einstein, Marie Curie, the electron, and radioactivity, among other topics, or browse for a variety of written resources and images.

American Physical Society. A Century of Physics. Available online. URL: http://timeline.aps.org/APS. Accessed April 25, 2006. Wonderful, interactive timeline describing major events in the development of modern physics.

———. Physics Central. Available online. URL: http://www.physicscentral. com. Accessed April 25, 2006. Updated daily with information on physics in the news, current research, and people in physics.

CWP and Regents of the University of California. "Contributions of 20th-Century Women to Physics." Available online. URL: http://cwp.library. ucla.edu. Accessed April 25, 2006. Highlights 83 women who have made original and important contributions to physics prior to 1976.

Fermilab Education Office. Available online. URL: http://www-ed.fnal.gov/ ed_home.html. Accessed April 21, 2006. Official Web site of the educational outreach organization founded by Leon Lederman at Fermilab.

Feynman Online. Available online. URL: http://www.feynman.com. Accessed April 3, 2006. A tribute to Richard Feynman with many useful links to all aspects of his life and science, including streaming video of four lectures on QED in New Zealand in 1979.

Garwin, Richard L. "Memorial Tribute for Luis W. Alvarez." In *Memorial Tributes*, National Academy of Engineering, vol. 5. Washington D.C.: National Academy Press, 1992. Also available online. URL: http://www. fas.org/rlg/alvarez.htm. Accessed April 20, 2006. A detailed obituary and memorial tribute for Luis Alvarez.

Lawrence Berkeley National Laboratory. Nuclear Science Division. "The ABCs of Nuclear Science." Available online. URL: http://www.lbl.gov/ abc. Accessed April 25, 2006. Introduces the basics of nuclear science—nuclear structure, radioactivity, cosmic rays, antimatter, and more.

———. Particle Data Group. "The Particle Adventure: The Fundamentals of Matter and Force." Available online. URL: http://particleadventure. org/particleadventure. Accessed April 25, 2006. Interactive tour of quarks, neutrinos, antimatter, extra dimensions, dark matter, accelerators, and particle detectors.

National Inventors Hall of Fame. Available online. URL: http://www. invent.org. Accessed April 18, 2006. Search Web site by name of inventor or invention.

Nobelprize.org. Available online. URL: http://nobelprize.org. Accessed March 27, 2006. The official Web site of the Nobel Foundation contains brief biographies of Nobel Prize winners, summaries of their prize-winning work, and their acceptance speeches.

Reyer, Steve. 1954–2004: The TR-1's Golden Anniversary. Available online. URL: http://people.msoe.edu/~reyer/regency. Accessed September 19, 2005. Describes the world's first transistor radio.

Robbins, Stuart. *Journey through the Galaxy*. Available online. URL: http://home.cwru.edu/~sjr16/. Click "History" for "A Brief History of the Universe," or go to http://home.cwru.edu/~sjr16/advanced/cosmos_history.html. Accessed April 21, 2006. A Web site with a number of useful pages on cosmology.

Schwarz, Patricia. The Official String Theory Web Site. Available online. URL: http://www.superstringtheory.com. Accessed April 21, 2006. A comprehensive Web site about string theory, the physicists who have worked on it, and its history.

The Science Museum. Available online. URL: http://www.sciencemuseum.org.uk. Accessed March 27, 2006. A British online science education resource that includes useful exhibits on Atomic Firsts; Life, the Universe, and the Electron; Marie Curie and the History of Radioactivity; and many other topics discussed in this book.

The Science Shelf, Books for the World Year of Physics 2005. Available online. URL: http://www.scienceshelf.com/WorldYearofPhysics.htm. Accessed April 26, 2006. This page on the book review site of Fred Bortz has brief comments about a number of books published in recognition of the World Year of Physics, plus links to reviews of a number of other physics books for nonspecialist readers.

Sloan Digital Sky Survey. SDSS Sky Survey/SkyServer. Available online. URL: http://cas.sdss.org/dr4/en. Accessed April 21, 2006. The official Web site of the SDSS program.

Watt, Robert D., W. Peter Trower, M. Lynn Stevenson, Richard A. Muller, and Walter Alvarez. "Luis W. Alvarez, Physics: Berkeley." In Krogh, David, ed. *University of California: in Memoriam 1988*. Also available online. URL: http://ark.cdlib.org/ark:/13030/hb967nb5k3. Follow link to "View Options: Standard" and choose "Luis W. Alvarez." Accessed April 20, 2006. A memorial essay about Luis Alvarez by many individuals who knew him best.

Wilkinson Microwave Anisotropy Probe (WMAP). Available online. URL: http://wmap.gsfc.nasa.gov. Accessed April 21, 2006. Official WMAP Web site.

World Year of Physics 2005. Available online. URL: http://www.physics2005.org. Accessed March 27, 2006. An online resource developed in honor of the centennial of Albert Einstein's "Miracle Year."

Index